THE QUÉBÉCOIS ÉLITE:
PATRIOTS OR SCOUNDRELS?

Robert Sauvé

THE QUÉBÉCOIS ÉLITE: PATRIOTS OR SCOUNDRELS?

Copyright © Robert Sauvé, 1998
PO Box 20277
390 Rideau Street
Ottawa, Ontario, Canada
K1N 1A3

Second Printing 1999

Published by CanPub Information Technologies Inc.
Ottawa, Ontario, Canada
http://www.canpub.com

Printed and bound in Canada, 1999
Doculink International
Ottawa, Ontario, Canada

Jacket design and other illustrations by Richard Sauvé

Since the historical data used in this book were obtained from reputable sources, they are assumed to be accurate. The author intended that his conclusions flow logically from these data.

Canadian Cataloguing in Publication Data

Sauvé, Robert, 1934-
    The Québécois élite: patriots or scoundrels?

Includes bibliographical references and index
ISBN 1-894275-00-4

    1. Quebec (Province)--Economic conditions. 2. Quebec (Province)-- Social conditions. 3. Power (Social sciences)-- Quebec (Province). 4. Quebec (Province)--History--Autonomy and independence movements. 5. Quebec (Province)--Politics and government. I. Title.

FC2920.N38S38 1998   971.4   C98-900734-0
F1053.2.S276 1998

In this book I salute those discriminating individuals who not only can distinguish between politeness and political correctness but who also see the social benefit of promoting the first and discouraging the second. Among these admirable people are a few who commented on my work as I struggled with it. Especially helpful were my friends who reminded me that it wasn't necessary to refer to the Québécois élite as rogues in every sentence, that I should simply allow the evidence to condemn them. I tried to follow their counsel. This does not mean, however, that I will not pay vigorous homage to the people of Québec when they finally get around to settling accounts with their self-serving leaders.

Many thanks then to my son Richard, my wife Lois, her brother Paul Gallagher, and fellow curmudgeon Noel Rutland. Thanks are also due to my daughter Susan Meyer who tried to ensure that the quality of my arguments satisfied the rigorous standards she sets for her graduate students. If I failed, the fault is mine, not theirs. And, there are, of course, special bouquets for family friends Cathy Brown and Betty Smith, and for senora Margaret Gallacher from the Argentine side of the family, whose comments helped smooth more than a few rough edges.

Moreover, Anne, Susan, Richard and Paul Michael, and their partners, Milton, Sonia and Melissa, will recognize here some of the passion that marked the occasional discussion at the family dinner table. And some day, my granddaughter Hannah Ruth will read this book and realize that there was more to her grampa than corny jokes and the tendency to say "eh!"

Robert Sauvé
Ottawa, Canada
June, 1998

Nothing over the centuries has more often been urged than the social rewards of hardship-- urged by those who will not have to suffer it.

John Kenneth Galbraith

PREFACE

Since this book deals with the *Québec Question,* it is necessarily political. But then, some wags claim that everything in Québec is political. In fact, the more irreverent insist that even *Québécois* scientific texts on sub-atomic particle physics probably have political slants. In any event, since this book deals primarily--but not exclusively--with the devastating economic consequences to ordinary *Québécois* of the misguided leadership of their élite, and with the concurrent enrichment of these élite at the expense of the people being impoverished, it addresses the *Question* from a unique perspective. That is, because the history of Québec is usually discussed in terms of political power struggles between Québec and Ottawa, between French and English, this book presents a relatively unorthodox perspective.

Since few people enjoy seeing their sins described in public, the *Québécois* élite are not likely to appreciate this book, or even read it. However, if they do sneak a peek, and predictably remain unconvinced of their knavery, I hope that they are at least annoyed by it. On the other hand, I would dearly love to have it read by ordinary *Québécois,* the people whose well-being has been sacrificed to satisfy the whims of their élite. Unfortunately, since the historical record suggests that the *Québécois* masses tend to take direction from their leaders, I will probably be disappointed. And this is unfortunate since the ultimate resolution of the *Québec Question* is in the hands of *Québécois.* Moreover, if they do not reject, or at least ignore their mischievous leaders, they will continue to be cheated in the future as they have been in the past ... whether they live in Canada or in their very own independent country.

Then there are Canadians of the non-*Québécois* persuasion. Whether they are potential participants in this national debate, or are simply interested spectators, I hope that they find this book informative. So also, of course, for interested foreigners. Indeed, since the conclusions derived here are based on evidence and not on opinion, this book will arm them all very well. On the other hand, if they are seeking emotional counter-punches to the xenophobia that characterizes political discourse in Québec, they should simply give up and not read any further. But remember, if we are unable to counter emotion and myths with the truth, we might as well surrender now and get used to living with the sorry consequences.

Now, let's meet a few of the players in this drama.

Quebecers	Residents of Québec. Not synonymous with the French word *Québécois.* The proper English translation of *Québécois* is *Québécois.*
Catholic Church	Religious institution that has traditionally enjoyed the official allegiance of about 99.9999 percent of *Québécois* and about a third of non-*Québécois* Quebecers. Generally called the Church.

Francophones	People of French mother tongue.
Anglophones	People of English mother tongue.
Allophones	People in Québec whose mother tongue is neither French nor English.
Canadiens	19th-century term for francophones in Québec. Displaced by the term *Québécois* in the 1960s.
French Canadians	Synonym for *Canadiens*.
Québécois	Francophone residents or former residents of Québec, most especially those claiming to be uncontaminated descendants of the original 17th-century French colonists; or
	Immigrants to Québec who have chosen French rather than English as their official public language; or
	Residents or former residents of Québec whose political allegiance is to Québec rather than to Canada. Many of them enjoy giving occasional voice to the racist hymn "*Le Québec aux Québécois.*"
	Forms an oxymoron when combined with the prefix anglophone.
Nationalists	Those individuals, usually allied in political groups, who advocate independence or autonomy for their nation. Often an ethnic or language group that is sometimes given to disparaging fellow citizens in other ethnic groups.
Separatists	Those *Québécois* nationalists who strive to have Québec secede from Canada to form an independent state. Known also as secessionists.
Federalists	Synonym for Canadians who accept the legitimacy of the government of Canada in Ottawa. Includes many *Québécois* and most Québec anglophones and allophones.
Elite	Those who exercise the major share of authority and influence in the community.

Québécois Élite   Until about 1960, the Catholic clergy and those public officials who took their social and political direction from the Church. After 1960, secular nationalists, provincial politicians and their fellow travellers.

The People   The masses. Sometimes affectionately called the great unwashed.

Patriots   Those individuals who love, support and defend their country and its interests with great devotion. Particularly vociferous when their country is under pressure from an external source. Not to be confused with nationalists.

Scoundrels   Disreputable people who are sometimes called cads, knaves, villains or rogues. They prey upon the credulous by fraud, and tend to wrap themselves in the flag to conceal their knavery.

TABLE OF CONTENTS

STATISTICAL TABLES

Statistical Tables

1

INTRODUCTION

Since about 1960, political discourse in Canada has been overwhelmed by secession-related demands from Québec. This has created a national social climate that is both politically and economically disruptive to all Canadians. Crowning this discourse were two gut-wrenching referenda in Québec, the first in 1980, the second in 1995. Sponsored by the Québec government of the day, both sought the secession of that province from Canada; both were defeated. But who knows how many more referenda we will have to endure before:

.   The secessionists finally win one and Québec secedes; or

.. Ordinary *Québécois* finally tire of this economically disruptive secessionist rhetoric and begin to ignore it, turning their attention instead to other imperatives, such as putting bread on the table; or

... Canadians outside of Québec become fed up with these secessionists and seek to partition Québec into Canadian territory and the foreign country these 'patriots' seek.

But, that is the political side of the *Québec Question*, not the side of particular interest to me ... at the outset. Although I will not ignore the purely political, I will concentrate first on the economic plight of the people.

Thus, this book is not a call for love and understanding to solve Canada's national unity problems; nor is it a *touchy-feely* entreaty that abhors the judgemental. It is, instead, a finger-pointing polemic, an analysis of a controversial subject, where I take sides. For example, although in some families, uncle Jimbo's sour disposition is usually blamed on *his perpetual cold*, I will ascribe it instead to his perpetual addiction to whisky. You may detect a small measure of disdain in this not-so-subtle reference to the world's bleeding hearts. To be frank, I seldom miss an opportunity to dump on those who prefer to bleat rather than think. Seems to me that, if they fell into a pit of hungry alligators, they would not try to extricate themselves for fear of hurting the feelings of the ravenous beasts that were about to devour them. But I digress.

I will argue here that ordinary *Québécois* have been betrayed by those unique beings I call the *Québécois* élite. By élite I do not necessarily mean those who were to the manor born, or those whose wealth occasionally elicits envy, or even those whose skills place them at the summits of their professions. Those are the classical elites who belong to a social class common to all societies. Although not necessarily excluding them, I mean instead something else, something quite special: Those whose influence on the conduct of political, social and economic life in Québec was and remains strategic; those who, by aggressive pursuit of their own narrow interests, ruined the economic prospects of the people as they simultaneously enriched themselves.

This élite group includes the Church and its heirs among modern nationalists, provincial politicians and those attached to them in the public and parapublic sectors. Most of all, it includes the Montréal daily newspaper *Le Devoir*. On the periphery are those who have benefitted financially from various public policies implemented in Québec by these élite since 1960. For instance, although there is no evidence to suggest that the masses benefitted financially from Québec's language laws, it is clear that *Québécois* executives in the private sector did fairly well as a result.

And the people of Québec, how have they reacted to all this? What will they do in the future to protect themselves from their own leaders? If history is any guide, they will continue to protect themselves by reacting to the intolerable in well practiced ways. In the short term, some may try to emigrate, following the example of many before them; others will shrug their shoulders, hunker down and hope for better days. In the longer term, they might even deal with the current élite in the same way they eventually dealt with the Church: By ignoring them.

Be advised that this book will not be a lazy read. Since it is a polemic, I have two options. The first is simply to offer my opinions and then exhort the reader to accept them and reject contrary views. But, in a world of conflicting expert opinion, this approach is obviously untenable. This does not mean, however, that I will not occasionally quote expert sources to make a particular point. For instance, who better to quote than a bishop to suggest that the Church preferred an obedient flock to the discriminating variety. In the few cases where I quote unidentified sources, or where I resort to opinion, I submit myself to the judgement of the reader. The second option, the one favoured in this study, assumes that, if my arguments are fair minded and convincing, informed readers will accept them, contrary ideologies and political correctness notwithstanding. However, if they are weak, the same readers will reject them.

The second option obviously puts pressure on the reader, pressure to deal with and not avoid complex analyses, pressure to evaluate and not ignore evidence and argument that challenge sacred cows, pressure not to wallow in but to rise above the constraints of myth, legend and prejudice. As I said, not a lazy read. But the subject is worth the effort: I am offering here a perspective on Québec generally ignored by journalists and academics.

Finally, two technical points. First, for those who are more interested in my conclusions than in how I derived them, there are special summaries at the end of each chapter starting in Chapter 3. Second, I will develop my thesis much as a prosecutor develops a case in court: I will begin by setting out an indictment; then I will offer evidence to support it. It will then be up to readers to evaluate the evidence and decide whether the *Québécois* élite are indeed patriots or scoundrels.

Now into the fray.

2

INDICTMENT

"*Do as I say, not as I do!*" is a well known admonition that many of us heard as children from tobacco-addicted parents; they commanded us to be guided by their wise advice, not by their bad habits. Even though this proved, in retrospect, to have been good counsel, it seemed pretty suspect at the time. Consequently, our parents usually failed because we were sure that they were only trying to keep us from one more of life's great pleasures. There have been interesting variations on this theme involving some TV evangelists who, when caught with their pants down, confessed their sins, begged for forgiveness and urged their followers to keep the faith. Though severely wounded, some of the faithful forgave the sinners and kept the faith, others did not.

Closer to home, the historical record will show that the transgressions of the *Québécois* élite are even more egregious. Although the original clerical élite have been rejected, the current secular élite still enjoy the support of the people. Hence, it remains to be seen how they will be treated when they are eventually found out ... as they certainly will be.

The *Québécois* élite have traditionally called upon the people of Québec to make sacrifices to protect their francophone and Catholic culture which was allegedly at risk in anglophone and Protestant North America. First among these élite was the hierarchy of the Catholic Church: They urged the faithful to reject modernity by remaining isolated in the countryside. Better, apparently, to be Catholic, French, uneducated and poor on the farm than risk losing one's faith and language by going to school or by working in the wicked cities. It was in Québec's cities that the more educated Protestant English were developing a modern economy ... and enriching themselves in the process.

The Church was followed by Québec's secular nationalists who successfully implemented political and cultural policies that were and remain inimical to the economic interests of the people. That is, they subordinated the people's need for bread and butter to élite preferences for culture, language and secessionist politics. However, the average *Québécois* has always been more interested in bread and butter than in language, religion and political manoeuvring. Nevertheless, modern secular nationalists have succeeded in getting the various governments of Québec to pursue the interests of the élite at the expense of those of the people. To accomplish this, they followed the same ignoble path trod earlier by the Church. That is, they:

1.   Maintained control of, or at least a strong influence over, public policy;

2.   Kept the people under-educated and misinformed;

3.   Implemented public policies whose effect was to discourage job-creating business investment;

4.   Justified it all by associating it with ethnocentric Québec nationalism.

The members of this élite thus differ from traditional elites who generally see little need to ennoble their greed by cloaking it in the flag. But, the *Québécois* élite are not only greedy, they are duplicitous: While they preached solidarity with the people, they in fact betrayed them. They accomplished this by dominating the public and parapublic sectors where they not only implemented policies that impoverished the people, but where they also paid themselves the highest wages in Canada, wages paid by the taxes of the people they were impoverishing!

Included in this august group are the members of *l'Assemblée nationale du Québec*, politicians who awarded themselves the highest salaries paid to provincial politicians in Canada: 30 percent higher than their opposite numbers in neighbouring and more prosperous Ontario. But, their sense of generosity and fair play ran out when they set welfare benefits for disabled persons 29 percent behind Ontario. To paraphrase George Orwell in <u>Animal Farm</u>, some *Québécois* are clearly more equal than others. Moreover, workers in the Québec public and parapublic sectors benefit from taxpayer-paid salaries that are equal to or greater than those in Ontario. To make matters worse, there are about 30 percent more people on the public payroll in Québec than in Ontario ... and Québec is about 35 percent smaller than Ontario.

And what about the average *Québécois* who is unable to get his nose into the public trough, the guy who has to make a living in the competitive jungle called the private sector? Average family income from employment was 11 percent lower in Québec than in Ontario in 1960 and 20 percent lower in 1991. I will show that élite-driven public policies in Québec:

1.   Produced in Québec the highest rate of poverty in Canada;

2.   Produced one of the highest rates of illiteracy in Canada;

3.   Produced one of the least educated workforces in Canada;

4.   Produced a social environment that kept per capita job-creating business investment 15 percent below Ontario; as a result, unemployment rates are generally half-again as high in Québec as in Ontario;

5.   Saddled *Québécois* with the highest taxes and public debt in Canada.

But what about the fabled Quiet Revolution, you ask? Not only was it supposed to make *Québécois* masters in their own house, it was also intended to improve the economic lot of all *Québécois*. Indeed, some have done rather well by it: For instance, the news media are awash with stories of *Québécois* businessmen who have forged to the summit of, it is claimed, brilliantly successful Québec enterprises. Unfortunately, the same success has not been visited upon the people who toil for wages within those companies ... if they can find work at all.

Moreover, during this same period, while the *Québécois* élite built and made good use of the largest private school system in Canada, the average *Québécois* had to put up with what is demonstrably one of the country's least effective public systems. As a result, the levels of literacy and education in Québec are among the worst in Canada. Note that education, one of the most important keys to economic success, is under the constitutional control of provincial governments. In summary, as a result of delinquent behaviour by this élite during the first three decades of the Quiet Revolution, the typical *Québécois* family saw its economic position deteriorate relative to that of both Ontarians and anglophone Quebecers. Some revolution!

However, despite this sorry record in the social and economic fields, the *Québécois* élite succeeded magnificently in having the people of Québec advance steadily toward the political objective of this élite: The secession of Québec from Canada. That this secession would not improve the lot of the people seemed not to concern anyone. Moreover, to add insult to injury, these secession-related political policies will likely cause Québec to be partitioned: Those areas with secessionist majorities will be split from Québec to form the independent state of Laurentia(?). And, based on 1995 Referendum results, the poorest and least educated *Québécois* will find themselves living in Laurentia while the most affluent and best educated will remain in the residual Canadian province of Québec. Note that most secessionist leaders currently live in the Montreal area ... which will likely remain in Canada after partition. And, anyone who thinks that these élite individuals will do the honourable thing by emigrating from cosmopolitan Montréal to, say, hinterland Chicoutimi in Laurentia, is dreaming. Thus, the circle will be complete: After enriching themselves and impoverishing the people, and after selling the people a political mirage, the *Québécois* élite will abandon the masses to fend for themselves in Laurentia as the élite take comfortable refuge in Canada.

Table 2-1: Québec Compared to Ontario

Politicians' Salaries	30	%	Greater
Other Élite Salaries	15	%	Greater
Size of Public Service	30	%	Greater
Average Family Income	20	%	Lower
Welfare Benefits	29	%	Lower
Investment	15	%	Lower
Poverty Level	32	%	Greater
Tax Burden	22	%	Greater
Provincial Spending	18	%	Greater
Provincial Debt	23	%	Greater
Rate of Illiteracy	25	%	Greater
Less than grade 9	30	%	More
University graduates	21	%	Fewer

Élite-initiated ethnic cleansing in Québec.

The policies and leadership of the *Québécois* élite will likely result in the partition of Québec into the independent state of Laurentia and the residual Canadian province of Québec. The leaders of this élite will likely choose to remain in Québec, Canada, as they abandon their supporters to fend for themselves, poverty stricken and under-educated, in Laurentia. The scoundrels will be warm and cosy on the inside as their victims, fellow *Québécois*, suffer the traditional fate of suckers on the outside.

P.T. Barnum would have been proud of the *Québécois* élite: They treated, and continue to treat their own kin as suckers and hence deserve to be called scoundrels and dealt with accordingly.

And, to complement their record in the social and economic arenas, the current *Québécois* élite have disgraced themselves in politics as well. First, to neutralize the inconvenient non-secessionist voting tendencies of Québec's anglophones and allophones, they resorted to policies whose effect was to 'encourage' these recalcitrants to leave Québec. In other words, they resorted to ethnic cleansing ... and they appear to be succeeding. Second, to maximize the vote favouring secession, they set ambiguous referendum questions in 1980 and 1995 that clearly misled the voters into voting against their best interests. And, third, since the first two items were not entirely successful, they attempted to provide razor-thin winning margins to the secessionist side by cheating in both referenda: Their polling agents, the majority at every poll, simply rejected the valid votes of thousands of people who dared to vote against secession! The *Québécois* élite are obviously not very honourable.

That is the substance of the indictment.

Members of the jury, you are now invited to evaluate the evidence and argument advanced in the following chapters and decide if they support the indictment. I will argue that, even though they love to wrap themselves in the flag of Québec, the record proves conclusively that the *Québécois* élite are classical scoundrels. However, before you make up your minds, I invite you to question those being skewered in this book. But, be prepared for tough going: When under attack, they usually resort to the impregnable offended-virgin defense.

Thus, if you wish to question them on the merits of the evidence and arguments advanced here, be prepared for cries of humiliated rage. For example, sensible adults of good will should be able to advance an argument, any argument, if not to its logical conclusion, then at least to its next stage. To do this, however, both sides must be willing to admit the obvious and concede the arguments won by the other side. But this is not always possible with this lot. For example, if you try to open a discussion on the fact that the rate of illiteracy among *Québécois* is about the highest in Canada, wear heavy armour and be prepared to take cover!

Although an orthodox approach would be to first ascertain the accuracy of such a statement (it is accurate), and then to address the substance of the issue, this discussion would likely not even get off the ground: The statement would probably be described as ridiculous and dismissed out of hand; the claimant would then be accused of making racist allegations that humiliated all *Québécois*! And, if you think that I am merely resorting to hyperbole to make a point, think again. Better still, ask Esther Delisle.

Delisle is the author of <u>The Traitor and the Jew</u>, a well documented treatise on ιe virulent antisemitism of the fascist right in Québec in the 1930s. pecifically, she fingered four nationalist icons: The Reverend Lionel Groulx, ιe daily newspaper *Le Devoir*, and two nationalist groups that have since isappeared mercifully into the mists of time. Guess how *Québécois* academics nd journalists reacted to <u>Traitor</u> after its publication in 1993?

They either ignored it or savaged it because--get ready--Delisle ιad humiliated all *Québécois*! She was condemned for having resurrected ιomething disagreeable from the past that, they said, had no echo in modern Juébec (Who do they think is being targeted when modern nationalists chant the ιacist hymn *"Le Québec aux Québécois"?* Sounds like a related echo to me!) ?urthermore, added her critics, why was she pointing a finger at Québec when ιntisemitism was also common in English Canada at that time. Thus, they Iaimed, Delisle should have recognized that this quartet, especially Groulx, was ιnly reflecting the ideology and public sentiment of the 1930s. Whether Groulx ιnd company were following or leading the fascist parade is of course Iebateable: Delisle argued that they were leading.

On the other hand, <u>Traitor</u> was well received in English Canada. So also was <u>None is Too Many</u> which was published in 1982. Irving Abella and Harold Troper, the authors of <u>None</u>, cited chapter and verse to argue ιhat the government of Canada had acted abominably in the 1930s when it ·efused asylum to Jews fleeing Nazi Germany. As a result, those desperate ·efugees had to return to Europe where many eventually perished in Hitler's Ieath camps. That was an abomination, something that should have shamed us ιhen, but did not, and which should shame us now, and does. And that was ιrecisely how journalists and academics in English Canada reacted to the ιublication of <u>None</u>. Moreover, it became a best-seller. On the other hand, I ιm willing to bet the mortgage that <u>Traitor</u> is relatively unknown in Québec, ιxcept among those whose interests were best served by dumping on it.

Consequently, unless you are prepared to deal with the ιrrational, you might wish to avoid extended discussions with this type of *Québécois*: Facts cannot dislodge those who occupy the self-defined moral high-ground defending positions that make them impervious to the liberating effects ιf inconvenient facts! Furthermore, *Québécois* nationalists have been known to *invent* facts: I describe a few in this book. So, if you find yourselves debating with them, be prepared for the odd whopper ... and lots of flack!

Finally, although this polemic will help you better understand ιhe villainy of the *Québécois* élite, you will not be able to take direct corrective ιction ... unless you live in Québec. However, you can, and should, reject :ategorically the notion that *Québécois* have been victimized by anyone but their ιwn leaders. On the other hand, if you live in Québec, you can act more directly: The final arbiters in this matter are *Québécois* who will, some day soon, I pray, deal harshly with their leaders. Since less egregious chicanery has ιrovoked bloody revolutions elsewhere in the past, a vigourous condemnation ιf these scoundrels would be quite appropriate.

3

ANALYTICAL AIDS

Overview

Because the arguments advanced here are controversial, they must be supported by analyses that can pass muster with competent, fair-minded critics. My approach is not only based on sound principles, it uses the best data available in conjunction with appropriate analytical techniques. Thus, if someone objects to the conclusions that derive from this objective approach, offering no justification except subjective opinion, I would argue that the objective is more reliable than the subjective, no matter how exalted the objector may be.

Now, let us consider a few principles, the nature of some of the data that will be presented, and an analytical tool that will be used to help interpret these data. This is meant not only to address the valid concerns of fair-minded readers, but also to preempt those who bray: "*Liars figure and figures lie!*" At the risk of being blunt, let me set the record straight: Figures do not lie, liars lie, and only the analytically illiterate say silly things like "*Liars figure and figures lie!*" That said, let me acknowledge that this book will be more interesting to those able to distinguish between chop suey and chopped liver.

Principles and Other Guidelines

Among the principles and guidelines that figure in this study are the following:

1.   To resolve an issue, you must face up to it, even though avoiding it may be convenient. Similarly, to misrepresent an issue is contemptible. For example, to claim that the flight of Jews from Germany in the 1930s had nothing to do with antisemitism is preposterous.

2.   Similarly, if the action producing an allegedly unintended consequence is repeated, the consequence of the action must have been intended by its proponents. For example, pogroms that terrorized Jews in 19th-century Tsarist Russia were invariably followed by increased Jewish emigration. Since these pogroms had the support of the authorities, one should conclude that they approved the expulsion of these Jews.

3.   If you repeat an unchallenged whopper often enough, it stands a good chance of eventually being accepted as true. Note Herr Goebbels.

4.   People's actions over time are consistent with their true intentions. For example, although Québec is nominally Catholic, today's near empty Churches suggest that *Québécois* are more secular than religious.

5.   Reliable evidence and logical argument beat ideology, feelings and

error every time. For example, those who claim that the earth is flat must be in error since there is evidence to prove that it is not flat.

6.   To know Québec, you must understand its economy. And to do this, you must muck around in the numbers. The alternative is to place your faith in those who 'know better' and then be guided by them. To those who choose to avoid getting their hands dirty, I say, "*Bonne chance!*"

7.   To understand any economy, you must be able to discriminate between fact and fiction, and know how to follow an argument. You should also be ready to ask questions: Children do it all the time, and look at how omnipotent they become as teenagers!

8.   Everything is relative in economics. Hence, it would be silly to complain that Québec's welfare recipients in 1995 received twice as much as rookie engineers were paid in 1958: I bought a fine new Ford in 1958 for $2,000, about one-tenth what it would have cost in 1995! It would be equally silly to compare average incomes in Bangladesh and Canada. But, since Québec and Ontario have relatively similar economies, comparing them makes sense.

        Similarly, it is more significant that Québec's poverty rate went from Canada's second worst in 1961 to its worst in 1991 than that the Québec rate improved absolutely. In other words, it did not improve enough. For example, there is no point in fielding an army that has progressed from spears to bows and arrows when the enemy already has machine guns.

        Since many conclusions in this book derive from this principle, those who do not accept it should not waste their time reading any further.

Statistics and the Economy

Much of the data I shall offer as evidence are statistics supplied by, or derived from, reputable sources such as Statistics Canada (StatCan). Before plunging into this sea of evidence, it might be helpful to get a brief overview of one of the main statistical elements used in this polemic, the Gross Domestic Product or GDP, the measure that describes the size and composition of the economy. In Table 3-1 are listed the main components of Canada's Income-Based GDP which represents the income from all the goods and services produced in the economy. Its mirror image is the Expenditure-Based GDP.

        The absolute value of Canada's GDP in 1990 was about $670 billion. However, since the objective of the economy is to provide for the people in it, the per capita value of $24,128 is more relevant. Moreover, note that per capita income for "Farms" is determined by taking the total absolute

Table 3-1: GDP Income-Based 1990	
	$ Per Capita
Salaries	13,559
Small Businesses	1,306
Farms	120
Capital Allowances	2,731
Indirect Taxes	2,703
Interest	2,085
Corporate Profits	1,624
Total GDP	24,128
Source: StatCan 13-213 p. 2, 1986/90	

value of money earned by all farmers in Canada in 1990 ($3.3 billion) and dividing it by the population of Canada. The resulting per capita value obviously does not mean that each person living on a Canadian farm earned an average of $120. It is simply a convenient way of showing the relative importance of farming to the whole economy. Thus, when you look at Table 3-1, you would have to conclude that the small business sector was about eleven-times as important to the economy as farming.

Another valuable use of these statistics is in inter-provincial comparisons. For instance, when you compare Saskatchewan's 1990 per capita farm income of $1,143 to Newfoundland's $24, you would conclude that, where Saskatchewan's is a farming economy, Newfoundland's is not. Moreover, to determine income from employment of all kinds, we simply add together three of these values: Salaries ($13,559), Business Income ($1,306) and Farm Income ($120). That is, income from employment in Canada in 1990 was $14,985 per capita of which 90 percent came from salaries, 9 percent from small businesses and 1 percent from farming. Stated another way, about 62 percent of the GDP was paid to employed people for their work (14,985 of 24,128). Note that these figures only include income from employment, not from social benefits such as welfare and unemployment insurance. Confirming the supremacy of the individual in the Canadian economy is the fact that personal expenditures account for 59 percent of the Expense-Based GDP (14,212 of 24,128 in Table 3-2).

Conclusion? A healthy economy requires jobs, especially well paid jobs. And, jobs are created as a result of someone investing in something that requires workers ... which brings us to the difference between public and private sector investments.

Table 3-2: GDP Exp.-Based 1990	
	$ Per Capita
Personal Exp.	14,212
Govt Current Exp.	4,682
Business Investment	4,396
Govt Investment	614
Net Exports	224
Total Provincial GDP	24,128
Source: StatCan 13-213 p. 2, 1986-90	

Business investment accounted for 88 percent of all investment in Canada in 1990 (4,396 divided by the sum of 4,396 and 614 in Table 3-2). The reason why government investment makes up such a small proportion of total investment is not mysterious: As will be shown later, where $1 million of business investment creates, say, ten jobs, the equivalent government investment would do well to create one. Therefore, if you want to create jobs, you obviously need to encourage the private sector to invest. And, if you wonder what would happen to an economy where government investment is dominant, consider the now efunct Soviet Union where, between about 1917 and 1990, they relied xclusively on government investment. There they struggled valiantly to make :ate capitalism work, resorting to the totalitarian whip to help it along, before ankruptcy forced them to turn to private investors and international charity to ail them out. In this study, I will show that low business investment is one of 1e two main causes of poor employment income in Québec; the other is an nder-educated workforce. And, I will demonstrate that the *Québécois* élite are :sponsible for both deficiencies.

Although complex analyses are sometimes required to convert ome statistics into useful information, relatively simple groupings and ratios ke those cited above are often quite adequate. Still, the purpose of either imple or complex analyses is the same: To maximize the relevance of objective ·vidence and minimize that of subjective opinion.

:anada's Economy: Its Structure

\t the risk of revealing the obvious, let me state an important economic maxim: Vorkers are not all equal. For instance, automotive industry workers earn more han farm workers because assembling cars tends to be more profitable than rowing hay. Similarly, electricians working in an automotive plant earn more han their cousins who sell the same services to farmers. Consequently, salaries vill consume a greater share of the sales dollar in the automotive industry than n the farm. To extend the analogy, an economy dominated by the automotive ndustry will tend to be more prosperous than one dominated by farming. Remember this when we compare the Ontario and Québec economies.

Now, to move from the theoretical to the concrete, consider Table 3-3 where the provinces are ranked by population. Note that, Québec, the second most populous province, ranks fourth in per capita GDP. Although Employment Income here means the same as it did earlier, GDP is defined somewhat differently. Where the Income-Based GDP described the economy in terms of the income it generated for the people living in it, the GDP at Factor Cost describes the economy in terms of the value of goods and services it

Table 3-3: Canada 1990	GDP		Employment Income	
	$/Capita	Rank	$/Capita	% GDP
Ontario	23,447	2	17,386	74
Québec	19,163	4	13,682	71
BC	21,012	3	14,843	71
Alberta	26,006	1	15,063	58
Manitoba	18,830	6	12,687	67
Saskatchewan	19,151	5	11,023	58
Nova Scotia	16,114	7	12,161	76
NB	15,663	8	11,035	71
NFLD	13,385	10	9,689	72
PEI	14,744	9	10,427	71
Canada	21,331		14,985	70

Source: StatCan 11-210, T 6; 15-203, T1.

produces. Something like describing a cake by its baking ingredients instead o[its chemical structure. Same cake either way.

It should be noted that, although per capita GDP in industria[Québec was just marginally greater than that in agricultural Saskatchewan, pe[capita Employment Income was 24.1 percent higher in Québec. Sinc[Employment Income should be reasonabl[correlated with GDP, this apparent anomaly doe[not mean that inter-provincial GDP comparisons ar[irrelevant, it simply underlines the obvious: A[noted earlier, workers fare better in industrial tha[in agricultural economies. Hence, Québec shoul[normally only be compared with provinces having structurally similar economies. Thus, the nearly equal shares of GDP in the manufacturing sector (Table 3-4) make Québec and Ontario structurally similar to one another. Hence, it is legitimate to ask why per capita GDP was 18.3 percent lower in Québec than in Ontario in 1990, and why the related per capita employment income was 21.3 percent lower. These are the two main questions I address in this book.

Table 3-4: Manufacturing	
Manufacturing GDP as Percent of Total GDP	
Ontario	22
Québec	21
BC	13
Alberta	9
Manitoba	13
Saskatchewan	6
Nova Scotia	10
New Brunswick	14
NFLD	9
PEI	7
Source: StatCan 15-203	

Regression Analysis

Now that you have had a taste of the statistical data that lie ahead, let me describe the analytical technique to be used in the analysis of the more complex data. It is called regression analysis and is used to determine the degree of correlation between two or more items when the relationship between them is difficult to determine. Consider, for example, the correlation between lung cancer and the smoking of cigarettes. Since we know that some non-smokers also contract lung cancer, we know that there cannot be a perfect correlation between them. However, since scientists have found a reasonable statistical correlation between the incidence of lung cancer and the smoking of cigarettes, we can safely conclude that our chances of contracting lung cancer are greater if we smoke cigarettes than if we do not.

Regression analysis is a powerful analytical tool. Its correlation index (R^2) is an objective reference that can be very useful as we attempt to separate the wheat from the chaff in complex social studies such as this one. For example, I will use this technique to help answer questions such as: How well correlated are employment income and education? With the help of regression analysis, I will demonstrate that public investment in education was the best way to improve the financial lot of the average *Québécois*. Except for the particularly obtuse, of course, this conclusion will astonish no one.

Then when the historical record shows that Québec's

educational system has been and remains underfunded and inadequate, I will first assume that those responsible for the allocation of scarce public resources must have invested instead in more important areas. But, when the record shows that those areas of *higher* priority in fact advanced the interests of the élite rather than those of the people, I will conclude that the people have been cheated. To defend this type of conclusion before the predictable wrath of Québec's offended virgins, one needs to be properly armed with objective analytical measures.

The value of the correlation index (R2) can vary between zero (no correlation) and 1.0 (perfect correlation). For instance, a value of R2 equal to 0.80 means that the items in question are 80 percent correlated. In this study, I will be suspicious of correlations below 0.60. Those in need of more information on regression analysis should refer to Appendix I.

Correlations: The Economy, Investment and Education

I argue that the economy is driven, *inter alia*, by the level of investment in it as well as by the ability of workers to use that investment. For example, if you own a truck but have no driver for it, your truck is useless. A healthy economy clearly needs the proper investment mix complemented by competent workers.

If we ignore workforce competence for the moment, and test for the correlation between GDP and government investment across all provinces in Table 3-5, we find that the correlation index (R2) is almost zero. That is, the variation in inter-provincial GDP is hardly explained at all by the variation in government investment between provinces. On the other hand, when we test for the correlation between GDP and business investment, the value of R2 rises to an impressive 0.83. That is, the variation in business investment between provinces explains about 83 percent of the variation in interprovincial GDP. What this means is that, while the impact on the economy of public sector investment is insignificant, that of the private sector is considerable.

When we add to private sector investment the effect of education, defined here as the share of the population over age 25 with some post-secondary education, we find a minuscule improvement in correlation as R2 rises from 0.83 to 0.84. On the other hand, when the effect of education is

Table 3-5:   Investment and Education, 1986-1990

	Annual Investment $ Per Capita		% of Population Over Age 25 with:	
	Gov't	Business	Post Sec. Education	Univ Deg
Alberta	820	6,303	37	14
BC	664	5,161	38	13
Sask	644	4,567	32	10
Ontario	564	4,445	32	15
Québec	538	3,867	26	12
Manitoba	553	3,225	31	12
NScotia	688	3,188	33	12
NB	659	3,066	29	9
NFLD	657	2,845	30	8
PEI	753	2,601	34	9
Canada	614	4,396	32	13

Source: StatCan 93-328, 13213, T2.

defined as those with university degrees, R2 rises dramatically to a near perfect 0.95. Thus, we can conclude that healthy modern economies require very well educated workers capable of using a high level of business investment.

And what does this type of analysis reveal about Québec? Its GDP lagged 18 percent behind Ontario's in 1990. In the period 1986-90, Québec lagged behind Ontario by 13 percent in business investment and by 21 percent in university graduates. Revealing enough?

And, what about the next correlation, the one between income and GDP? About 76 percent of the inter-provincial variations in overall employment income in 1990 were explained by related variations in the overall provincial GDP. Although this correlation (R2 = 0.76) is not bad, it is not that good either. But then again, a less than optimal correlation is not surprising: Comparing industrial Québec and Ontario to agricultural Saskatchewan or aquacultural Newfoundland is like comparing apples with oranges. Can the correlation be improved by digging a bit below the surface to eliminate the apples/oranges distortion? That is, what is the correlation between overall employment income and the GDP in any one segment of the economy? Between overall employment income and farming, for instance? It depends of course: If farms accounted for, say, 90 percent of the GDP in an economy, the average wage would obviously resemble the relatively low wages paid to farm workers; the reverse would obtain if the higher wage automotive industry was dominant.

Turning this example on its head, if we see a low correlation between overall employment income and the GDP in any particular sector of the economy, we can conclude that that sector is relatively unimportant to the overall performance of the economy. By the same token, if we see a high correlation, we can conclude that that sector is very important.

Now, let's dig a little.

In Table 3-6, the Canadian economy is viewed as three independent groups. Within each, the component sectors are listed in order of the size of their per capita GDPs. The first group splits the economy into private and public sectors; the second into goods and services; the third into nine other sectors.

In the first group, there is a dreadful correlation (R2 is 0.06) between inter-provincial variations in per capita employment income and variations in public sector GDP: Only six percent of the variations in employment income are explained by variations in public sector activity. There is, on the other hand, a much better correlation with the private sector: 75 percent of the variation in per capita employment income is explained by variations in private sector GDP. In other words, the private sector is about twelve-times as important as the public sector. In 1990, Québec's per capita private sector GDP lagged behind Ontario's by 21 percent. Advantage Ontario.

In the second group, we see a strong correlation (R2 = 0.86) between employment income and economic activity in the services sector, a

| Table 3-6: | The Québec/Ontario Economies, 1990 | | |

| R2 = | Correlation of Overall National Employment Income with GDP in each Economic Sector | | |

	R2	Qué. GDP Compared To Ontario	
Private Sector	0.75	-21.0	%
Public Sector	0.06	- 5.4	%
All Services	0.86	-19.5	%
All Goods	0.54	-15.9	%
Services - Private Sector	0.82	-27.5	%
Manufacturing	0.72	-23.5	%
Services - Public Sector	0.27	- 7.2	%
Wholesale/Retail Trade	0.97	-22.2	%
Construction	0.50	- 7.6	%
Communications/Utilities	0.31	0.2	%
Transportation	0.28	-11.2	%
Natural Resources	0.06	-25.0	%
Farming/Fishing	0.15	13.3	%
All Sectors	0.76	-18.3	%

Source: StatCan 15-203, 1984-93

relatively poor correlation ($R^2 = 0.54$) with the production of goods. That is, the provision of accounting services, for example, is more important to the overall economy than the manufacture of widgets. Since Québec lagged significantly behind Ontario in both sectors, it is still advantage Ontario.

Then, when we split the services sector into its private and public sub-sectors, we see that R^2 is 0.27 in the public sub-sector, 0.82 in the private sub-sector. Thus, workers are much better off in service economies dominated by the private sector. In 1990, Québec's private sector services sector lagged 27.5 percent behind Ontario's. Advantage Ontario.

Moreover, it would appear that the best economy for workers is one dominated by Private Sector Services and Manufacturing because the combined correlation between overall employment income and the combined GDP of these two sectors is very high ($R^2 = 0.95$). In 1990, the combined per capita GDP of these two sectors in Québec ran 26 percent behind Ontario. Advantage Ontario.

Finally, when we consider the other sub-sectors in Table 3-6, Québec's general economic malaise becomes more evident. If we look at this list through the eyes of the average worker, we are looking for two things: A reasonably high value of R^2 in sectors of reasonable size. Thus, we can conclude from this third group that, apart from the relatively insignificant fifth and eighth-place sub-sectors (Communications-Utilities and Farming-Fishing), Québec's economy lagged substantially behind Ontario's in every area. Game, set and match to Ontario.

Summary

The guiding principles followed in this study are of the common sense variety, and hence should find favour among fair-minded readers. For instance, I hold that reliable evidence and logical argument beat emotion every time. Further, central to my case is the notion that, since the economies of Québec and Ontario are structurally similar, they are thus comparable. Moreover, Québec's relative economic performance is more significant than its absolute performance. For example, it is more significant that Québec's poverty rate went from Canada's second worst in 1960 to its worst in 1990, than that the rate improved at all. In other words, the rate did not improve enough.

Much of the evidence I shall offer is in the form of statistical data supplied by reputable sources such as Statistics Canada. I shall also enter into evidence calculations derived from those data. Moreover, since the purpose of an economy is to provide for people, I will use per capita rather than absolute values. For instance, it is more informative to describe Canada's economy as equal to about $24,000 per capita per year rather than $700 billion per year in absolute terms. It also permits us to ask questions such as: Why were per capita GDP and employment income so much lower in Québec than in Ontario?

As regards structure, about 62 percent of Canada's GDP was paid to people for the work they performed. About 90 percent of this employment income came from salaries, 9 percent from small businesses and 1 percent from farming. Moreover, job-creating business investment accounted for 88 percent of all investment in 1990, job-poor government investment for only 12 percent.

One of the main analytical tools used here is called Regression Analysis. It is a technique that is used to determine the degree of correlation between two or more items when the relationship between them is not only uncertain but difficult to determine. For example, we are all familiar with the correlation between lung cancer and the smoking of cigarettes: Our chances of contracting lung cancer are greater if we smoke cigarettes than if we do not.

Regression's correlation index (R2) can vary between zero (no statistical correlation) and 1.0 (perfect correlation). In this study, I will tend to be suspicious of correlations where the value of R2 falls below 0.60. When we use regression analysis to analyze real life, we obtain some very interesting information. For example:

1.   The correlation between GDP and government investment is close to zero; that between GDP and business investment is an impressive 0.83.

2.   Then, when we add the level of university education to the level of business investment, this correlation rises to a spectacular 0.95. As will be shown later, Québec lags significantly behind Ontario in business investment and the production of university graduates.

3.   The best economy for workers is one dominated by Private Sector Services and Manufacturing. Québec lags very badly behind Ontario in both areas.

4

BACKGROUND

Overview

Hugh MacLennan's great novel, <u>Two Solitudes</u>, was first published in 1945. It dealt with the social stress caused by the conflicting objectives, assumptions and prejudices in the late 19th and early 20th-centuries of Québec's two main ethnic groups, the English and the French. To put it another way, it dealt with the social stress between English Canadian Protestants and French Canadian Catholics, between *les anglais* and *les canadiens*. On the one hand, the largely urban English pursued objectives where commercial imperatives ruled the roost; on the other, the agricultural French tried to protect their religion, language and culture by isolating themselves in their rural parishes where the Church and xenophobia shielded them from the English. Better to be Catholic, French and poor than risk losing one's soul consorting with Jezebel. Or so said MacLennan's characters. The term *Two Solitudes* has since come to describe the cultural divide between the French and English in Canada.

But, however accurate MacLennan's description may have been, or still be, there have been, and still are, two other solitudes in Québec ... and they both speak French. On the one hand are the special *Québécois* élite who have generally attempted to increase their political power at the expense of anglophones within Québec and the federal government in Ottawa; on the other are so-called ordinary *Québécois* who, like the masses everywhere, have done their best to come to terms with their environments, to care for their families, to keep the wolf from the door. Fairly routine and apparently non-conflicting goals. But, as I will demonstrate shortly, pursuit of the élite's goals has in fact been detrimental to the interests of the people.

By special élite, I refer first to one institution, the Catholic Church, and second to a relatively heterogenous class of secular nationalists who have been bolstered by various hangers-on. These hangers-on are not unlike their relatives in other societies, people on the make who are driven by routine self-interest. Before I deal specifically with the sins of this élite, let me first provide a glimpse of the strategic influence they exercised over their fellow *Québécois* and how this influence differed from that of traditional elites.

Influence of the Québécois Élite

It has long been known that members of this special élite have exerted a compelling influence over their less fortunate kin, the great unwashed. They have done this by restricting the social, political and economic options made available to the people. Some insist that the relationship between this élite and the masses has been relatively coercive, like that between feudal lord and serfs. Although this judgement may seem harsh, few doubt that this particular *Québécois* élite has been and remains more influential than traditional elites.

In Ontario, for example, the political elite seem to be driven less by ideology than by the uncomplicated urge to exercise political power. They thus tend to deal with the electorate at a practical bread-and-butter level. To advance a constitutional issue, for instance, would likely bore voters in Ontario. (Not like Québec where babies are born with the ability to carry on complex constitutional discussions. Just kidding!). On the other hand, the economic elites in both Ontario and Québec appear to be motivated simply by uncomplicated greed. They, in effect, say to the people, "*Imitate us if you can, but we will not lose much sleep if you do not.*" Not so transparent are the special *Québécois* élite: Their avaricious self-interest is well camouflaged.

Moreover, the *Québécois* élite have traditionally urged their kin to make the financial sacrifices required to protect their common distinctive culture from the corrupting influence of modernity in general and anglophones in particular. That is, they preached collective action to protect and promote the common good. This is not unlike the leadership role taken by revolutionary and forward-looking elites in other lands and other times. When you contrast this apparently noble attitude with that of traditional, self-centred and socially disinterested elites, you are inclined to applaud one and dump on the other. But do not jump to hasty conclusions, something ignoble lurks beneath this Québec veneer, some of which is cloaked in the garments of the Church.

Let us now address two questions that might be perplexing to the reader. First, the *Québécois* élite seem to have made a fine living preaching a gospel, according to which Québec's unique culture must be protected. What culture are they trying to protect, and why should it, or need it be protected? Second, the influence of the élite described here suggests that *Québécois* are, to put it charitably, more than a mite gullible. If this is so, what accounts for this gullibility? *Québécois* culture and history may suggest an answer.

Québécois Culture

The definition of *Québécois* culture depends very much on one's perspective. At the sociological level, culture is "*the sum total of ways of living built up by a group of human beings and transmitted from one generation to another.*"[1] Moreover, since most modern societies tend to be driven by relatively common socio-economic imperatives, they similarly tend to possess some common cultural characteristics. Therefore, since Québec is a modern society, one must determine what unique items distinguish its culture from others' if one is to know what to protect. For instance, how is Québec's uniqueness to be distinguished from Newfoundland's?

Until about 1960, the answer was clear: Québec was distinct because it was massively Catholic and francophone, and was governed by its unique code of civil law. Since the civil law is unique to Québec and can only be amended by the sovereign Québec legislature, it obviously needs no protection. Moreover, since *Québécois* have largely abandoned the Church, the province's historic Catholicity is no longer an issue. This leaves the French language as the only item needing protection, assuming first, that it needs protection, and second, that the people want it protected.

And on this matter, let me not mince words: There is nothing in the historical record to suggest, first, that French needs protecting, or second, that the people want it protected. That is, since the francophone share of Québec's population has tended to increase, not decrease, over the past 125 years, how can one conclude that it logically needs protection? For instance, in 1901, about 80 percent of the population of Québec was francophone; in 1961 it was 81 percent; and, in 1991, about 83 percent. Looks like a non-menacing trend for francophones.

Moreover, the record also suggests that, when forced to choose, the people of Québec tend to opt for bread and butter over language. How else do we explain the fact that the original French settlers have almost as many descendants living today in the United States as in Québec? Who then is making the fuss over language? The *Québécois* élite, of course, the people whose objectives obviously differ from those of the man in the street!

And this brings us to the definition of culture that would probably find favour with the *Québécois élite*: "*An ethnic group is a group of people who share a common and distinctive culture.*" At first blush this seems fairly innocuous. After all, who would deny that, because *Québécois* share a common language, they must also share a common culture? Most reputable scholars would dispute this assumption since they know there is no necessary correlation between language and culture.

The Scots and Irish, for example, had to give up their native Gaelic and accept the language thrust upon them by the conquering English. Yet, they remain culturally Scottish or Irish, not English. On this there is no argument. Still, some might insist that Scottish culture, for instance, might have evolved in a different way had the English language not been imposed upon them. Perhaps, but I doubt it: If the Pacific Ocean could not prevent American culture from invading and thriving in Japan, how could anyone prevent equally compelling social and economic imperatives from crossing the border into Scotland from adjacent England, no matter what language was spoken by the Scots? In any event, the sloppy-of-tongue should beware: It is said that to claim that a Scot is culturally English is to insult him. Their cousins across the Irish Sea in Ireland are no less contemptuous of the English. In fact, the Irish like to say that, even though the English language was forced upon them, the Irish nevertheless perfected it. How else, they say, do you explain the fact that Ireland has more Nobel Prize winners in literature than England! Or what about the Jews? They speak all the languages of the world yet remain culturally Jews. Moreover, the French of France are obviously not cultural mirrors of the francophones of Belgium, Québec, Switzerland, Africa or Asia. All this to conclude that there is no necessary correlation between language and culture.

Moreover, there is an important reason for not looking kindly upon those who espouse and promote the ethnic definition of culture. To begin with, in a pluralistic society like Québec's, where racially similar inter-ethnic marriages have been common for almost three-hundred years, who is to determine membership in the dominant *Québécois* ethnic group? And how? Even if it was possible, what would be done with this determination apart from being able to establish the technical definition of a non-*Québécois*? Ever hear of ethnic cleansing? If you think that this horrible notion cannot apply in modern Québec, ask your neighbourhood anglophobic nationalist what he and his fellow thugs mean when they chant *"Le Québec aux Québécois."* And if you do not believe that ethnic cleansing has in fact taken place in Québec, have a look at the statistics on the massive anglophone exodus from Québec since the 1970s. Those figures, about which more later, do not lie: Ethnic cleansing in Québec is an historical fact.

At another level, culture means *"the quality in a person or society that arises from an interest in and an acquaintance with what is generally regarded as excellent in arts, letters, manners and scholarly pursuits."*[2] Since excellence here is the result of individual effort (unless you wish to argue that Molière's plays were composed not by Molière but by the people of France), you would have to conclude that culture is first of all personal. However, because of the influence of individuals, it can become collective. For instance, because of the brilliance and influence of Austrian musicians such as Mozart, it is claimed by some that Austrians became music lovers. I would also argue that societies motivated by excellence-related culture would: (1) tend to be influenced more by the personal efforts of individuals, past and present, than by group-related legends, and (2) tend to rank individual rights ahead of group rights. This type of society often turns out to be a popular democracy. I would conclude from this that popular democracies thus tend to embrace modernity while ethno-centric democracies do not.

Furthermore, in societies where personal freedom and the pursuit of excellence are nurtured, culture, by any definition, is more likely to be diverse than monolithic. In Québec, for instance, the *Québécois* nuclear physicist and the Gaspé fisherman might share a common language, perhaps even common ancestors and the same religious faith, but what else would encourage them to make common cause? On the other hand, if this same fisherman broke bread with his Newfoundland counterpart, I am sure that their language divide would soon be overcome by their common interests.

Here, the two definitions of culture collide, the ethnic with the individual, legend with reality, the present with the past, neither one finding comfort in the other. And if the nuclear physicist was a Muslim immigrant from a francophone country, he would have nothing in common with the Gaspé fisherman except language. Clearly, as Québec integrates increasing numbers of immigrants, friction between ethnic and non-ethnic definitions of culture is inevitable. Thus, it should be clear that the promotion of ethnically-motivated cultural policies in a multi-ethnic society is a prescription for social disaster. So, why are such socially disruptive policies being promoted in Québec?

Because, say the nationalists, if you do not protect French in Québec, French culture will disappear and that is bad. I would argue, however, that this notion is absurd. First, as argued previously, there is no necessary correlation between culture and language. Second, what is so bad about one language being displaced by another? Without wishing to be insensitive, let me be frank: Assimilation into other language groups has been going on since the beginning of time. As people move from one circumstance to another, they change; as new environments impose new demands, people evolve. They may look back at the old ways with some nostalgia, but seldom with regret. Why? First, in life there is no going back, and second, people are generally better off in the new circumstances than they were before. And, for most people, that is what counts. If you look at the fate of the millions of Americans descended from expatriate *Québécois*, you will find that they are generally better off than their cousins who remained in Québec. American culture with all its grandeur and warts has displaced the French customs and language inherited from their ancestors. Those who wail at the loss of culture would have to argue that American culture is inferior to French; that Shakespeare is inferior to Molière; that Dostoyefski is superior to Dickens, and so on. And that would be silly.

Clearly, when *Québécois* nationalists fuss over language, they are on shaky ground, and they know it. That is why I would argue that preserving the French language is in fact not their goal, that increasing their political power is. Thus, their objectives differ from those of the people: Where the people seek bread, butter and peace, the élite seek power and influence. And, of course, the main consequence of the pursuit of the élite's goals is the enrichment of the élite and the impoverishment of the masses.

Gullible Québécois

So, are *Québécois* really gullible? Consider the historical record.

1. For 200 years, most *Québécois* followed the Church's instructions to reject modernity, to shun economic temptations, to remain poor and under-educated to protect their French language and Catholic faith.

2. Despite the fact that the francophone share of Québec's population has been growing for over a century, the *Québécois* élite have had no trouble selling the mischievous notion that francophones are losing ground demographically to non-francophones.

3. Despite the fact that Québec receives *more* from Ottawa than it pays in taxes, the élite have succeeded in selling the lie that Québec receives *less* than it pays. More on this later.

4.   Despite the fact that the economic wounds suffered by *Québécois* have
        been self-inflicted, the élite have very successfully deflected the blame
        onto anglophones in general and Ottawa in particular.

5.   About one-third of those who voted for secession in the referenda of
        1980 and 1995 did not believe that they were voting for secession.
        They thought that they were simply giving their political leaders more
        clout for use in their never-ending confrontations with Ottawa. But
        evidence that came to light after the 1995 Referendum shows clearly
        that the Premier of Québec intended to make an illegal unilateral
        declaration of independence almost immediately after a successful
        Referendum vote. More on this in Appendix III.

Conclusion? *Québécois* certainly appear to be gullible.

But what made *Québécois* so unquestioning of their élite? I would argue that
there are two related explanations: Their feudal origins and the 200-year
promotion by the Church of the main social characteristic of feudal societies,
loyalty to one's social betters. It is no wonder then that this produced an
obedient and gullible people waiting to be had by their own leaders. For those
unfamiliar with how feudalism affected the historical evolution of Québec, let
me offer a few explanatory paragraphs.

In feudal Europe, wealth, authority, prestige and their related perquisites
depended on the exploitation of land, all of which was owned by the king. The
monarch granted the use of his lands to those nobles he favoured in return for
an obligation to provide resources and arms to the king whenever he needed
them. In turn, landlords permitted peasants to farm the land in return for annual
fees and a promise to serve in the landlord's army when called upon to serve the
king. The landlord also promised to protect and care for his peasants.
        The Church was among those benefitting from the king's land
grants. Hence, we see here a natural hierarchy: Peasants at the bottom with
nobles and the Church in the middle and the monarch on top. Moreover, the
Church figured a second time in this hierarchical equation because of its august
position as God's representative on earth, a considerable benefit in a world that
defined itself in religious terms. Thus, the feudal system can be defined in two
ways. The first is economic in that it defined how the bounty from the king's
lands was allocated; the second is socio-political in that it established a class
system with rights, obligations and perquisites dependent upon one's position
within it. By either definition, peasants came out on the short end of the stick.
        Furthermore, because of the obligation of the landlord to care
for his peasants, there developed a sense that there was no need for the peasants
to provide for themselves anything more than the bare necessities of life. I
would argue that this attitude persists to this day in Québec. How else do we

explain the fact that Quebecers are the least generous people in Canada? Statistics Canada reports regularly that Newfoundlanders are Canada's most generous contributors to charities while Quebecers are at the bottom of the list.[3]
However, explaining the origin of this fact is a matter of interpretation. To claim that it is because Quebecers are mean spirited tightwads is a gratuitous slander that is supported only by conjecture. What is supported by evidence is, first, the fact that this attitude is consistent with traditional feudal behaviour, and, second, that the spirit of medieval feudalism has not been extinguished in Québec. Thus, goes the argument, since the government, or the Church, is supposed to provide social services out of taxes or tithes, why should Quebecers pay twice by donating to charities as well? Although I consider myself personally obligated to be my brother's keeper, my tax load notwithstanding, I still find that the implicit counter-argument prevalent in Québec is logical. Whether it justifies a reduced level of charitable donations is, of course, another matter. But back to feudalism.
In Europe, all countries were feudal at one time or another, some more than others, some for longer than others. For example, while feudalism was on the wane in England in the 16th-century, it was still relatively strong in France. And there is no mystery to explain this divergent socio-economic evolution. While England was experimenting with a whole range of new labour saving farming innovations, France stuck with the old, tried and true labour intensive system. As a result, where the English farmer began to use new technology and better farming practices to improve farm yields, the French peasant was stuck in the past using traditional methods that were less productive and hence less rewarding financially; where English landlords realized that running valuable wool-producing sheep on their lands was more profitable than collecting fees from peasants, French landlords stuck with the peasants. Thus, as England threw its unneeded peasants off the land (via ethnic cleansing) to create a pool of surplus people, many of whom ended up emigrating to the Americas, France retained its peasants to work the land in the time honoured, labour intensive fashion ... preserving the class system in the process.
This explains why, in 1760, the population of the English colonies in the Americas was about 30-times that of New France even though the population of England was then less than half that of France.[4] Moreover, where colonists from France brought the class-defined feudal system with them to New France, their British cousins were fleeing the same system to seek a new life in British North America where personal liberty was more esteemed than feudal rights and obligations. Thus, where feudal practices remained strong in New France, they tended to be much weaker in Britain's American colonies.
In New France, this produced, *inter alia*, an authoritarian, higherarchical society with peasants fairly obedient to the Church, and a classical aristocracy that mirrored *ancien régime* France. Since the Québec Church successfully promoted this hierarchical social order until well into the 1960s, it should come as no surprise that ordinary *Québécois* today might tend to be

accepting of the pronouncements of their current lords and masters. Custom, like a cockroach, can be difficult to kill.

Illiteracy, lack of education, not to mention education of inferior quality, also help to explain this gullibility. Just in case the reader is not aware of it, the rate of illiteracy among *Québécois* is the highest in Canada outside of Newfoundland. Also, *Québécois* have been and remain less educated than other Canadians. Interestingly, the most literate and best educated appear to be Québec anglophones ... and the *Québécois* élite.

Although the illiterate and uneducated might naturally tend to be gullible, you would not expect the educated to suffer from this affliction. But, even educated *Québécois* may be gullible, or at least unconvinced by inconvenient facts. It has to do with what is taught in French schools.

For example, to improve the teaching of French, the Québec Ministry of Education decided to use textbooks that would encourage students to embrace their studies with vigour and joy instead of bored disinterest. And what made these textbooks joyous to read? They described the joys of astrology and numerology in the lives of the students! These two subjects are without doubt quackery of the first order, something that might have interested Barnum but which should have appalled competent pedagogues. *Le Devoir* was thus justifiably outraged and the Québec Minister of Education suitably embarrassed when this became known to the general public. But not embarrassed enough, it seems. About a year later, *Le Devoir* became apoplectic when it discovered that the same quackery was used in still other texts in French schools. This time Ministry officials said that new text books would make no mention of astrology or numerology ... when they became available in a few years.[5] Existing stocks either had to wear out or run out. Until then, *Québécois* students will continue to be taught quackery. Clearly, the most vulnerable will leave school to test their mettle in our modern economy thinking that astrology and numerology are as legitimate as mathematics and literature!

Moreover, as they enter today's competitive economy, these same students will no doubt impress prospective employers with their parochial world-view. That is, according to historian Jack Granatstein, poor performance by *Québécois* in a national history test (they came last) is explained by the fact that they knew almost nothing of historical events outside Québec. He was not surprised: Québec's schools do a good job promoting *Québécois* nationalism by ignoring anything at variance with that ideology.[6]

There is more.

Economics is taught in Québec high schools, presumably to provide the economy with well informed workers, people who are capable of helping their employers sort their way through the jungle of modern business life. Statistics on government finances are of course central to these economics programs. One

Table 4-1:	Federal Expenditures	
% of Federal Revenues		
	1961	1991
Alberta	118	84
BC	111	95
Ontario	85	111
Québec	75	123
Manitoba	146	172
Sask	200	175
NB	242	187
NS	278	189
PEI	336	249
NFLD	281	259
Canada	104	123

Source: StatCan 13-213S 1991

of these statistics concerns the exchange of taxes and services between taxpayers and tax collectors. According to the economics text used in Québec's high schools as I write (1996), Québec taxpayers pay more to the federal government than Québec receives back in one form or another. The facts of course prove that the reverse is true. However, since the calculation and understanding of this balance require the ability to comprehend grade three arithmetic, it might prove too difficult for some. It would appear that *Québécois* politicians and their cohorts in the Ministry of Education are either deficient in this skill or are intent on spreading baloney.

Clearly, even if we did not know where the truth lay, we would know that someone had to be in egregious error on this one. Unfortunately, since you do not know which side to trust, and since neither journalists nor pedagogues seem to be interested in, or capable of, deciphering this mess, you have no choice but to do it yourself. Either that or ignore it and hope for the best. If you choose not to ignore it, your first step would be to ask Statistics Canada to direct you to the appropriate public documents dealing with this subject. Your next step would be to spend an hour or so studying these documents. If you do this, you will find the data summarized in Table 4-1, a 30-year overview of how the provinces fared in this federal revenue-expenditure balance.

Note that these expenditures do not include federal spending overseas for things such as peacekeeping, embassies and foreign aid. If we were to completely balance all federal revenues and expenditures, each province would have to accept an appropriate allocation of this foreign spending. But, even without this allocation, it is clear that the feds spent 23 percent more in Québec in 1991 than they took in. So, whose nose should be growing?

Moreover, in Newfoundland, for instance, federal expenditures in 1961 were almost three-times as high as federal revenues from that province. But, by 1991, federal expenditures there had declined from 281 to 259 percent of federal revenues. Hence, during that period, Newfoundland's federal deficit declined a little. So did that of six other provinces. During this period, only Ontario, Québec and Manitoba increased their federal deficits. In Québec, for example, federal spending went from 75 to 123 percent of federal revenues. Advantage Ontario, Québec and Manitoba. So, where is Québec's beef?

Let's consider another comparison, this time between federal transfers and federal revenues (Table 4-2). Transfers are payments by the federal government to individuals in the form of pensions, and grants to provincial governments to support various social programs. In Québec, federal

Table 4-2: Federal Transfers		
% of Federal Revenues		
	1961	1991
Ontario	36	45
Alberta	72	53
BC	68	57
Québec	40	76
NS	135	103
Manitoba	82	117
NB	145	128
Sask	150	132
PEI	207	170
NFLD	215	200
Canada	53	68

Source: StatCan 13-213S
1991

transfers amounted to 76 percent of the federal revenues extracted from that province in 1991. Perhaps that was what was meant in the Québec high school textbook where it was claimed that Québec pays more to Ottawa in taxes than it gets back. I suppose that there is nothing technically inaccurate with this if you ignore federal spending in Québec on pencils, paper and public service salaries, or if you assume that Québec does not have to bear its share of Canadian government spending overseas. Although you might be technically correct, you would also be an ignorant ass. Imagine shovelling such mischievous nonsense at impressionable high school students!

In any event, here we see the same trends: Federal spending as a percent of revenues declined in seven provinces between 1961 and 1991; only in Ontario, Québec and Manitoba did the percentage increase. As before, advantage Ontario, Québec and Manitoba. Again, where is Québec's beef?

Finally, let's look at equalization payments. This is a program where Ottawa recognizes that some provinces are poorer than others and hence require extra financial assistance from the federal treasury. According to the criteria in current use, Ontario, Alberta and British Columbia (the haves) are considered relatively rich; the other seven provinces (the have-nots) are considered relatively poor. In 1991, Ottawa distributed $7.7 billion to the have-nots in the form of equalization payments, of which 45 percent went to Québec, 13 percent to New Brunswick, the next largest recipient, and so on down to PEI which received 2.4 percent.[7] Advantage Québec.

Conclusions?

I would argue, first, that there is no evidence to suggest that any province was mistreated by Ottawa in this period; second, to claim that Québec paid out more than it received is demonstrably incorrect. To insist that it is true means that the claimant is either thick or suffering from lengthening of the nose.

That this obvious inversion of the truth might interest some politicians, I have no doubt. I might even accept it as part of the normal cut and thrust of partisan politics. But, what of the pedagogues in the Québec Ministry of Education? They must have been asleep when this infamous economics text was evaluated. Or, did they approve it knowing it contained lies? They are of course condemned in either case. Clearly, misinformed and gullible students would be the normal products of such a system.

And was the system ever successful! A public opinion poll in

May 1997 revealed that 69 percent of *Québécois* believed that the federal government takes more out of Québec than it puts back. This share rose to 90 percent among those who voted for secession in the 1995 Referendum but dropped to 44 percent among those who said no.[8] So, those responsible for misinforming the people of Québec can take a well deserved bow: They succeeded wonderfully. Even Herr Goebbels would have been impressed.

There is still more.

High school students periodically write standard exams set by the Québec Ministry of Education. For students in English schools, the exams are translations from the French originals. Complaints about the poor quality of the translations finally boiled over in 1995: Honour students in English schools were failing because they could not understand the questions on the exams, the translations were that bad.[9] Although teachers in the English schools wanted to use the original French exams, the Ministry refused. Hence, English schools were required to use the pitiful translations provided by the Ministry of Education. And this in a country with the best translators in the world! Makes one wonder how many other school texts, teaching methods and administrative practices are similarly corrupted in Québec.

Last one.

Just in case the reader may be inclined to think that these horror stories apply only to elementary and secondary schools, think again. There is in Québec a post-high school and pre-university educational institution called *Le collège d'enseignement général et professionel (Cégep)*, an institution that is criticized by some and lauded by others. I belong in the second camp. So impressed was I with the outstanding education received by my two daughters at a Montreal Cégep (Dawson College) that I later sent my son to a *Cégep* in Hull, Québec (Heritage College) even though we were then living in Ontario. Unfortunately, not all *Cégep* students are so fortunate.

I am familiar with one deplorable textbook that is in current use in some Montreal French *Cégep*s. How many other similarly bad books are circulating in this milieu is anybody's guess. But, judging by this case and the examples cited previously, one may fear the worst. The textbook in question is entitled *"L'Invention d'une minorité: Les Anglo Québécois."* The author, Josée Legault, apparently teaches political science and history at *L'Université du Québec à Montréal* (UQAM). This book figured in her MA program at UQAM. Some readers may be familiar with her political musings which appear regularly on the editorial pages of *Le Devoir* as well as on English radio.

In my review of Legault's book, I argued that, not only did she appear to be driven by vicious anglophobia, her book was also riddled with very poor analysis. For example, she admitted that the Church had shepherded the post-Conquest French into secure isolation from the commercially-driven British in order to protect their Catholic faith, French language and race (nation). The logical economic consequence of this was a class of relatively prosperous British businessmen and workers at the top of the economic heap with relatively poor and unskilled francophones at the bottom. Although one may be dismayed at such an outcome, who could have expected any other result? But whom did Legault blame for this condition? The Church? The Québec Ministry of Education? No, she pointed her accusing finger at discrimination by Anglos! As a result of continuous exposure to such hateful trash (Legault is not alone), it is hardly surprising that so many *Québécois Cégep* and university students believe nonsense such as this.

Legault also claimed that only with the Quiet Revolution of the 1960s were francophones liberated from Anglo-Saxon (Legault's term) economic domination. This was not only mischievously anglophobic, it was factually wrong. First, had she consulted the historical record, she would have discovered that the wage gap between Québec and Ontario workers had been narrowing since early in the 20th-century. By the time the Quiet Revolution rolled around, wages in Québec had almost climbed to parity with Ontario. Second, it would have been more logical to argue that educational reforms brought about during the Quiet Revolution had improved the income-generating potential of francophones. With better schooling they would have become more competitive with their better educated anglophone cousins, and so on. Third, I am told that proportionately more anglophones than francophones voted in 1960 for the Lesage Liberals, the people who gave birth to the Quiet Revolution. Hence, the Quiet Revolution can hardly be called a victory over Anglo-Saxons. Clearly, Legault's interpretation of the Quiet Revolution is just plain wrong. But, she is in good company: This anglophobic misinterpretation of the Quiet Revolution is an unchallenged *fact* among *Québécois*.

Then, she went on to claim that, only with the advent of language laws, did francophones start to overcome the effects of anglophone economic discrimination. Choosing not to recognize the responsibility of the Church-run school system, she said (my translation) "*Bill 101 (the language law) brought to an abrupt end the social, cultural and economic apartheid that had lasted more than two centuries.*" Moreover, said she, the anglophone community has yet to admit its guilt for this sorry state of affairs.[10] Unfortunately, for Legault, the historical record does not support her accusations. As she admitted herself, and as all informed people

Table 4-3:	Average Annual Incomes, Montreal			
	1961	1970	1980	1985
Francophones				
Unilingual	2,975	5,636	14,351	20,699
Bilingual	4,201	7,686	19,411	27,160
Anglophones				
Unilingual	5,749	9,123	19,840	27,601
Bilingual	5,931	9,367	19,920	29,071

Source: *Les Anglois Québécois, p. 216*

:now to be true, the Church was responsible for isolating the francophone :ommunity from economic opportunity. In addition, the recent historical record loes not support her claim that language laws had a beneficial effect on the wages of francophones.

Consider as evidence of this, Legault's own data (Table 4-3). Bear in mind that the first language laws were enacted in the early 1970s. Where the average annual incomes of unilingual (lower paid) francophones increased by 89.4 percent between 1961 and 1970, those of unilingual anglophones increased by 58.7 percent. **Advantage lower paid francophones.** Among bilingual, or higher paid workers, francophone incomes increased by 83.0 percent versus 57.9 percent for anglophones during the same period. **Advantage higher paid francophones.** Hence, it is clear that, according to Legault's own data, all francophones fared better than anglophones between 1961 and 1970, thereby closing the wage gap between the two groups ... **without benefit of language laws.** If you continue these comparisons, still using Legault's data, you find that unilingual, lower paid francophones continued to increase their incomes more rapidly than anglophones after 1980 when language laws **were** in effect. Thus, with or without language laws, Legault's data show that lower paid unilingual francophones were closing the wage gap with their unilingual, anglophone neighbours. Hence, Legault's claim, that closing the wage gap was due to language laws, is not supported by her own data.

And what about higher paid bilingual workers? As mentioned above, the incomes of bilingual francophone workers increased by 89.4 percent between 1961 and 1970, a period well before the advent of language laws. Comparable anglophone incomes increased by 58.7 percent. **Again, advantage higher paid francophones.** But when you compare performance among bilingual workers between 1980 and 1985, when language laws *were* in effect, you find, *mirabile dictu*, that incomes increased more rapidly among anglophones (45.9 percent) than among francophones (39.9 percent). **Advantage higher paid anglophones!** Did the language laws thus favour bilingual anglophones? Not bloody likely! Were the language laws more beneficial for unilingual francophones than for bilingual francophones? Perhaps, but not likely. So what explains the advantage of bilingual francophones before the language laws and their relative disadvantage thereafter? There is only one sensible response for a prudent analyst: Since these data and Legault's hypothesis produce ridiculous answers, one cannot conclude that the language laws were of economic benefit to anyone!

Legault, is obviously neither very prudent nor a very good analyst: Her conclusions derive from her fertile imagination and anglophobic ideology, not from her data or from discriminating analysis. But again no matter, it seems: Legault's weird conclusions are generally accepted among *Québécois*. Let us hope that Legault has little to do with the teaching of diagnostic skills to *Québécois* brain surgeons, tax accountants or engineers.

While we are on the topic, I would argue that there is no single reason to explain the fact that francophone workers fared relatively well during this period. That having been said, I would argue that, apart from the economically beneficial effects of ethnic cleansing, the foremost reason was the undeniable fact that the francophone workforce was becoming better educated. Thus, more economic opportunities were becoming open to them. Then, serendipity probably took over: As francophones moved into management, they naturally tended to favour their own. And francophones were reasonably well represented among business managers: Legault claimed that about 40 percent of senior managers in Québec were francophone in 1961.[11] Not bad considering that the Church had laboured long and hard to keep the flock away from business. In any event, these higher shares of francophone managers probably led inevitably to increased hiring of lower level francophones, whether unilingual or bilingual.

The very same preferential hiring practices became ever more evident among anglophone managers as well. Businessmen gradually realized that the use of French was becoming increasingly imperative in all areas of business life in Québec. Thus, the need to be bilingual was gradually shifted from francophone workers to anglophone managers. For instance, when I was hired as a sales engineer in Québec by Esso in 1958, it was understood that I would have to be able to work in French with both co-workers and customers.

But mine, of course, is an unsubstantiated, though probable, anecdotal hypothesis. Thus, I will settle for the uncontestable conclusion that derives from Legault's own data: There is no evidence to support the notion that language laws helped francophone workers improve their economic conditions ... which reminds me of a joke. There was a psychologist who was studying the behaviour of flies. When they lighted on his arm, he would say: *"Fly off"* and they would obediently fly off. He then removed one wing from each fly. When he said: *"Fly off"* they still flew off. But when he removed both wings, they did not fly off when commanded. The psychologist's conclusion? Removing both wings makes flies deaf. Sounds like Professor Legault.

I hesitate to even speculate about what other textbooks at other Québec *Cégeps* and universities may be similarly corrupt, or what other teachers and professors may be as mischievous as Legault.

Another explanation for the apparently unquestioning deference of the *Québécois* masses toward their élite, may be other linguistic, cultural or historical factors. For instance, in English there is but one term for the pronoun *you*, whether you are addressing a peasant or the Queen. But in French there are two, the formal *vous* and the intimate *tu*. It is common practice to use the formal *vous* when addressing an older person or someone in authority. This applies, with some exceptions, even when the conversationalists become well known to one another. In English, although, there is no strict comparison, there is an analogous reverse tendency to use someone's nickname, even in formal situations. The French are simply more formal and deferential than the English.

Moreover, where but in France or Québec do we find institutions such as *l' Académie française*, an institution that decides which words are approved for inclusion in the dictionary and are thus admissible in proper conversation. Whereas in English, common practice over time decides how words are used, the French insist that only the most accomplished literary people should do this with *l'Académie* as arbiter. Among the French, there is no doubt that authority prevails over the popular will.

Some cultures, on the other hand, are less deferential than others. It is said, for instance, that Israelis tend to be disputatious: Two Israelis, six opinions, all contradictory, you know the stereotype. It is not surprising therefore that Israelis are apparently prone to challenging their leaders. In Iran, on the other hand, my informants tell me that similarly disputatious behaviour is less evident. Moreover, I would argue that societies dominated by religious leaders are more likely to be accepting of authority than those with secular traditions. Furthermore, societies dominated by authoritarian religions will tend to be more accepting of authority than will those blessed with the less authoritarian. Thus, Catholic societies will tend to be more accepting of authority than will Protestant communities. For example, since the Catholic Church has traditionally been associated with the notion of infallibility, Catholics have grown accustomed to subordinating their doubts to the authority of the Church. Protestants, on the other hand, follow another tradition. They claim (I simplify) that truth is to be found in the Bible, and that the faithful should study Scripture themselves and not seek interpretations from intervening priests. Québec, obviously, falls into the Catholic category, thus helping to explain the relatively ease with which the *Québécois* élite have been able to sell fluff.

Finally, when we consider the composition of this élite (nationalist groups, politicians, public school teachers and university professors, the information media, public sector unions and various consumer and producer associations, as well as public and para-public sector bureaucrats, etc.), it should give us pause. Who else of any social or political significance remains? Clearly, when these warriors take to the field, it can hardly be called a fair fight. The *Québécois* masses did not and do not stand a chance. They were and remain, as Barnum might have said, suckers waiting to be taken.

Summary

Although Hugh MacLennan identified the two solitudes in Québec as the French and the English, there are in fact two other solitudes in that province and they both speak French. On the one hand are the special *Québécois* élite who strive to increase their economic and political power at the expense of Québec anglophones and the federal government in Ottawa. By special élite, I mean the Catholic Church, the newspaper *Le Devoir* and a relatively heterogenous group of secular nationalists who are bolstered by various groupies and hangers-on. On the other hand are ordinary *Québécois* who, like ordinary people everywhere, do their best to provide for their families with the cards that God dealt them.

This special *Québécois* élite has traditionally called on all *Québécois* to make economic sacrifices to safeguard their common distinctive culture, to protect it from the corrosive influence of anglophones and modernity. Where this distinctive culture was once defined principally in terms of the Catholic faith and French language, the religious dimension is no longer relevant, most *Québécois* having abandoned the Church.

Current nationalist orthodoxy insists that *Québécois* culture and the French language are synonymous and at risk. That there is no evidence to support the necessary correlation between culture and language seems not to concern these nationalists at all. Nor is this notion of French-at-risk at all buffeted by the fact that, during the past 125-years or so, the francophone share of Québec's population has *increased.* Nor do they appear to be concerned that the historical record suggests that, given a choice, *Québécois* have consistently chosen bread and butter over language. It would appear then that the élite's concern for the French language has less to do with its protection than with its use as a political tool.

Clearly, the élite have succeeded in getting their kin to act against their own (kin's) economic interests. The fundamental reason for this gullibility is first, that unquestioning loyalty to one's social betters is an essential characteristic of feudal societies, and second, that Québec is still socially feudal. A complementary reason is an educational system that is dedicated more to the promotion of secessionist ideology, misleading textbooks and touchy-feely pedagogy than to the production of informed and discriminating students. No surprise then that *Québécois* tend to be unquestioning of their elites. Nor that, as a result, they tend to get screwed a lot.

Notes

1.   Random House Dictionary of the English Language, 1969, p. 353.

2.   Random House, p. 353.

3.   StatCan reported that in 1995, Newfoundlanders led the country with an average donation of $250 per taxpayer; Québecers were last with an average of $100; the average Ontarian donated about $175. In a list of 26 Canadian cities, the 5 lowest in donation terms were cities from Québec; Sherbrooke was the highest Québec city in this list, tied with 5 other cities from outside Québec for 16th place. News item reported in the Ottawa Citizen, p. A4, Nov. 7, 1996.

4.   M. Conrad et al, History of the Canadian Peoples: Beginnings to 1867, (Copp Clark Pitman, 1993), p. 206.

5.   Le Devoir, 10/11 février, 1996, p. A4.

6.   *Ottawa Citizen*, June 30, 1997, p A1. The national survey was financed by the Donner Canadian Foundation. The poll was conducted by Angus Reid. Also reported on CBC National News, June 30, 1997.

7.   Unpublished document from Finance Canada, Oct., 1996.

8.   COMPAS poll reported in the *Ottawa Citizen*, May 13, 1997, p. A1.

9.   *Ottawa Citizen*, Dec. 23, 1995, p. A4 and May 4, 1996, p. A10.

10.   Josée Legault, *L'Invention d'une minorité: Les Anglo Québécois*, (Montréal: Boréal, 1992), pp. 88, 91.

11.   Legault, pp. 229, 261.

5

The First Élite: The Church, 1760 - 1960

Overview

Though this may astonish some and scandalize others, the Catholic Church's vocation in Québec was more than spiritual. Until about 1960, the Church was the most influential social and political institution in that province. Remember as well that Catholics, many of whom were either devoutly obedient or easily cowed, accounted for virtually all *Québécois.*

Testifying to its ubiquitous presence is the fact that about two-thirds of the hospital beds in Québec in 1960 were in hospitals founded, controlled and managed by francophone Catholic religious orders. The remaining third were in institutions managed by the various non-francophone communities.[1] The Church also financed, managed, and staffed all Catholic elementary, secondary and post-secondary schools. Note that Québec's public schools are legally either Catholic or Protestant, not neutral. Moreover, the Church controlled access to the then rudimentary welfare system. Finally, it used its bully pulpits unashamedly to direct the personal and public lives of the faithful, and often not in the interests of the people. For instance, it promoted rural life even when agricultural economies were giving way to the industrial variety throughout the western world, and when their own flocks were fleeing the countryside in search of jobs in the cities of Québec and the United States. By focussing on the training of priests, lawyers and doctors, it also hobbled the public education system when Québec's growing industrial economy was crying for engineers, economists and other skilled workers; it intimidated socially vulnerable women into having large families when poor economic conditions screamed for restraint; it reminded voters that they must vote for the *blue* Conservatives, not for the *red* Liberals since *"Heaven is blue and hell is red."*

To those who have never lived in a society dominated by an omnipotent religious institution, this type of influence may be difficult to grasp. But believe it, just look at Poland or Ireland today, more Catholic than which it is difficult to imagine.

The Cassock in Poland and Ireland

Some political commentators claim that the Church was partly responsible for the overthrow of Communism in Poland in the 1980s. Don't scoff! During World War II, when Stalin mockingly asked *"How many military divisions has the Pope?"* he obviously underestimated his adversary. As a result, some argue that he paid the ultimate price for his folly: While Communism has fallen into the dustbin of history, the Catholic Church is triumphant in Poland today. So triumphant in fact that the liberal abortion laws of the Communist regime were *adjusted* to conform to Catholic orthodoxy. As a result, abortion in Poland is effectively prohibited. The point is not that the Polish Church's attitude toward abortion was right or wrong, but that it was able to impose its will on secular legislators, politicians whose constituents wanted to retain communism's liberal abortion laws. The Church obviously had enough divisions in Poland.

In Ireland, the Church has always fought tooth and nail to maintain its controlling influence over state social policy, and it has generally succeeded. For instance, while the rest of Europe has enacted relatively permissive legislation on birth control, abortion and divorce, this most Catholic of countries still considers (or did until very recently) these acts, not only illegal, but unconstitutional. Whether this puts the Church in Ireland on the side of the angels or not is not the issue here. After all, there is nothing unorthodox about its position in these matters. But, Church orthodoxy is not at issue. What is, as it was in Poland, is the success of the Church in imposing its will on a secular state, something considered quite unusual in other western countries.

Even though public opinion polls in Ireland showed a definite trend toward popular rejection of this clerical totalitarianism, the Irish Church soldiered on, admonishing Irish politicians to ignore the wishes of the people and to legislate instead in the interests of the Church. The Irish clergy (154 priests per 100,000 people) kept the pressure on these politicians by appealing from their bully pulpits to their relatively obedient flocks who still attend Church services in large numbers.

The Cassock in Québec

If the Irish clergy could successfully promote retrograde public policies with 154 priests for every 100,000 of the faithful[2], the related success of the more numerous *Québécois* clergy should start to make more sense. I take it for granted that an institution, such as the Church, that has access to influential pulpits, will be more effective with more rather than with fewer priests.

In Table 5-1 is a list of the historical presence of Catholic priests in Québec.[3] Bear in mind that the importance of these data lies not so much in their absolute size, but (1) in their trend, and (2) in their comparison with the Irish benchmark of 154 priests per 100,000 of the faithful. Note how the number of priests per 100,000 people in Québec declined from a maximum of 1,000 or so in the earliest years of the French colony to a minimum of about 54 in 1830, 70 years after the Conquest of New France by the British, then rose to a new maximum of 198 in 1950, after which it began to decline gradually before starting to plummet toward near oblivion in the 1970s.

The very high ratios in the early years of the French colony simply confirm the missionary objectives of those responsible for early colonization. Then, the gradual decline in this ratio until the Conquest in 1760 is explained by two factors: (1) there were relatively few priests among later arrivals from France, and (2) the offspring of the residents of New France tended to prefer careers in the secular world to those in the Church.

The post-Conquest decline until about 1830 is explained by

Table 5-1: Priests in Québec Per 100,000 people	
1992	59
1970	192
1950	198
1930	176
1910	153
1890	176
1870	152
1850	84
1830	54
1810	73
1780	133
1760	200
1710	625
1680	833
1660	1,000

Sources: Hamelin, Canadian Council of Bishops

two other factors: (1) since there were no bishops living in the colony after the Conquest, it was some time before a bishop became available to consecrate new clergy, and (2) until the Church reasserted itself in the post-Rebellion period after 1839, it might be argued that the growing influence of Québec's secular politicians may have made politics a better career choice than the priesthood. Afterward, the record suggests a relatively steady rise in Church influence between about 1840 and 1960. According to these data, the Church in Québec must have been at least as influential in social and political matters in this period as its Irish sister is today. And that influence was considerable.

After 1960, the influence of the Church dropped dramatically, again for two reasons: (1) since many priests simply gave up their ministry, and fewer young men entered the priesthood, there were fewer priests available to influence the faithful, and (2) people simply walked away from the Church in droves. The reasons for these two related phenomena are interesting but of little relevance here. Suffice to say that they both reflected the consequences of secular-religious tensions in the western world after WW II.

The Feudal Church in Québec

The impact of this large cohort of priests was heightened by the very favourable social environment in which the Church operated. Let's consult the historical record for a taste of this environment.

As described in the previous chapter, the original French colonists brought the feudal system with them from France. Among other things, this included the class system with the crown at the top, the clergy and the nobles in the middle, and the peasants on the bottom supporting everyone above them. After the Conquest of 1760, only the Church, land agents (*seigneurs*) and peasants remained. This left the Church in a position to use its historic feudal power and prerogatives to influence the overall development of the colony. The exercise of this power was facilitated by the traditional feudal tendency of peasants to defer to authority.

Although the conquering British accorded the *seigneurs* more social status than they previously enjoyed, effective leadership of the abandoned colonists fell by default to the Church. And, according to the Reverend Lionel Groulx, about whom more later, the Church's leadership was indeed effective: Where New France before 1760 was driven by the allure of the western fur trade, the Church pushed post-Conquest Québec toward a more pastoral life.[4]

Though I find it difficult to acknowledge any redeeming

qualities in Lionel Groulx, he did make a useful technical point when he lamented the dispersion of the people at the time of the Conquest: Of the 85,000 or so French colonists who remained in North America after 1760, about 25,000 (30-percent), were engaged in the fur trade beyond the confines of New France. According to some demographers, this expatriate share increased steadily thereafter, reaching 50-percent in the 1980s. They claim, for example, that the original 10,000 French colonists produced about 10 million descendants in North America, about half of whom currently live outside of Québec, and most of them in the United States.[5] This suggests first, that the migration of francophones in search of bread and butter started before the Conquest and continues to this day, and second, that the non-agricultural economy has exercised a much greater pull on ordinary *Québécois* than Groulx and his disciples cared to admit.

From its earliest years, therefore, Québec was torn between two apparently irreconcilable imperatives: The drive by the masses to make a living anywhere they could, and the desire by the Church, the dominant élite at the time, to pursue its divine mission through an agriculturally-based economy in that province. That the founding of New France, and by extension Québec, was divinely inspired, was a dominant notion in Québec until at least the 1940s when it reached its apex under Groulx.[6]

Although Groulx insisted that the Church's leadership was unchallenged after 1760, such was not the case. It would appear that there was a struggle between 1760 and 1840 between the sacred and the profane with the Church dominant in the early years. For instance, when the British colonies in Canada were faced in 1775 with a potential invasion from the then revolutionary Americans, the bishop of Québec, Jean-Olivier Briand, issued a pastoral letter reminding his ambivalent flock that "*your religion requires you to defend your country (Canada) and your king (the British monarch) with all your might.*"[7] He even promised to refuse the sacraments to the disobedient, a not inconsiderable threat at that time. To no one's surprise, he was successful: The *Canadiens* refused the blandishments of the American emissaries, and instead simply sat out the American revolutionary war doing nothing.

As the post-Conquest period wore on, secular politicians gradually acquired the relative political advantage, going so far as to foment the Patriotic Rebellion in 1837-38, during which the rebels actually proclaimed the independence of Québec! This not only drew a vigorous military response from British forces (the rebellion was put down, as was its companion insurrection in Ontario), it also elicited a horrified reaction from Church leaders. First, they objected to the overthrow of legitimate secular authority, not only because one does not overthrow the crown in a feudal regime, but also because the conquering British had treated the Church and its flock with considerable respect. This included allowing the Church to retain all of its pre-Conquest assets and feudal prerogatives. The British also granted the *Canadiens* freedom of religion, a significant gesture since that freedom had not yet been granted to Catholics in England. Second, the Church must have been apoplectic at the heretical temerity of the Patriots who included in their declaration of independence a promise to effect the separation of church and state in an independent Québec.[8] When the rebellion was put down, Church officials in Québec must have heaved a collective sigh of relief.

Clearly, the Church's influence, although considerable, was not unfettered. Because of emerging socio-economic factors, the Church's hold on the people was less than it would have liked, certainly less than it was accustomed to in feudal Europe. Eventually, the feudal obedience of the people was tempered by countervailing social imperatives: By industrialization and urbanization, for instance. But, rather than adjust to the inevitable, the Church grieved. Lionel Groulx, for instance, mourned the passing of this feudal society in Québec. What he really lamented was the growing exodus of people from the farm, where the influence of the Church was great, to cities where it was weak.

Québec according to Lionel Groulx

Lionel Groulx was a francophone Catholic priest (1878-1967) whose hagiography is revered by Québec nationalists. So influential is his memory that schools, a Montréal subway station and other monuments have been erected to honour him. Note, however, that his fame derives more from his eulogizing of the early French settlers than from the precision of his historical analysis.

For instance, his insistence that the first settlers spoke an impeccable French is simply absurd: Most were not only illiterate, many may not even have spoken French since they came from parts of France where French, if spoken at all, was spoken only as a second or third language. Or, how about his insistence that neither cripples nor the impotent were permitted to settle in New France. The impotent? Since the Church was not then, and is not now, in a position to make such determinations, this claim is simply stupid.[9] Almost as stupid, and certainly as irrelevant, was his insistence that the women sent over to breed with the lonely bachelors who preceded them were virgins. First, how could anyone tell who was a virgin and who was not; and second, why did Groulx consider virginity so important? If their virginity was important, which it obviously was not, it was not as important as the fact that they were more educated than the men with whom they bedded in New France. In fact, since most came from francophone Paris, they probably introduced French to many of the colonists who may not have spoken French at all.[10] Moreover, that Québec's nationalists celebrate a man whose writing drips with xenophobia in general and anglophobia and antisemitism in particular, seems not to concern them *outre mesure*. Esther Delisle argues that Groulx reacted to liberalism by adopting the ideologies of the French racists Maurice Barrès and Gustave LeBon. She claims that:

> *From Barrès and LeBon, Groulx acquires and defends a thesis brutal in its simplicity: socio-psychological characteristics are*

> *transmitted through the blood, and (sexual) union between*
> *people of different races (includes races as such as well as*
> *nationalities, ethnic and language groups) engenders firstly,*
> *the degeneration of the individual, and ultimately, on a larger*
> *scale, the degeneration of the race itself.[11]*

Thus, ever mindful of this ideological dictum, Groulx insisted that:

> *there lived in New France a white and French population, not*
> *at all like elsewhere in America where there was a mixed*
> *population, semi-indigenous .... only one type was possible*
> *here, it was a colony of the white race.[12]*

He was, however, wildly wrong: His notion of racially pure *Québécois* obviously derived more from his fertile imagination and biases than from the historical record. Consider the evidence.

Western Canada is full of the offspring of the adventuresome French colonists who coupled so vigorously with Indian women in the West that they produced a half-breed people, a people we today call the Métis nation. Moreover, even within the French colony, men outnumbered women by a considerable margin. And how did Groulx imagine that these surplus males responded to nature's call? By remaining celibate or by courting the Indian women among whom they lived and worked? Groulx would have us believe that this unattached surplus male cohort remained celibate!

Clearly, since French males outnumbered European women in New France by a margin of about 6 to 4 during the whole colonization period, it should be obvious that about one-third of the conjugal unions in New France must have been between French males and Indian women. Hence, we might expect that a substantial proportion of *Québécois*, perhaps one-third, must have Indian blood in their veins and hence technically be considered Métis. And this does not include the progeny of the thousands of unions between *Québécois* and later immigrants such as the Irish, Scots, English, Italians, Americans and Algerians. But, since fact and logic cannot displace a more convenient myth, Groulx and his disciples have succeeded in spreading the unsupportable notion that *Québécois* are the racially and ethnically pure descendants of the original French settlers. So well established is this notion that most white *Québécois* claim to be *Québécois pure laine* (pure blood *Québécois*).

Groulx made his support for this absurd notion abundantly clear in his literary masterpiece, L'appel de la race. It deals with the unhappy consequences of a mixed marriage between an anglophone Protestant wife and a francophone Catholic husband. Only with the breakup of the marriage and the return of the husband to his French roots was the husband redeemed in Groulx's eyes. What a curious conclusion from a priest whose Church insists still on the indissolubility of marriage! Clearly, even though Groulx was a devout servant of the Church, his primary loyalty was to French Canadians (Groulx's term) whom he considered a chosen race.[13] So chosen in fact that Groulx, hiding behind the pseudonym Lambert Closse, cited the discredited <u>Protocols of The Elders of Zion</u> to prove that French Canadians should beware of the Jews. Said he, Lambert Closse, in <u>La réponse de la race</u>:

> *Since they (Jews) apparently haven't succeeded with `Protocol'*
> *no 2, `destroy the life of the family life through the preaching*
> *of liberalism', they chose to pull out all the stops. The police*
> *have seized bacilli, microbes, the germs of venereal diseases*
> *in Jewish laboratories, with which sanitary napkins were to be*
> *infected. Is that criminal enough?*

And, if you think that Groulx's literary bark was an aberration, consider what he said about Herr Hitler the year following Hitler's rise to power:[14]

> *Happy Austria (sic) to have found its leader and, with him the*
> *road to resurrection! How we too (in Québec) need a*
> *National Front and a man who, like the young and captivating*
> *chancellor of Austria (sic), would dare to say these moving*
> *words: "I want to reconstruct my country on the basis of the*
> *Quadragesimo Anno encyclical (of the Pope).*

Groulx's heroes were not very admirable.

One more thing: When the antisemitic <u>La réponse de la race</u> was published in 1936, it bore the *imprimatur* of Cardinal J. M. Rodrigue Villeneuve, Catholic Archbishop of Québec.[15] For those unfamiliar with the Church's hierarchy, only the Pope outranks a cardinal. In other words, a cardinal is a very important Church official, a real *mensch*! Moreover, the *imprimatur* is one of the designations used by the Church to signify its approval of a text. For instance, to signify disapproval, a book can be condemned from the pulpit or be officially banned by being placed on the Index. To signify neutrality, a book may be accorded a *nihil obstat*, meaning that the Church finds nothing objectionable in it. But, if the Church really likes a book, it would accord its ultimate seal of approval, the *imprimatur*. Moreover, in Québec in the 1930s, when the Church's influence was riding high, an *imprimatur* must have been treasured. But why would the Church accord its valuable *imprimatur* to <u>La réponse de la race</u>?

Well, we might conclude that the Church approved the book knowing it was antisemitic, or that it approved it not realizing its true character. If you defend the first option you would then have to conclude that the Church in Québec was antisemitic. Since it did in fact look favourably upon antisemitic fascist movements in Italy, France and Spain, it would not be surprising then to find antisemitism in the Québec Church. If, however, you defend the second option, you would have to argue that Church officials did not know of its true character because they had not read it before granting their approval. This would suggest that they were either careless administrators or that they were simply accommodating its author, a respected colleague. If you defend this last option, you would have to conclude that they made their decision on the basis of their knowledge and approval of Groulx's past writings. Since racism, fascism and antisemitism were not unknown in Groulx's writing, we might conclude that Church officials must have approved this particular work knowing or assuming it was also antisemitic. Seems to me that our assessment of the Church and its officials must range from sloppy and incompetent at the benign end of the scale to hateful and antisemitic at the other. Reader's choice.

To put this into a more recent context, can you imagine the Cardinal Archbishop of Toronto granting his *imprimatur* in the 1990s to the works of Ernst Zundel, the Holocaust-denier? No? Well, remember that someone of equivalent rank did just that in Québec in 1936. Furthermore, if Zundel had received this *imprimatur*, can you imagine the public and journalistic outrage that would have ensued? Well, remember that there were no riots in the streets of Montreal following the granting of the Church's *imprimatur* to the equally antisemitic La réponse de la race. Moreover, to the extent that it was noticed then by the *Québécois* press, it was with favour rather than sorrow or outrage. Some pretty disgraceful things are done in the name of God.

Although Groulx was despicable by any test, he nevertheless remains beloved of Québec nationalists. That he could have redeeming values sufficient to justify their adulation, then or now, escapes me. For another view of Québec's history, let us turn to F. X. Garneau.

Québec according to F. X. Garneau

The Patriotic Rebellion of 1837 marked a turning point for the Québec Church. Before then its influence was being challenged by increasingly aggressive *Canadien* politicians; afterwards its influence went essentially unchallenged until about the 1960s. It was during the immediate post-rebellion period that the Church sowed seeds whose bitter fruit we are harvesting still. But, before dealing with the return to dominance of the Church at that time, it might be instructive to take note of the social, economic and political dynamics then prevailing in Québec. And what better interpreter of that period than François-Xavier Garneau, French Canada's first major historian. In 1859 he wrote:[16]

> *Since the (1760) conquest, they (Canadiens) resisted distractions by philosophers and those who proclaimed the rights of men (during the French Revolution of 1789). In addition, they rejected other ideologies with which city dwellers amuse themselves in order to base their policies on their own survival. ..... They turned inward, gathering their*

*children about them, sticking to the ways of their ancestors
despite the sarcasm of their (English) neighbours.
Consequently, they have conserved their religion, their
language and a foothold in English North America. .....
Canadiens have survived to this day (1859) as a farming
people in this hostile climate.*

Note that Garneau seems not to have considered political secession a solution
to the problems of *Canadiens*. Not that he may not have preferred independence
to living in a British colony; he apparently saw isolation from the English-
dominated commercial world, *within* that British colony, as a more practical way
to protect their Catholic religion and French language at that time. In other
words, Garneau concluded that, given their situation within the English-
dominated commercial regime, only by being cocooned within an effective
feudal system could their *Canadien* culture be preserved. He thus celebrated the
survival of feudalism in Québec (Lower Canada) as well as the concurrent
rejection of modernity. The conclusion to draw from Garneau is not only that
feudalism survived in Québec but also that the *Canadiens* themselves chose to
withdraw from the developing industrial economy of the time, leaving the way
clear for the English who were not similarly inclined.

That the Church was responsible for this unfortunate choice is
not evident in Garneau's observations but is crystal clear from other sources: As
mentioned earlier, Lionel Groulx credited the Church with having diverted the
post-Conquest colonists from the external fur trade to an internal pastoral society
within the protective bosom of the Church. What is also to be noted in
Garneau's remarks is the fact that this rejection of modernity took place very
soon after the Conquest, thereby supporting Groulx's contention. That was the
social environment, but what of its political and economic consequences? For
that we now turn to Lord Durham.

Québec according to Lord Durham

One of the best commentaries on Québec during the first half of the 19th-century
is the <u>Report on the Affairs of British North America</u>." Published in 1839, its
author was John George Lambton, Earl of Durham. He had been sent to British
North America to investigate and report on the state of British colonial affairs
in 1837.[17] The report, universally known today as the <u>Durham Report</u>, is
scorned in Québec: Durham had dared to recommend that the *Canadiens* be
done a favour by being assimilated into the English community by the simple
expedient of merging Québec (Lower Canada) and Ontario (Upper Canada) into
one legislative unit, the United Province of Canada. By so doing, the
Canadiens, a majority in Québec, would then become a minority in the
combined province, and assimilation of the *Canadiens* by the English would thus
necessarily take place over time. Or so Durham assumed. That attempt to

legislate the assimilation of *Canadiens* by English Canadians is viewed by modern *Québécois* commentators as a crime of heinous dimensions. On the other hand, they see no logical contradiction in their current attempts to compel (via restrictive language laws) the similarly involuntary assimilation of immigrants into Québec's francophone community.

In any event, although the union of the two colonies was effected in 1841, the assimilation strategy failed because of an unforseen political alliance: *Canadiens* from Québec and reformers from Ontario combined to form the majority political party thereby frustrating Durham's intentions. The *Canadiens*, in effect, bartered French language protection in Québec for political reform in Ontario. But rather than celebrate this victory over Durham, *Québécois* historians prefer to castigate him because he dared to even think of assimilating Québec's francophones into the English community. They also take vigorous umbrage at Durham's derision of Québec's literary heritage.

All things considered, I feel that the Durham Report is a brilliant record of that period. Admittedly, it is flawed in that some of the implications that Durham drew from his observations were wide of the mark. In addition, his main objective, assimilation, was not realized, and some of his very arrogant remarks were obviously irritating. Clearly, Durham's powers of observation outstripped his forecasting abilities. And that suits me since his observations are of much greater import in this analysis.

Sent to Canada by the British government to determine why its colonies in Québec and Ontario were in revolt in 1837, Lord Durham found *"two nations (in Québec) warring in the bosom of a single state."* He said:

1.   *Every contest is one of French and English.*

2.   *The French and English have an invincible hostility toward each other.*

3.   *Arguments (in newspapers) which convince one (race) are calculated to appear utterly unintelligible to the other.*

4.   *The partiality of grand and petty juries is a matter of certainty; each race relies on the vote of its countrymen to save it harmless from the law.*

5.   *They thus live in a world of misconceptions, in which each party is set against the other not only by diversity of feelings and opinions, but by an actual belief in an utterly different set of facts.*

6.   *Because cessation of their ancient antipathy to the*

> *Americans is now admitted, an invading American*
> *army could rely on the cooperation of almost the*
> *entire French population of Lower Canada.*

7. *Since the resort to arms in 1837, the two races have*
    been distinctly and completely arranged against each
    other.

If his observations were accurate, we can conclude that the English and French in Québec were, to say the least, not enamoured of each other at that time. And if we fast-forward to the 1990s, we might be tempted to conclude that this inter-ethnic hostility has not changed appreciably in the intervening 160 years. But what explained this acrimonious state of affairs in 1837?

Part of the explanation may derive from the normal hostility of any vanquished people toward their conquerors--the suppression of the 1837 rebellion was, after all, fairly ruthless. Maybe so, but this level of hatred existed before 1837. Could it have been a holdover from the 1760 Conquest? Perhaps, but then again, although it is reasonable to assume that the colonists who chose to remain under British rule after 1760 may indeed have been apprehensive, even fearful, there is no evidence to suggest that this developed into the visceral hatred that Durham described. In fact, if Groulx is to be believed, the transition from French to British rule was pacific and without rancour. He said:

> *The colonists retained from the old order all that could be*
> *retained under the circumstances. ..... There was no social*
> *decapitation created by the Conquest since the clergy filled the*
> *leadership gap (created by the departing French military and*
> *public officials). ..... The occupying British forces paid the*
> *habitants in cash for their produce using a sound currency*
> *(unlike the near valueless money used by the previous French*
> *colonial administration). ..... Religious freedom was*
> *guaranteed to the conquered French colonists by the British,*
> *quite a departure from the norm in England where practice of*
> *the Catholic faith was proscribed by law.*[18]

Supporting Groulx are some historians who claim that the colonists were better off after the Conquest than they had ever been during the French régime. For instance, the American historian Francis Parkman said: "*A happier calamity never befell a people than the Conquest of Canada by British arms.*"[19] There are, of course, *Québécois* historians who claim that the trauma of the Conquest was so terrible that it has never been forgotten, that it made such an impact on the psyches of *Québécois* that it haunts them still. There is so little evidence for such a far fetched notion that it must be rejected as puerile nonsense.

Thus, it is difficult to see here the seeds of the hatred Durham described. In addition, 1837 was more than two generations removed from 1760. Moreover, said Durham,

> *A large part of the Catholic clergy and a few of the principal proprietors of the Seigneurial families support the Government against the revolutionary violence.*

Nevertheless, Durham's evidence suggests that, despite the pacifying and considerable influence of the Church and bourgeoisie, a more political and less pacific secular élite was able to find nourishment in Québec immediately after the Conquest. Part of this dislike of English settlers by the *Canadiens* may have developed in reaction to British arrogance. As Durham reported,

> *It was not until recently that this society of English civil and military functionaries ceased to exhibit towards the higher orders of Canadians an exclusiveness of demeanour, which was more revolting to a sensitive and polite people than the monopoly power and profit (that was enjoyed by the English).*

And there can be little doubt that the British at that time were indeed arrogant and might very well have annoyed *Canadiens* more than a little. To cite G.M. Craig, the editor of <u>Lord Durham's Report: An Abridgement,</u>

> *No man of Durham's time, who was caught up as he was in the on-rushing material and political progress of the English-speaking peoples of the British Empire and the United States could be expected to sympathize with an allegiance to conservative and traditional values (i.e., to sympathize with French Canadians).*

On the other hand, could part of this hatred be explained by simple misunderstanding? As Durham noted:

> *It was not until some years after the commencement of the present century that the population of Lower Canada began to understand the representative system which had been extended to them (by the English).*

Since the British system was a significant departure from Québec's feudal past, it may indeed have taken the people some time to forgo the comfortable practice of feudal obedience in favour of the rough and tumble of representative democracy. This could have generated unrealizable expectations and the frustrations that must inevitably have followed. Although this is a plausible explanation, I am not inclined to grant it much weight. A more probable explanation for this hostility may have been simple jealousy. Durham claimed:

> *They (Canadiens) looked with considerable jealously and dislike on the increase and prosperity of what they regarded as a foreign and hostile (English) race.*

Moreover, because of the lack of *Canadien* investment capital or even of interest in business, Durham reported:

> *The active and regular habits of the English capitalist drove out of all the more profitable kinds of industry their inert and careless competitors of the French race, and created employment and profits which had not previously existed. Furthermore, the large mass of the labouring population are French in the employ of English capitalists. The more skilled class of artisans are generally English.*

This, of course, gives rise to two more questions: First, why were *Canadien* investors so *inert and careless?* Second, why were *Canadien* workers so unskilled? The short answers are, first, that, given their feudal history, *Canadien* businessmen probably had not yet developed either enough surplus capital for investment or the competitive culture required to make risky investments; second, that, as I will argue in due course, given their poor educational system which was more attuned to the needs of a simple pastoral society than to those of a more demanding industrial economy, *Canadien* workers would naturally have tended to end up near the bottom of the skills hierarchy.

If, however, you are not persuaded by any of these arguments, how about two more. The first is conflicting political visions, the second frustration over limited access to the fruits of the public trough.

Simply put, where the British Imperial government wanted to create an east-west economic axis in Canada by improving navigation along the St. Lawrence River between Québec and Ontario, the *Canadien*-controlled Québec legislature wanted instead to improve its north-south links with the USA. How? By providing Québec with better access to the Erie canal system just south of the border in New York. No surprises here: Even during the French régime, many French fur traders preferred to sell their beaver pelts at premium prices to Dutch or English merchants in New York.

Furthermore, why would Québec voluntarily spend its money improving the navigation system between Québec and Ontario when that was certain to cause a decline in its revenues from import duties, its principal source of revenue? Remember that cargo from overseas' ships destined for Ontario had to be offloaded in Québec for trans-shipment in smaller ships to Ontario. Consequently, import duties had to be paid by Ontario importers at the port of entry in Québec to the government of Québec.

Although no doubt galling to English Ontario and the British Imperial government, there was not much they could do about it ... for the moment. Thus, improvements to the St. Lawrence River navigation system that would have permitted these overseas' vessels to bypass ports of entry in Québec and sail directly to Ontario, would have transferred the receipt of these import duties from Québec to Ontario. And who but the simple minded would voluntarily invest in a venture that was certain to reduce their income? Since the *Canadiens* were not simple minded, they did not act against their financial interests ... especially to further British political interests.

Coupled with this was the practice then common in all of Britain's colonies in North America, political patronage on a grand scale. Thus, in Québec there was a never-ending battle over who controlled access to this lucrative pot of gold, the minority English who controlled the executive wing of the government or the majority *Canadiens* who controlled the legislative assembly. Durham reported that:

> *While the Lower Canada (Québec) Assembly was wasting the surplus revenues of the Province in jobs for the increase of patronage, it left untouched those vast and easy means of communication which deserved and would have repaid the application of the provincial revenues. The state of New York made its own St. Lawrence from Lake Erie to the Hudson (by building the Erie canal), while the government of Lower Canada could not achieve, or even attempt, the few miles of canal and dredging that would have made its mighty rivers navigable almost to their sources (in Ontario).*

Durham's British-centred vision, one shared by the English in Québec and Ontario, obviously differed from that of the *Canadien*-controlled legislature in Québec. In my view, Durham should have blamed this stalemate on the absence of a federal government, not on a province refusing to act against its interests.

In summary, therefore, there existed in the 1830s great animosity between *Canadiens* and English in Québec and Ontario, a condition that was exacerbated by the conflicting interests of the two colonies. Its cause can be attributed to any one or combination of three possibilities:

1.   The normal hostility that might arise between conquered and conqueror;

2.   The political and social objectives of *Canadiens* that differed greatly from those of the English in Québec and Ontario;

3.   Jealousy by *Canadiens* of their prosperous English neighbours.

The weight you are prepared to grant any one of these options depends very much on your perspective. For instance, some *Québécois* historians, more influenced by ideology than by evidence, would cast most of their votes for the first option, the balance for the second, rejecting the third out of hand. Others, more respectful of the role of evidence, would cast a few votes for the first option, most for the second, but also reject the third.

But those without an axe to grind would have a less categorical view of things. They would, first of all, tend to minimize the effect of the first option without of course trivializing it. Then, they would divide the population of Québec into two categories: On the one hand the political classes where the second option would tend to find favour, on the other the masses who would probably fall into the third category. In other words, we see here clear evidence of the early emergence of Québec's two francophone solitudes. Now that we have put this ethnic hostility into some perspective, let us carry on with Durham's other observations.

After the Conquest, said Durham, the Catholic Church was the only institution available *"to preserve the semblance of order and civilization in the community."* In fact, *"the Church has been left in possession of the endowments it had at the conquest."* Moreover, said Durham:

> *In the general absence of any permanent institutions of civil government, the Catholic Church has presented almost the only semblance of stability and organization, and furnished the only effectual support for civilization and order. The only institution in the nature of local government is the fabrique (for the repair of churches).*

Even Groulx supported Durham here. Thus, continued Durham:

> *The religious observances of the French Canadians are so intermingled with all their business that the priests and the church are the centres of their little communities. Consequently, the priest continues to exercise over him (the Canadien) his ancient influence except in the district of Montreal.*

Except in the district of Montreal? Do we see here the beginning of cracks in Québec's social fabric? Whereas the Church reigned supreme in rural Québec, its influence was on the wane in urban areas, even in 1837. As a matter of fact, from that period until the mid-20th-century, the bishops of Québec issued regular pastoral letters urging the flock to *stay on the farm*, to shun *Babylon* in the cities. More later on the bishops. Durham continued:

> *The French Canadian priests have an almost unlimited*

influence over the lower classes of Irish.

This crossing of the linguistic battle-lines by the largely anglophone Irish was not surprising. As recent immigrants from a land where Catholics had long been under the thumbs of their English Protestant conquerors, where Irish priests had stood by the people during perilous times, these Irish immigrants naturally felt comfortable being ministered to by Catholic priests, no matter what language they spoke. In fact, many of these Irish immigrants gradually became assimilated into the majority francophone community, some eventually becoming true blue *Québécois*. Thus, it is not uncommon today to see *Québécois* with Irish family names shouting the most strident of nationalist slogans, castigating anglophones, with equally Irish names, for having *oppressed* them! But, to get back to Durham, he also said:

> *No general provision was made for education, that alone among the nations of the American continent, it (Québec) is without a public system of education."*

As a result, said Durham:

> *They (Canadiens) remained the same uninstructed, inactive, unprogressive people; habitants are almost universally destitute of the qualifications even of reading and writing. Nevertheless, we find every village in Lower Canada filled with notaries and surgeons, with little practice to occupy their attention.*

This is at the heart of the charge brought against the Québec education system from that day to this: Controlled by the Church, it favoured the few but provided little for the majority who were thus condemned to economic penury and feudal subservience to their élite. In fact, the school system in New France, which continued relatively unchanged until well into the 20th-century, was geared to meet the Church's need for priests and nuns, not the economy's need for carpenters, engineers and businessmen. And because the Church maintained control of the province's Catholic schools until 1964, (yes, 1964!), the secular needs of Catholics were only gradually provided for in Québec's schools. Fortunately for most anglophones, the Church had no jurisdiction over Protestant schools. Consequently, those attending English schools were exposed to a course of study that more or less prepared them for the then developing industrial-commercial world. Inadequate education, said Durham, helped to contribute to an economy where *Canadiens* simply could not compete.

> *Rude manufactures are carried on in the cottage by the family of the habitant; and an insignificant proportion of the*

> *(Canadien) population derived their subsistence from the barely discernable commerce of the province.*

In other words, manufacturing and its attendant commercial endeavours were all but absent at a time when industry and commerce were the twin engines of economic growth and social progress throughout the western world. Whether this was the result of people inadequately attuned to the imperatives of the commercial world or the result of inadequate business investment is, of course, arguable. Both conditions seem to have applied in Québec at that time. As mentioned earlier, because of the lack of *Canadien* investment capital or business interest, English businessmen ruled the roost. Moreover, said Durham:

> *The large mass of the labouring population are French in the employ of English capitalists. The more skilled class of artisans are generally English.*

This suggests that, not only could the *Canadiens* not compete with the English in existing commercial areas, they could not be counted upon to innovate with new business endeavours. In fact, said Durham:

> *Whatever energy existed among the population was employed in the fur trade and hunting* (occupations that were destined to occupy insignificant positions in the Québec economy in very short order). *Further, the mass of the community exhibited in the New World the characteristics of the peasantry of Europe. The Conquest has changed them but little.*

Perhaps more perceptive than he realized at the time, Durham added:

> *Accustomed to rely entirely on the government, the French population has no power of doing anything for itself.*

As I argued earlier, this type of behaviour, still evident in Québec, is quite consistent with that found in feudal societies. Moreover, even in agriculture, the *Canadien* was deficient according to Durham:

> *The English farmer very often took the very farm which the Canadian settler had abandoned, and, by superiour management, made that a source of profit which had only impoverished their predecessor. ..... The entire wholesale, and a large portion of the retail trade of the Province, with the most profitable and flourishing farms, are now in the hands of the English.*

Etienne Parent, a leader among the *Canadien* Patriots, was to make the same point soon thereafter. And the reason why English Canadians were better farmers than their *Canadien* cousins was not complicated: The former were beneficiaries of a tradition of agricultural innovation in England while the latter were still following farming practices that their ancestors had brought over from agriculturally backward 17th-century France. Here again, Parent made the same point. As additional proof of weakness in the agricultural sector among *Canadiens*, Durham said that, although the overall population of the province had increased about seven times between 1760 and 1837,

> *There has been no proportional increase in cultivation or of produce from the land already under cultivation; and the increased population has been in great measure provided for by mere continued subdivision of estates.*

In addition, he cited a report that claimed that, between 1784 and 1826,

> *The population of the seigneuries had quadrupled, while the number of cattle had only doubled, and the quantity of land in cultivation had only increased one-third. Complaints of distress are constant, and the deterioration of the condition of a great part of the population is admitted on all hands.*

In other words, Durham claimed that even the agricultural sector, the dominant economic sector, was having a hard time feeding even the local population. This was quite a charge since it was the rural life that the Church was promoting to safeguard *Canadien* culture. And to make matters worse, Durham said:

> *From the French portion of Lower Canada there has, for a long time, been a large emigration of young men to the northern states of the American Union, in which they are highly valued as labourers, from which they generally return to their homes in a few months or years. ..... The stationary habits and local attachments of the French Canadians render it little likely that they will quit their country (permanently) in great numbers. ..... Above all, the French population's attachment to its Church has produced the effect of confining it within its ancient limits.*

Although Durham's observation of the exodus of workers was quite perceptive, his conclusion that this was, and would always be, only a temporary exodus proved to be dead wrong. In fact, as I outlined previously, the number of expatriate *Canadiens/Québécois* rose from about 30-percent of the descendants of the original French settlers in 1760 to about 50-percent in the late 1980s.

This suggests that, until the Québec economy starts providing for its own, its people will continue to emigrate in search of the necessities of life.

Finally, as regards the relations between the masses and their secular élite, between the two francophone solitudes of that period, Durham said:

> *The persons of most education belong to the same families as the illiterate habitants. To this singular state of things I attribute the extraordinary influence of the Canadian demagogues. The most uninstructed population anywhere trusted with political power, is thus placed in the hands of a small body of demagogues.*

I would argue that this deferential attitude cited by Durham can be explained, at least in part, by the traditional feudal deference of the people toward their leaders. That these demagogues chose to pursue their own narrow interests rather than lead the people toward modernity, is of course a tragedy, but still consistent with the feudal practices of earlier times. Moreover, said Durham:

> *The entire neglect of education by the Government has thus contributed to render this people ungovernable. ..... Those who were not even entrusted with the management of a parish, were enabled, by their votes, to influence the destinies of a State.*

Now, what major conclusions can we derive from Durham's observations? It seems clear to me that French-English relations must appear at the top of the list. Moreover, notwithstanding the clearly enormous social influence of the Church, *Canadien* politicians pursuing objectives not shared by the Church had obtained close to the upper hand by the 1830s. Although not reported by Durham because it followed his investigation, the suppression of the Patriotic Rebellion had the effect of restoring the Church to its position atop the influence ladder in Québec. That said, I would conclude that:

1.   Notwithstanding the temporary success of secular *Canadien* politicians, the Church remained the most influential institution in Québec between 1760 and the 1840s ... and on into the 1960s;

2.   The Church was responsible for an educational system which produced nuns, priests, lawyers and doctors;

3.   The mass of *Canadiens* were uneducated and unskilled, and consequently remained poor;

4.   The existence of two francophone solitudes was very much in evidence

at that time;

5.   The prevailing social and political attitudes in *Canadien* society at that time were clearly feudal;

6.   The English, who not only controlled business but also tended to occupy the more skilled trades, were more affluent than the *Canadiens*.

If you stand back and compare Durham and Garneau from a distance, you would find that their observations were largely congruent. Where Garneau described a people who chose to be inward-looking, Durham reported on the social and economic consequences of their choice. Moreover, Garneau (and others such as Groulx) accepted the adverse economic consequences of this choice as a minor price to pay for the protection of *Canadien* culture.

In any event, the suppression of the rebellion convinced some Patriots to go underground and wait for better days ... which finally arrived more than a century later; others allied themselves with the Church as it set about to reassert its influence in *Canadien* society. William Johnson argues that the anglophobia that characterizes *Québécois* literature today first saw the light of day in this post-rebellion period.[20] The plots in Québec's novels remained essentially unchanged until about the 1940s as if they followed a prescribed formula: The farm boy leaves for the city where he becomes contaminated by the English and is redeemed only when he returns home to his *Canadien* rural roots in the protective embrace of the Church. That this type of literature served the interests of the Church is clear. Moreover, there should be no doubt that this type of literature served the interests of the secular nationalists who went underground in the late 1830s to surface again only during the 1960s. Others, not wishing to throw in their lot with the Church, redirected their energies, abandoning the *futile* pursuit of secession in favour of the more practical pursuit of political power within British-controlled Québec. A few even tried to improve the economic lot of *Canadiens*.

Now, before anyone jumps to the conclusion that pursuit of the economic interests of ordinary people was implicit in the political choices of the élite, let me point out the obvious from the historical record: First, the Church was prepared to sacrifice the economic interests of the people in order to achieve its own institutional interests; second, there is no evidence to suggest that those who seek political power necessarily care a fig about the well-being of their constituents. All that can be said is that, although those who lust after power always promise that, once elected, they will alleviate the travails of the poor, the facts often reveal quite another story: Many power seekers, certainly those in Québec, have ignored the interests of their gullible constituents in the pursuit of their own, sometimes contradictory objectives. Étienne Parent (1802-74) was among the few *Canadiens* who tried to improve the economic lot of the people.

Québec according to Etienne Parent

To some, Étienne Parent was the leading intellectual in the Patriot camp. As a journalist and lecturer in the 1840s and 1850s, he tried to convince those in power first, to improve the Québec educational system, and second, to encourage more *Canadiens* not only to invest in business, but also to start sending their sons to business and engineering schools instead of to the more traditional law and medical schools.[21] He was of course rebuffed by the Church and politicians of his day. In fact, the record shows that the attitudes decried by Parent in the 1840s still prevailed in the 1990s!

Although Parent was a man ahead of his time in some matters, he was not so well advanced in others. For instance, since he did not support the notion of the sovereignty of the people, he certainly was no democrat.[22] But then, how many unconditional democrats were there at that time? He also held that *Canadien* culture could only be protected within the caring embrace of the Church, a very orthodox position for that time. Although some of his ideas would not find much support among modern analysts, others would. In fact, I would argue that we should ignore his orthodoxy and instead respectfully doff our hats to him for his revolutionary attempts to save Québec from the smothering embrace of the Church.

He felt that "*there are three ways to conserve our (Canadien) nationality: religious, political and social.*" Since the first was under the care of the Church, and the second that of *Canadien* politicians, Parent became a champion of the third, the orphan no one seemed to care about. He said:

> *I urge you (Canadiens) to pay more attention to industry than you have heretofore done. Our inattention in this area is the cause of the lamentable (economic) state in which we find ourselves in our own country (Québec). Let us admit that we abhor industry, an unfortunate attitude that we inherited from our motherland in France.*[23]

One does not have to be a rocket scientist to acknowledge the political courage required to make public statements such as this at that time. After all, he was promoting a social program diametrically opposed to that desired by the Church, the most influential institution of the day. I can think of no similar example in Québec today. And not that there is any lack of opportunity. For instance, have you ever heard of any member of the secessionist *Parti* Québécois admitting that the average *Québécois* would be better off if their politicians spent more time trying to improve Québec's education system than in provoking constitutional confrontations with Ottawa? For those not aware of matters constitutional, education is a provincial responsibility in Canada, a responsibility guarded jealously in Québec. No, there are few modern versions of Étienne Parent.

He went on to say that industry, not agriculture, was the source of social power in America; that the nobles on this side of the ocean were industrial workers and businessmen; that, although the priest had an important role to play in society, he must not usurp the legitimate role of others. This said, Parent then declared that *Canadiens* were very un-American in this respect:

> *We (instead) become merchants to avoid manual labour; we become lawyers, notaries and doctors to show off our diplomas; but our education in industrial matters is almost non-existent.*

Consequently, concluded Parent, *Canadiens* had become second class citizens in their own land. And, as Durham had observed earlier, the *Canadiens* became resentful of the relatively wealthy English. Parent argued that this resentment was misplaced because *Canadiens* were the cause of their own misfortune. Although the same argument can be made today, hell will of course freeze over before 'heresy' such as this issues from the lips of any *Québécois* nationalist!

To help break out of the economic *cul de sac* in which he found his fellow *Canadiens*, Parent felt that they had to improve the quality of their public schools. Remember that Durham had earlier reported on the sorry state of education in Québec. To effect this improvement, Parent recommended that *"it is better to have one or two good schools in each parish than the eight or ten we have now."* Although having ten schools in a parish seems improbable, the parishes were geographically much more dispersed at that time which might account for this apparent proliferation. But no matter, Parent was really pushing for better education. To pay for better schools, he recommended an increase in taxation, a noble gesture for which he was rebuked by both property owners and the Church.

Canadien politicians resolved the education issue by refusing to deal with it: They ceded responsibility for education to the Church in 1874, a responsibility it maintained until 1964. No need to point out that Parent's recommendations were not implemented in Québec's Church-run schools.

Québec according to the Bishops

So much for the forward looking but doomed prophets and analysts of mid-19th-century Québec. But where the Church ignored inconvenient prophets, it co-opted some politicians and cowed others who could not be ignored. For instance, the political leader of the Patriots, Louis-Joseph Papineau, although apparently a closet atheist, still chose not to challenge the hegemony of the Church. This may explain his model for *Canadien* society, a rural society based on subsistence agriculture, a mirror image of the socio-economic model favoured by the Church.[24] This model also found favour in other secular circles. For instance, in 1884, the lawyer Charles Thibeault wrote:[25]

> *In the country-side, everything is green, joyous and gracious*
> *... (But) consider our towns with their princely residences,*
> *their grandiose monuments, their huge buildings, their wide*
> *avenues, their noise, their disarray, their social discord, their*
> *misery, their wealth, their commerce, their uncertainty, their*
> *speculative stock markets, their financial catastrophes, do you*
> *think that happiness reigns there? That people feel safe*
> *there? That the police can really protect people from danger?*
> *Do not fool yourselves; behind the silk curtains flow more*
> *tears in a day than you will see in a whole year (in the*
> *country)! The smile on the face of a businessman often masks*
> *his anxiety; the sweetness on the lips of a city dweller often*
> *covers the bitterness in his heart. It is in the heart of large*
> *cities that we find desperation, crushing remorse, trouble,*
> *unrest and insomnia that country people do not experience in*
> *this country. Suicide, this morbid weakness of lazy and*
> *deranged people, is the product of feverish urban life.*

Although this anti-urban attitude in the mid-19th-century may have been well founded--I make no case for or against it--it was nevertheless out of step with the prevailing economic imperatives of the day: The western world was industrializing rapidly in urban areas. Yet, the Church still resisted the trend with its biggest guns. In an 1894 pastoral letter, the bishops of Québec said:[26]

> *We are right in saying that agriculture is the real foster*
> *parent of all people, its principal source of wealth; it is in the*
> *land that we find the real wealth of a nation, wealth that is as*
> *stable and certain as God's bounty, which always renews itself*
> *and which is less subject to the disastrous fluctuations that*
> *afflict business and industry.*

It would appear that these bishops had never heard of, or perhaps had chosen to ignore, the disastrous consequences that follow crop failures, almost certain regular occurrences in agricultural economies. And, if Durham is any guide, Québec agriculture in the 19th-century was so inefficient as to make crop failures almost inevitable. Nevertheless, the same bishops went on to say:

> *People rush foolishly toward Babylon (corruption?) in our*
> *cities; seeking happiness, they find ruination. This exodus*
> *from the country-side over the recent past has brought great*
> *unhappiness to our people, duplicating what happened in*
> *Europe (Dickens?). This abandonment of the country-side is*
> *a definite threat to public prosperity; it is also a moral*
> *disaster. In the big cities, in the factories, the farmhand finds*
> *himself quickly in contact with the most impious people, with*

> *perverts; as a result, he gradually loses the (Catholic) faith*
> *which had nourished him until then; his beliefs and his morals*
> *crumble sadly, and he acquires only misery and dishonour for*
> *his old age.*

With the passage of time, anti-urban attitudes within the Church seemed to remain unchanged. In 1902, theologian Louis-Adolphe Paquet said:[27]

> *Our (Canadien) mission is not so much to concern ourselves*
> *with money but to develop ideas; it is not to be concerned*
> *with factories but with spreading the social influence of our*
> *homes, homes that are illuminated by religion and ideas. .....*
> *It is futile to struggle against American or English (Canadian)*
> *economic power. Our vocation lies elsewhere. And what*
> *would be more appropriate then than to follow the leadership*
> *of our religious élite, who, having been concerned with the*
> *future of the French-Canadian collectivity since 1760, propose*
> *that we turn our backs on the material world to follow a more*
> *noble spiritual path.*

Note that the message here is to forgo the material for the greater rewards of the spiritual. Since Paquet served as theological counsel to the bishops, his opinions must have reflected theirs in this area. Conclusion? The Church in Québec clearly used its considerable influence to discourage *Canadien* participation in the then developing industrial economy. Moving on to 1920, the bishops made clear that their attitude toward education was still consistent with this social objective. Louis-Nazaire Bégin, the bishop of Québec, said:[28]

> *Because ignorance has saved our people from assimilation in*
> *the past, we intend to save ourselves in the future in the same*
> *way. Therefore, we can state publicly that French Canadians*
> *need only know their (Catholic) catechism and a little*
> *arithmetic.*

In 1923, in another pastoral address to the faithful the bishops declared: [29]

> *We are addressing ourselves to those who live in the country-*
> *side, among whom we always recognized the source of our*
> *religious and national heritage. It is there in contact with the*
> *soil where our motherland is rooted, ... there where are*
> *affirmed the characteristic virtues of our people which make*
> *us the most religious and happiest people on earth. ..... For a*
> *small amount of easy money, factories sap the physical energy*
> *of your children; the promiscuous city, with its unhealthy yet*

*attractive activities, exercises on them a disastrous influence
for which their simple education did not prepare them.*

This is another clear rejection of modernity; it is also an admission that the
education provided by the Church simply was not intended to prepare Catholics
(mostly francophones) for the then developing modern industrial economy. In
1944, the Jesuit Richard Arès wrote:[30]

*The (modern) economic life does not help us, it hinders us. .....
It is this source of life, stability and patriotism (in the country-
side) that urban living tends to tarnish for its own benefit.
The city consumes men and disturbs family and parish life. ....
Big cities mix up working people and destroy them in physical,
social, moral and national terms.*

Clearly, the evidence suggests that the position of the Church on rural/urban
matters remained essentially constant from the years of the French régime in the
18th-century to at least the mid-20th-century: It preferred a society that was
more rural and agricultural than urban and industrial. But, since there is many
a slip betwixt the cup and the lip, the central question remains: Did the Church
succeed? Was it able to impose its will on *Québécois* politicians, the people
who were in a position to translate Church preferences into public policy?
Moreover, was it able to arrest the trend toward urbanization and
industrialization, a trend that was then in full swing throughout the whole
western world? Although the short answer to both is a qualified yes--it was able
to impose its will on politicians and it did succeed in slowing down migration
from farm to city--let us seek support for this answer in the historical record.

The Church Triumphant

In 1866, reflecting the widely held notion that the state should take its direction
from the Church, Bishop Lafleche said:

*A Catholic legislator cannot vote for a law that goes against
the teaching of the Church.*[31]

Sounds like something you might hear today from some 'fundamentalist'
religious leaders. Although I am not certain that the Church was as bold in
Québec then as, say, ascendant Islam is today, I think its influence was probably
at least as great. For instance, rare were the political or social gatherings that
did not pay homage to the local clergy. Bishops, of course, merited respect
from politicians that bordered on the sycophantic. And with good reason. The
historical record shows that any politician in Québec foolish enough to work
against the interests of the Church--until at least the 1960s--usually found

himself in mortal danger at the next election. This I can attest to from personal experience. Elected as a school commissioner in Montréal in 1977 with the support of the Church, I was soundly defeated three years later because Church authorities supported my adversaries. The reason? I had had the temerity to vote for some administrative measures that had displeased the bishop.[32]

But the influence of the Church extended to well beyond the relatively parochial world of school politics. In a 1958 budget speech, Maurice Duplessis, the premier of Québec, said:[33]

> *The government of the Union Nationale (Duplessis' party) has always understood that agriculture is the economic foundation of nations. Moreover, the traditions, customs and folklore that provide a people with its character, are nurtured in the country-side.*

Since Québec had been urbanizing steadily for some time, passing the 50-percent mark in 1915, you would have thought that a politician of Duplessis' stature would have been able to realize that his political objectives and the Church's rural goals were no longer as congruent as they once were. But no, Duplessis was either of the same rural mindset as the Church or very reluctant to oppose it. That he harboured the same rural notions was not improbable: His political strength in fact lay in rural Québec. In addition, although his sometimes illegal and often brutal suppression of the civil rights of those who opposed him attest to his well deserved reputation for the ruthless abuse of power, his attitude toward the Church was one of caution. Not that he was afraid to oppose the Church when he had to: When Cardinal Charbonneau of Montreal sided with some striking workers, the Pope suddenly reassigned Charbonneau to a minor position in rural British Columbia, it is said at the request of Maurice Duplessis.

But before anyone criticizes M. Duplessis, remember that, in the old days prior to the 1960s, when priests successfully directed the devout, they did so with the omnipotent authority of Holy Mother Church and therefore of God Herself. The faithful knew that disobedience certainly meant social rejection within their xenophobic communities and probable condemnation to an eternity in hell for the particularly obtuse. For example, some of my more irreverent kin insist that they were present (or knew someone who was) when the *curé* berated unfruitful married women who were not doing their duty. Unfruitful meant having only three children! So numerous are these apocryphal tales that some must be true: Where there is smoke there must be fire, and all that. As a result, most listened attentively to their *curés* and obediently produced larger families. This was the so-called *revenge of the cradle*, the Church-inspired plan to overcome British domination through the wombs of the faithful. Although the demographic result was positive--the dominant *Québécois* share of the provincial population was never challenged--the economic consequences were clear and predictable: Poverty. That is, if you start with low wages, because the economy produces relatively low-paying jobs, and you then require those wages to support large families, the result has to be economic stress for the families concerned. Fortunate it was for the people of Québec that the Church's assault on modernity failed eventually, but unfortunately, not before it inflicted considerable economic and social harm on the people.

Hence, it is no stretch to conclude that the people must have listened respectfully to the Church's message on the joys of rural life. However, the extent to which they translated this message into action is, of course, arguable. For example, the record shows first, that the rate of urbanization increased in Québec despite the Church's rural message, but second, that it took place at a slower pace than elsewhere in Canada. So, was Québec's continued urbanization a direct rejection of Church directives by the people or were other imperatives at work? Let's consider the demographic record.

The Church and Demographics

Table 5-2: % Urban		
	Qué	Ont
1991	78	82
81	77	82
71	81	82
61	74	77
51	66	71
31	63	61
21	56	58
11	48	53
1891	34	39
71	23	22
51	15	14
1844	12	
Sources: Censuses 1931-1991		

In 1844, about 12 percent of the population of Québec lived in urban areas: 5 percent of francophones and 33 percent of anglophones.[34] So, even in those early years, there was a clear language split along rural/urban lines. By 1931, despite almost a century of admonitions from the Church, Québec's overall urban concentration had risen to 63 percent: 58 percent of francophones, 79 percent of anglophones and 88 percent of allophones. Twenty years later in 1951, 66 percent of Québecers were living in urban areas: 63 percent of francophones, 83 percent of anglophones and 87 percent of allophones[35]. The 1991 Census showed that 78 percent of the people lived in urban areas: 75 percent of francophones, 84 percent of anglophones and 93 percent of allophones. Clearly, from these and other data we can conclude that:

1.   Francophone Québec's urban concentration puts it behind Ontario, British Columbia and Alberta, and just ahead of rural Manitoba.

2.   Allophones are the most urbanized group in Québec; anglophones are second; francophones are the least urbanized.

But, what is the economic significance of this lag in Québec's rate of urbanization? Well, we know that urban societies are more prosperous than the rural variety. To cast more light on this situation, let's look at the record.

Note that, though Québec was originally more urban than Ontario (Table 5-2), it became relatively more rural than Ontario in the 1870s and remained essentially that way from then on. Also to be noted is the little appreciated fact that, not only was Québec absolutely *more* urban than Ontario in 1851 (137,000 to 134,000), it was also absolutely *less* rural (754,000 to 818,000). What these data tell us is that relatively urban Québec was well positioned in the late 19th-century to lead Canada into the industrial age. The answer to why it did not is hidden within the historical record. So let us dig a little deeper to unearth the answer from beneath these dry statistics.

Despite the fact that the birth rate was *higher* in Québec than in Ontario between 1851 and 1921, Québec's total population increased *less* rapidly, 1.4 percent per year versus 1.6 percent in Ontario (Table 5-3). Since greater fertility usually produces greater rates of population growth, it is curious that this did not happen in Québec in this period. Before dealing with this anomaly, let us consider another related anomaly. Since Ontario was industrializing more rapidly than Québec at that time, we might have expected its pace of urbanization to be more rapid as well: And the record shows that this indeed happened--urban populations increased at the rate of 3.7 percent per year in Ontario between 1851 and 1921 versus 3.3 percent in Québec. But, by the same token, a faster rate of urban growth in Ontario should have been accompanied by a slower growth rate in its rural areas. But that did not happen: Ontario's rural growth rate marginally exceeded Québec's, 0.6 percent per year versus 0.5 percent. That was the second anomaly. So, what explains these two anomalies, that both urban and rural growth rates were greater in Ontario between 1851 and 1921?

First of all, there is only one anomaly, not two; second, the anomaly is in Québec, not in Ontario. Although emigration of Quebecers to the United States in search of work had been going on since the days of the French colonial régime, there was a hemorrhage in the period 1850-1930 when about 500,000 mostly rural Quebecers emigrated to nearby New England in search of jobs in its textile mills.[36] Remember that Lord Durham reported this practice in his 1837 report. Moreover, it was a hemorrhage since it represented an emigration rate about nine-times the rate that prevailed almost a century later in the early 1990s! In addition, although this started as a seasonal migration, where *Canadiens* worked in New England for part of the year, returning to Québec for the balance, it soon became permanent: Families emigrated to set up permanent residence in New England. This rural exodus explains why Québec's rural population grew more slowly than Ontario's between 1851 and 1921.

Then, sometime in the 1920s, economic

Table 5-3: Population Growth Rates - % Per Year					
	Total		Rural		Urban	
	Que	Ont	Que	Ont	Que	Ont
1961-1991	0.9	1.6	0.4	0.9	1.0	1.8
1931-1961	2.0	2.0	0.8	0.2	2.6	2.8
1921-1931	2.0	1.6	0.2	0.8	3.2	2.1
1851-1921	1.4	1.6	0.5	0.6	3.3	3.7

Sources: Censuses 1931, 51, 61, 71, 91

conditions weakened in the United States, drying up the demand in New England for low-skilled *Canadien* workers. Instead of emigrating then, this rural *Québecois* proletariat tended to migrate to Québec's cities. This explains the relatively high urban growth rate in Québec in the 1921-31 period (3.2 percent per year in Québec versus 2.1 percent in Ontario) as well as the offsetting rate of rural growth (0.2 percent per year in Québec versus 0.8 percent in Ontario). The Great Depression of the 1930s stopped this urban trend by discouraging migration to jobless cities. This, coupled with the attraction of the farm for those wishing to avoid military service during the 1939-45 world war, accounted for Québec's relatively high rate of rural population growth in the 30-year period ending in 1961 (0.8 percent per year versus 0.2 percent in Ontario).

The period 1851-1961 coincides almost precisely with that period of Québec history when the socio-political hegemony of the Church was relatively unchallenged. In the post-1960 period, the leadership torch passed to secular nationalists who gave birth to the Quiet Revolution, about which more later. But what about the Church? To what extent was it responsible for keeping Québec rural relative to many other provinces, especially neighbouring Ontario?

Since the Church did unquestionably promote a rural life style, and since Québec did remain more rural than Ontario, one might be tempted to conclude that the Church indeed succeeded in imposing a rural life style on Québec. Although many of the faithful obeyed the Church's call to remain on the farm, the evidence suggests that, for most, the search for bread and butter was more compelling. Hence, it is inaccurate to place the blame for Québec's tardy urbanization only on the Church's pastoral preferences.

Without wishing to split hairs, I would argue instead that lack of jobs in Québec's cities was more properly to blame for this tardy urbanization. And I would argue further that this dearth of jobs was caused, *inter alia*, by a workforce whose skills did not measure up to the demands of a growing industrial economy. Thus, companies would simply have set up shop in Ontario where skilled people were relatively more abundant. And since the basis for skills-development is a sound public school system, this suggests that Québec's schools were less effective than Ontario's. I will offer evidence later to show that this was in fact the case. And remember, the Church was responsible for education in French in Québec until 1964. Hence, although its pulpits may have been marginally effective in keeping Québec rural, its schools were even more responsible. Because these schools were deficient in the quantity (and quality?) of their graduates, they kept Québec relatively uneducated and hence industrially uncompetitive with Ontario. Thus, although it might not be reasonable to suggest that the Church's sermons kept Québec rural, the record will show that it is quite reasonable to conclude that its schools did the job instead.

The Church and Education

One of the important tests of the success of any modern democratic society is the literacy of its people. That is, democracies are effective only when electorates are literate and informed, and hence able to make intelligent choices; a prosperous economy cannot exist without a literate workforce; and so on. And the historical record is brutally clear: Until Newfoundland joined Canada in 1949, Québec's rate of illiteracy was the highest in Canada. In 1891, for instance, 30.7 percent of Québecers could neither read nor write versus 11.3 percent in Ontario.[37] Although the definition of illiteracy has changed over time, the facts never vary: The highest rate of illiteracy in Canada outside of Newfoundland is to be found in Québec. Moreover, as will be shown later, since Québec anglophones tend to be among the most literate people in Canada, this indicates that *Québécois* must therefore be the least literate in the land. And what explains this miserable condition? Look no further than Québec's social investment in its libraries and public schools.

I would argue that a decent network of public libraries is an important indicator of the literacy of any modern society. What then would you conclude from the fact that, since 1960, per capita operating expenditures for public libraries in Québec have lagged about 75 percent behind those in Ontario?[38] That, for all practical purposes, means that Québec does not have a modern public library system. Although I have seen no comparable data for earlier periods when the Church ruled supreme, I would assume that the situation could not have been any better then. In fact, since the very influential Lionel Groulx castigated *Québécois* for belonging to organizations such as the Québec Library Association in the 1930s, we might safely conclude that public libraries could not have figured very prominently in Québec cultural life at that time. Thus, Québec did not have then, and does not have now, one of the most elementary building blocks of a literate society, a decent public library system.

| Table 5-4   Public Schools |||
| Enrolments per 1,000 People |||
Qué	Ont	Québec vs Ont
1991	162	194	- 17 %
75	214	239	- 10 %
60	213	227	- 6 %
45	156	166	- 6 %
40	179	171	+ 5 %
30	192	197	- 3 %
15	181	210	- 13 %
1900	168	226	- 25 %
1885	152	249	- 39 %
70	168	273	- 38 %
1866	168	256	- 35 %

Source: StatCan 81-568 T9

Moreover, when a clearly inadequate network of public libraries is coupled with a less-than-adequate public school system, high rates of illiteracy and other related social ills are almost guaranteed. For instance, consider the history of enrolments in elementary and secondary schools in Québec and Ontario (Table 5-4). Clearly:

1. Apart from the temporary blip in 1940, enrolment in Québec's public
    schools has always lagged behind Ontario's. Since Canada's war
    machine was reluctant to draft students, Québec's schools may have
    experienced an anomalous increase in enrolments in 1940.

2. Since enrolment in Québec's English schools was similar to Ontario's,
    enrolment in Québec's French schools must have been lower than the
    overall Québec figure shown here.

3. Many school-age children must not have attended school at all,
    especially in Québec. As a result, in the years prior to the turn of the
    20th-century, when the Church reigned supreme, this probably
    accounted for the very high illiteracy rate cited for 1891. Moreover, in
    the period 1911-32, 14 percent of children went without schooling in
    Québec versus about 10 percent in Ontario.[39] Not surprising then that,
    in 1961, near the end of the Church's reign, 57 percent of the adult
    population had elementary schooling or less in Québec versus 46
    percent in Ontario.[40] Moreover, in 1961, 48 percent of the workforce
    had elementary schooling or less in Québec, 38 percent in Ontario.[41]

4. The narrowing enrolment gap with Ontario from 1900 to 1960 can
    probably be explained by the increasing urbanization of Québec and the
    declining influence of the Church.

5. The worsening enrolment gap after 1960 suggests that the reforms in
    education brought about during the Quiet Revolution simply have not
    worked. More later on the Quiet Revolution.

Making this already bad situation worse in the period prior to 1960 was the
effect of the curricula in this Church-dominated school system. Québec's unique
classical colleges had been established by the Church to provide candidates for
its seminaries. And since the same course of classical studies was suited to the
preparation of doctors, lawyers and notaries, these future members of the
Canadien secular élite took their intellectual nourishment at the same altar as
their religious kin. Although this may have suited the liberal professions and the
Church, its suitability for other professions is not so certain.

    For example, my secondary school, Loyola, an English-
language Jesuit institution in Montréal, provided a modified classical program.
That is, while the top students followed a course loaded with classical Greek and
Latin, the 'not-so-brilliant' were required to put up with physics and chemistry.
I was among the lucky ones permitted to study Greek and Latin. You can
imagine how prepared I was for my university science program! No surprise
then that the 'dummies' got better marks than I in university. Still, I thank my
lucky stars that I was not required to follow the full classical program then

Table 5-5: Universities

Enrolments Per 1,000 People

	Qué	Ont	Québec vs Ont
1975	12.1	19.2	- 37 %
1968	10.9	12.8	- 15 %
1967	13.4	11.1	+ 21 %
1966	13.0	9.9	+ 31 %
1960	7.4	5.3	+ 40 %
1945	4.9	5.4	- 9 %
1940	3.5	3.3	+ 6 %
1930	3.3	3.6	- 8 %
1920	3.2	3.2	

Source: Historical Statistics, 2 ed.

common in French equivalents to Loyola. Fortunate as well were the graduates of other English secondary schools where the best students were not required to study Latin and Greek at the expense of physics and chemistry. Small wonder then that graduates of Church-run secondary schools and classical colleges tended to be under-represented among university students studying engineering and the sciences. Before considering evidence that demonstrates this under-representation, let us first examine the trend of university enrolments.

First, let me point out that the data in Tables 5-4 and 5-5 are apparently contradictory. That is, if the data for elementary and secondary school enrolments are accurate, and I believe they are, those for university enrolments do not make sense. For instance, while the data in Table 5-4 follow an orderly progression, as they should, those in Table 5-5 are unusually erratic. While part of this unusual pattern may have been caused by mistakes in data reporting, the major part is explained by the fact that Québec changed its system of education in the 1960s, a change which required it to report its statistics differently.

To put it very simply, Québec's classical colleges were abolished in the mid-1960s, and most of their functions reassigned to pre-university junior colleges (Cégeps). That is, where university enrolments in Québec up to 1967 included students at classical colleges as well as those in orthodox universities, the data after 1967 excluded classical colleges. Thus, we are looking at two unique data sets, the first up to 1967, the second since then. And since we are interested in education during the Church's period of hegemony, we will concentrate here on the period up to 1960.

By doing some rough averaging for the period 1920-1960, we find that, where proportional enrolments in Québec's elementary and secondary schools lagged about 5 percent *behind* Ontario's, enrolments in its universities and classical colleges ran about 5 percent *ahead* of Ontario. This would indeed be considered an anomaly--if both provinces had comparable school systems and similar university configurations. But we know that they were different.

This apparent anomaly can be explained by the effect of high enrolments in Québec's classical colleges: Ontario had no equivalent to these Church-dominated schools. Moreover, as mentioned earlier, these classical colleges were originally intended to prepare candidates for priestly studies in the Church's seminaries; and, based on the statistics cited previously, they succeeded admirably. Since classical studies also suited the early educational requirements of other liberal professions such as medicine and law, Québec's post-secondary school system tended to produce a curious mix of graduates: Relatively more priests, lawyers and doctors than engineers and economists, for instance. Ontario, on the other hand, tended to produce the reverse mix. To paraphrase Lord Durham and Étienne Parent, Québec's post-secondary system of education made it long on graduates that the economy did not need.

Stated still another way, while the Québec system produced administrators who stood *above* the modern economy, producing income for themselves but creating few jobs for others, Ontario produced graduates capable of working within the wealth-producing economy, thereby generating income for themselves *and* jobs for others. Clearly, while the Ontario system was geared to the needs of the economy, Québec's was not. This may explain why Québec's classical college system did not survive the early years of the Quiet Revolution.

Furthermore, this suggests a class system in Québec where educational opportunity was effectively restricted to a minority. On the one hand were the religiously devout and the sons of professionals who had access to higher education. On the other were the majority who came from less wealthy families or who may have been interested in science rather than in the liberal professions. Since the majority must have realized early that the classical system was not for them, they may simply have abandoned their studies before completing elementary or secondary school. At any rate, it would appear that the post-secondary system of education in Québec was geared to satisfy the Church's demand for priests, and the demands of the well-off for entry to the socially prestigious liberal professions; it obviously did not meet the needs of those with other social, economic or professional interests.

For example, consider Québec's universities in 1959-60. At that time they were still officially called Protestant or Catholic, designations that were to change shortly thereafter to English or French, anglophone or francophone. Although francophones accounted then for about 81 percent of the provincial population, French/Catholic universities accounted for only 63 percent of university enrolments. French institutions also accounted for 97 percent of theology students, 83 percent of law and medical students, 69 percent of commerce students, and 53 percent of engineering students.[42] Notice how little had changed from the time of Durham and Parent: Where, in the 1830s, priests, doctors and lawyers dominated the francophone educated class, they remained equally dominant in 1959; where francophones had shunned the commercial and technical professions in the 1830s, their participation in these areas still lagged significantly behind anglophone participation in 1959. Statistics for later years show that this same trend continued unchecked into the 1990s, the reforms of the Quiet Revolution notwithstanding.

Finally, the overall performance of Québec's post-secondary system of education was, by any test, pretty shoddy up to 1961: 3.4 percent of adult Québecers had university degrees versus 3.9 percent of Ontarians; an additional 40 percent of Quebecers had completed some high school studies versus 50 percent of Ontarians; and, as cited earlier, 57 percent of Quebecers had not progressed beyond elementary school versus 46 percent in Ontario.

Consequences

To its successors, the secular nationalists, the Church bequeathed first, an uneducated and inward looking people struggling in an economy where average family income lagged about 11 percent behind Ontario; second, a credulous people vulnerable to the demagogic appeals of unscrupulous hucksters; and third, a giant diaspora of dispossessed *Canadiens* that its policies had driven into economic exile. Moreover, as the faithful prepared to abandon its suffocating embrace, the institutional Church was left on the edge of the precipice leading to its social oblivion. Its efforts, however well intentioned, obviously went for naught. It is a pity that so many had to suffer for nothing.

Summary

From 1760 to the 1960s, the Catholic Church was the most important socio-political institution in Québec. It controlled the schools, hospitals and welfare systems; it influenced social, political and economic choices through its very effective bully pulpits. For instance, it promoted rural life when other agricultural economies were industrializing, when the faithful were fleeing the Québec countryside in search of jobs in the factories of urban Québec and New England; it geared its schools to the production of priests, doctors and lawyers when the economy was screaming for engineers, economists and carpenters.

As a result of two-hundred years of its leadership, the Church's legacy to the incoming secular nationalists of the Quiet Revolution in Québec was an under-educated and inward looking population whose average family income lagged 11 percent behind Ontario; a credulous people ripe for plucking by the less honourable among their leaders; and a huge diaspora of economically exasperated *Canadiens* almost as large as the current population of Québec. That it also neutered itself is no consolation to those who suffered at its hands.

But how could the Church have been so influential in areas beyond the spiritual?

From its earliest years, Québec was torn between two irreconcilable imperatives: On the one hand, the drive by the people to make a living anywhere they could; on the other, the desire by the Church to pursue its divine mission in a pastoral economy. Since France's strong feudal influence carried over to New France, and persists in Québec to some extent to this day, the Church was able to use its historic feudal power to influence the evolution of the colony after the British conquest in 1760. It was assisted in this endeavour by the traditional feudal tendency of peasants to defer to their leaders. For instance, so influential was the Church that it was able to keep the faithful from siding with the Americans during the American war of independence.

Moreover, in the mid-19th-century, F. X. Garneau told us that not only did feudalism survive in Québec, but that *Canadiens* chose not to participate in the new industrial economy, leaving the way clear for their English compatriots. Garneau's observations were not inconsistent with those of Lord Durham whose 1837 report on the turmoil in Québec must have been known to Garneau. Durham described a society where *Canadiens* remained illiterate and uneducated; where the feudal class system of haves and have-nots was obvious (early evidence of the existence of Québec's two francophone solitudes); where *Canadiens* had become so accustomed to relying on their government that they were unable or unwilling to provide for themselves; where *Canadiens* eschewed modernity even on their farms; where *Canadiens* resisted investing or working in modern industries; where educated *Canadiens* were drawn to the liberal professions rather than to business and science; where *Canadiens* were less skilled than English workers; where *Canadiens* were jealous of their more prosperous English neighbours.

Lest the reader be tempted to dismiss Durham for perhaps being partisan and biased, consider the views of Etienne Parent, the intellectual leader of the Patriots who rebelled against the British in 1837. In the 1840s and 1850s, Parent essentially repeated Durham's observations. In fact, said Parent, because *Canadiens* had chosen not to participate in the modern industrial economy, they had become second-class citizens in their own land. His recommendations to correct the situation were ignored by both the Church and the political system it controlled.

Furthermore, in addition to being in the right place at the right time, the Church also had the troops to do the job. For example, when we see how influential the Irish Church is today, and note that, until the 1960s, Québec had proportionately more priests than Church-dominated modern Ireland, the historic social influence of the Québec Church becomes more intelligible. No surprises then that, when the bishops spoke, everyone listened. So much so that even the powerful Maurice Duplessis, Premier of Québec, supported the Church's traditional preference for the rural over the urban ... in 1958!

But, did the Church succeed in its promotion of rural life? The short answer is a complex no and yes, but only partly.

To begin with, since about half of the descendants of the original French colonists now live outside of Québec, and most of them in the United States, we might conclude that the lure of bread has always been more influential than the rural preferences of the Church. Therefore, this suggests that the Church failed. But then again, Québec is in fact proportionately more rural than Ontario, British Columbia and Alberta, and only slightly less rural than rural Manitoba. This suggests instead that the Church succeeded.

Moreover, it appears that this resistance to urbanization in

Québec had more to do with the lack of jobs in Québec's cities than with admonitions from the pulpit. And, since the lack of job-creating investment can be attributed in part to the poorly educated Québec workforce, the product of the Church-controlled school system, we can thus credit the Church's schools for having thrown Québec urbanization into low gear.

Specifically, the overall performance of Québec's post-secondary system of education was clearly inadequate during the period of Church hegemony. In 1961, for instance, Québec lagged about 13 percent behind Ontario in university graduates per thousand people. This is important since, as I will show later, the health of the economy and the production of university graduates are closely correlated. Thus, the economy must have been significantly less robust in Québec than in Ontario. In fact, average family income in 1961 was 11 percent lower in Québec!

Finally, two class-related conclusions leap from the data. First, among francophones, the evidence suggests that those at the upper end of the social system always had better access to post-secondary education than did those nearer the bottom. Second, among those attending universities, francophones tended to dominate in the liberal professions, anglophones in engineering, science and business. No surprise then that the former dominated among lawyers, the latter among businessmen and industrialists, the people who controlled the economy.

Clearly, while Ontario schools, as well as anglophone schools in Québec, were geared to the needs of the economy, Québec's Church-dominated francophone schools were not. And generations of *Québécois* have paid dearly for this folly.

Notes

1.   "Femmes et religion," Le Devoir, 22 avril, 1996.

2.   Derived from Statistical Abstract of Ireland, 1989. Central Statistics Office, Dublin, Ireland.

3.   L.E. Hamelin, Évolution numérique seculaire du clergé catholique dans le Québec, (Québec: Recherches Sociographiques, vol 2, Université Laval, 1961), pp 189-241.

     Statistics of the Catholic Church in Canada, 1992-93, Canadian Council of Catholic Bishops, Tables 1 and 5.

4.   Lionel Groulx, Lendemains de conquête: Cours d'histoire du Canada à l'Université de Montréal, 1919-1920, (Montréal: Bibliothèque de l'Action française), pp. 49, 186.

5.   G. Lanctot et Georges Robitaille, Les Canadiens français et leurs voisins du sud, (Montréal: Valiquette, 1941), p. 241.

New Canadian Encyclopedia, vol 3, 2 ed., 1988, Hurtig, (New France).

6.   Roberta Hamilton, Feudal Society and Colonization: The Historiography of New France), (Gananoque: Langdale Press, 1988), p. 26.

7.   Denis Vaugeois et Jacques Lacoursière, Histoire 1534-1968, (Montréal: Boreal Express, 1968), p.227.

8.   J. Mathieu et J. Lacoursière, Les Mémoires Québecoises, (Québec: Les Presses de l'Université Laval, 1991), p. 272.

9.   E. Delisle, The Traitor and the Jew: (Montréal: Robert Davies, 1993), p. 72.

10. Jan Noel, "New France: Les Femmes Favorisées," Atlantis, VI, 2 (Spring 1981).

11. Delisle, p. 25.

12. Delisle, p. 27.

13. Delisle, p. 58.

14. Delisle, p. 84.

15. Delisle, p. 45.

16. François-Xavier Garneau, Histoire du Canada, tome 3, (Québec, 1859), pp. 359-60. Cited in Les Mémoires Québécoises, 1991.

17. References to the Durham report were derived from Lord Durham's Report, An Abridgement of: Report on the Affairs of British North America (Jan. 1839), Edited by G.M. Craig, Carleton Library Press, 1982/92.

18. Lionel Groulx, Lendemains de conquête, (Montréal: 1920), pp. 49, 66, 71, 140, 143.

19. Hamilton, note 1 p. 17.

20. William Johnson, L'Anglophobie: Made in Québec, (Montréal: Stanké, 1991).

21. P. E. Gosselin, Étienne Parent (1802-1874), (Ottawa: Fides, 1964)

22. Gosselin.

23. Gosselin, pp. 9, 52.

24. Johnson, p. 66.

25.   Mathieu/Lacoursière, p. 257, taken from Charles Thibault, avocat, dans Biographie de Charles Thibault, suivie de son discours prononcé aux fètes des noces d'or de la Saint-Jean-Baptiste, à Montréal, le 27 juin 1884.

26.   Johnson, p. 67.

27.   Mathieu/Lacoursière, p. 255.

28.   Mathieu/Lacoursière, p. 222, cited from Le Pays, 25 septembre, 1920.

29.   Le Mirage, p. 39, quoting Lettre pastorale du Cardinal Bégin de Québec, 25 mai, 1923.

30.   Johnson, p. 282, quoting Notre question nationale, Montréal, Éditions de l'Action nationale, 1944, p 107.

31.   Johnson, p. 58. Citation is from "Louis-François Laflèche, Quelques considérations sur les rapports de la société civile avec la religion et la famille, Montréal, Eusèbe Sénécal, 1866, p. 136.

32.   For more information, consult Durand et Proulx, La Déconfessionalisation de l'école: Le Cas de Notre-Dame-Des-Neiges, (Montréal: Libre Expression, 1980).

33.   Johnson, p. 187.

34.   D. J. Bercusan et al, Colonies: Canada to 1867, (Toronto: McGraw-Hill Ryerson, 1992), pp. 226-227.

35.   1931 Census of Canada.

36.   Gustave Lanctot, "Le Québec et les États-Unis, 1867-1937" pp. 290-310 in G. Lanctot (publisher), Les Canadiens français et leurs voisins du sud, (Montréal: Valiquette, 1941).

        New Canadian Encyclopedia, (New France)

37.   1931 Census of Canada, vol 1, Table 63, p. 1064.

38.   StatCan 81-205, 1962 and 1991 Census of Canada.

39.   1921 Census of Canada, Table 100, p. 693.

40.   1991 Census of Canada, 93-328, Table 1.

41.   1961 Census of Canada, VIII - Part 1, Table 17.

42.   Annuaire Statistique de Québec, 1960.

6

The Current Élite: Québécois Nationalists, 1960 - 1997

Overview

Modern Québécois nationalists can be considered either as the resurrection of the suppressed Patriot rebels of 1837 or as the natural inheritors of the Church's leadership mantle after 1960, or both. I would argue, first, that the hegemony of the Church did indeed pass over to today's nationalists during the Quiet Revolution, and second, that these nationalists are driven by the same secessionist motives that inspired the mid-19th-century rebels. Moreover, their secessionist bias seems to be fuelled by the noxious fumes of an ideological culture drawn from three historical sources.

      The first source was the anglophobia that characterized the literature of Québec for more than a century following the suppression of the 1837 Rebellion; the second was *Le Devoir*, the ultra-nationalist daily newspaper which catered so well to the antisemites of the 1930s, and caters today to Québec's anglophobes and the cultural idiots spawned by the Quiet Revolution. By cultural idiots I mean those who are more interested in suppressing English than in promoting French, even as they thus compromise the economic interests of the man in the street. The third source of this secessionist bias was the Marxist-inspired ideologies underpinning the anti-colonial turmoil in Africa and Asia after WW II. For example, many of the intellectual leaders among the current crop of *Québécois* nationalists equate the plight of *oppressed Québécois* with that of Algerians who had to resort to civil war to obtain the same political rights already enjoyed by *Québécois* for over two-hundred years! Got that? Some are so convinced of their oppressed status that they refer to *Québécois* as white niggers! Not only are both claims ridiculous, the second is blasphemous.

      In addition, Québec's Quiet Revolutionaries were enamoured of the notion that Québec's economy would be driven more by state economic power than by private sector investment. That this classical socialist model has not been very successful elsewhere seems not to perturb them *outre mesure*. Complementing this silly notion is the equally silly concept of Legislated Joy. That is, where success is normally associated with some measure of personal effort, *Québécois* have been led to believe that, if the government of Québec legislates, the problem is solved. This silly idea reached its apex during the 1995 Referendum when secessionist leader Lucien Bouchard promised that all of Québec's economic ills would vanish magically once Québec became independent. Snicker if you will, but, not only did *Québécois* not laugh him into submission, they voted massively to support him!

Québécois Nationalists and the Quiet Revolution

Although there is some truth to the notion that all *Québécois* are nationalistic in one way or another, I refer here to those who bridle at the mere presence within

Québec of anything English. You will find them especially in nationalist organizations such as *La Société Saint-Jean Baptiste, Le Mouvement Québec-Français, Le Mouvement National des Québécois*, and who knows how many other similarly august agglomerations of *oppressed* individuals.

Nurtured within these chauvinistic organizations is an anglophobic culture that has come to dominate Québec politics and poison social discourse. Although this culture is common to all political parties in Québec, it has found its natural home in the secessionist *Parti Québécois* (PQ).[1] However, let it not be assumed that there exists any Québec political party that is truly non-secessionist. For example, the allegedly pro-Canada Bourassa Liberals of the 1970s, 1980s and early 1990s made a fine living threatening to leave Canada every time Ottawa said no. But then, there was a certain political logic to Bourassa's manoeuvring: He could not appear to be less nationalistic than the secessionist PQ, the party that had cleverly associated itself with the soul of Québec by calling itself the *Parti Québécois*. Nor could Daniel Johnson, Bourassa's successor, afford to appear less nationalistic than the PQ. Thus, it was quite normal for Johnson to say that his party still considered the threat of secession as a legitimate political strategy for his pro-Canada party![2]

Supporting this secessionist bias is the notion of Québec-as-victim, a myth that is so well established that it should be recognized as an official psychological condition and be called the Poor-Québec-Syndrome. According to this notion, true nationalists insist that *Québécois* culture is under siege from anglophone Canada and must be protected at all costs. For many *Québécois* leaders, this protection can only be realized in a two-step process: First, by legislation that suppresses the use of English and the influence of anglophones in Québec; and second, by the political secession of Québec from Canada. And if, in the process, non-*Québécois* happen to leave Québec in massive numbers, few within this nationalist cohort will be surprised. Not that they intend this *de facto* ethnic cleansing to be the desired consequence of either step. Of course not! But, if a truly *Québécois* state was the natural consequence of the democratic decisions of non-*Québécois* to emigrate, why shouldn't the remaining *Québécois* feel good about the result, a state where *Québécois*, by ridding themselves of the English, are truly masters in their own home?

They would, of course, consider it a humiliating insult to suggest that this *democratic* exodus was in any way the inevitable result of the passage of anglophobic language laws; or that it may have been caused by the inability of even bilingual anglophones and allophones to find work within the huge Québec public service, a place of work obviously reserved for *Québécois*; or that the private sector, recognizing the real intentions of the language laws, had adjusted its hiring practices to discriminate in favour of *Québécois*; or that this exodus may have been caused by the dearth of private sector jobs for anyone, the necessary consequence of never-ending secessionist threats that discouraged job-creating business investment; or that the exodus was a simple desire by some Canadians in Québec to live in peace in a political environment where their very existence did not offend their neighbours.

Though you might properly argue that most *Québécois* tend to be mildly and perhaps innocently xenophobic, these nationalists are dangerously anglophobic. Moreover, their hatred extends to the federal government in Ottawa, the example *sans pareil* of English perfidy and oppression. If you think I exaggerate, speak to any of these so-called patriots and judge for yourself. But be prepared to nurse a splitting headache when all is said and done: Their memories are long, very selective and their *facts* often dead wrong. Some also tell fibs and humungous whoppers from time to time. So, wear your thickest skin and arm yourself with a stiff drink before engaging them in debate.

Cheering on these true-blue nationalists is a motley crew of fellow travellers whose careers have been well nourished within this xenophobic culture. I refer here to people such as journalists, public school teachers, university academics and artists. Also included are those employed within the bloated provincial bureaucracy, in addition to unions such as *La Fédération des travailleurs et travailleuses du Québec* (FTQ), *Le Conseil des syndicaux nationaux* (CSN), *La Centrale des enseignants du Québec* (CEQ), and associations such as *L'Union des Producteurs de lait du Québec*.

And then of course there is *Le Devoir*, than which no Québec daily newspaper is said to be more influential. So revered is it that, whenever it encountered the financial difficulties that occasionally afflict similar low circulation newspapers, the faithful always assembled dutifully to save it. And the social and political composition of these devoted saviours is amazing: Politicians and business people of every stripe, unions, even competing newspapers! After all, one does not allow to founder the newspaper whose publisher was often called the Pope.

When *Le Devoir* was founded in 1910, its mission was not merely to report and interpret the events of the day, that being the normal role of newspapers everywhere. Nay, its mission was to instruct French Canadians (the term *Québécois* not having been invented) in their civic duty, especially as regarded their obligation to defend their French, Catholic and rural heritage. This presumably made *Le Devoir* the self-proclaimed custodian of nationalist orthodoxy. Today, of course, Catholic and rural no longer figure in the definition of *Québécois* culture. Nevertheless, *Le Devoir* soldiers on, promoting the cause and editorially scolding those who offend the Pope, which means anyone who dares harbour contrary views. But, if scolding is not effective, *Le Devoir* majestically ignores them. Sounds like how the other Pope deals with the inconvenient and the impertinent.

It was these nationalists who gave birth to and directed the Quiet Revolution. They were hence responsible for both its successes and its failures, of which there is an ample supply of both.

The Quiet Revolution: General Assessment

The Quiet Revolution was born when the Liberals under Jean Lesage defeated the *Union Nationale* in 1960 and then initiated a series of reforms meant to reverse the consequences of two-centuries of Québec history. I remember still the exhilaration of voting for the Liberals in *Trois Rivières*, the home of the then recently deceased Maurice Duplessis, long time leader of the despised *Union Nationale*.[3] The Quiet Revolution was a true revolution in that it set out to break with the past, arguably producing the greatest period of social and political upheaval in Canada since WW II. And, like most revolutions, its accomplishments are a mixture of fact and fiction. For example, contrary myths notwithstanding, the historical record suggests that the Quiet Revolution failed to improve the economic lot of the average *Québécois* relative to Ontarians.

As mentioned previously, the Church's gift to the incoming secular nationalists was an under-educated and inward-looking people whose average family income languished 11 percent below Ontario's. It also bequeathed a sorry history of xenophobia, anglophobia and antisemitism. Although antisemitism no longer looms large in nationalist discourse, xenophobia and anglophobia do.
        That these primitive and ignoble notions would have survived the early days of the Quiet Revolution was not obvious at the time. It seems to me that two political slogans were then current. The first was "*Maitres chez nous*" (Masters in our own house) which clearly sought to dump all of Québec's ills onto the anglophone scapegoat; the second went something like "*Il faut s'instruir*" (One must be educated ... to earn a living) which was not anglophobic. The second slogan recognized that the major cause of the miserable financial condition of *Québécois* was the inadequate, Church-run public school system. Although I do not remember who was in either camp, the historical record is clear: The anglophobes won. That is not to say that Québec's educational system was not subject to reform since 1960. In fact, the reformers fell all over each other, and still do, in attempts to save Québec's schools from the egregious errors of their predecessors. But, despite their efforts, they failed miserably: Relative to Ontarians, *Québécois* remained as uneducated in 1991 as they had been in 1961. Moreover, *Québécois* were relatively poorer than Ontarians in 1991 than in 1961. More later on both these points.

But, *Québécois* poverty was only in part the fault of the educational system: Also responsible was a lack of job-creating business investment. And this can be attributed first to the strategic decision of the early Quiet Revolutionaries not to court business investment, but to rely instead on the economic power of the Québec state. Since this public investment model had not worked anywhere before, it is not surprising that it has not worked so far in Québec. I will show later that *not even* the most sacred of public ventures in this period, the nationalization of private hydro-electric companies to form Hydro-Québec, was particularly successful. And, more recently, it certainly did not make much sense to use quasi-public funds to purchase the economically sick asbestos mines and their processing plants in Québec to protect a few jobs. That industry was sick because demand for asbestos had been declining since asbestos had been identified as carcinogenic! Not surprisingly, this *great social investment* became a great economic white elephant. Moreover, the excessive administrative controls inflicted on business by the Quiet Revolution's earnest reformers simply discouraged potential investors. And, finally, the abrasive language laws enacted to protect an allegedly fragile French culture also had the effect of discouraging business investment--to say nothing of being in part responsible for cleansing from Québec the best and brightest anglophones and allophones (and some *Québécois*), people who decided to pursue careers in more hospitable environments elsewhere. Hence, Québec has remained job-poor.

The Quiet Revolution: Literacy

Table 6-1: Reading Skills 1991	
% of Population Above Normal	
Ontario	62
Québec	57
BC	69
Alberta	71
Manitoba	65
Sask.	72
NS	57
NB	56
NFLD	39
Canada	62
Anglophones	71
Francophones	58
Source: StatCan 89-515E, 1991 Tables 3.3, 4.1	

Until recent times, literacy was defined simply by the ability to read and write. In 1891, about 31 percent of the population of Québec over the age of five could neither read nor write versus 11 percent in Ontario. By 1931, Québec and Ontario had improved these sorry statistics to 9 and 5 percent respectively. Although this was a commendable improvement in Québec, it was still not enough to make it competitive with Ontario.[4] If we fast forward to 1991 when we had more sophisticated definitions, we nevertheless see the same story. In 1991, measurements of literacy dealt with three items: Reading, writing and numeracy. Since so little is known about how to grade writing, this element was side-stepped in the reference study on which my comments are based.[5] In reading, 57 percent of adult Quebecers scored above normal versus 62 percent of Ontarians (Table 6-1); in numeracy, the score was 54 for Québec, 64 for Ontario. Advantage Ontario. At the national level, 71 percent of anglophones scored above normal in reading versus 58 percent of francophones. Moreover, when reading literacy was measured against levels of schooling (Table 6-2) anglophones came out on top at all levels of education. Advantage anglophones.

Given the importance of language in Québec, it would help if we could distinguish anglophones from *Québécois* in Table 6-1. Unfortunately, the reference study provides no such data split, at least not explicitly. But, it did provide a national linguistic split which might help us decipher Québec linguistically. To do this, let's dig a little and see what language-related conclusions for Québec we can tease from these data.

Table 6-2: Literacy versus Schooling

% of adults able to read at the highest level by mother tongue in Canada

	English	French
Elementary		
Some/none	15	10
Secondary		
Some	52	44
Completed	77	70
Post Secondary		
Pre-Univ.	85	81
University	93	90

Source: StatCan 89-525E
1991 Table 4.5

From a strictly mathematical perspective, the Canadian average of 62 percent with reading skills above normal makes sense in that it sits between the values of its national linguistic components, between 71 for anglophones and 58 for francophones. I must admit, however, that I would have expected an overall national average closer to the anglophone 71 than to the francophone 58: The mysteries of statistics, I suppose. Now, here is where the digging becomes sticky, so pay attention.

If, for the moment, we assume that the 71 national average for anglophones was derived only from anglophones in provinces outside of Québec, we encounter a mathematical impossibility. That is, only Saskatchewan had a value above the anglophone national average of 71 while Alberta was right on the national average. Given the relatively small populations of these two provinces (combined they account for only 13 percent of Canada's total), it is mathematically impossible to derive an anglophone national average of 71 from these data. Therefore, there must have been a sizeable and very literate anglophone population somewhere else. And there was ... in Québec.

In 1991 there were about 1.2 million Québec anglophones (actually about 0.6 million anglophones and an equal number of allophones), greater than the populations of all provinces except Alberta, British Columbia and Ontario. Thus, in order to make any sense of a national anglophone average of 71, something like 73 percent of Québec anglophones must have had above normal reading skills. (I was initially baffled by Ontario's relatively low reading score of 62. However, other sources seem to confirms this low score.) And, for Québec to have had an overall above normal average of 57 in reading skills, with Québec anglophones at 73, the related score for *Québécois* must have been somewhere in the low-50s. Thus, assuming the data on numeracy skills mirror those on literacy, these data suggest that:

1.   Québec anglophones are much more literate/numerate than *Québécois*;

2.   Québec anglophones are more literate/numerate than other Canadians;

3.   *Québécois* are less literate/numerate than Canadians everywhere save Newfoundland.

Clearly, the Quiet Revolution did not do much to help *Québécois* close the overall literacy/numeracy gap with other Canadians. Moreover, since I always get a perverse chuckle pointing out interesting unintended consequences, let me finger a beauty: It would appear that the Quiet Revolution did more to improve the literacy/numeracy of Québec anglophones than that of *Québécois*!

The Quiet Revolution: Libraries

When we attempt to explain this alarming level of *Québécois* illiteracy/innumeracy, we have no choice but to confront the heart of the Quiet Revolution, the reforms to education. That having been said, I would argue that a necessary precondition to any efforts at educational reform is a literate society where the people have reasonable access to public libraries. Here, the historical record does not treat Québec very kindly. At the outset of the Quiet Revolution, per capita expenditures on Québec's public libraries were the lowest in Canada, 73 percent behind fourth-place Ontario (Table 6-3). Then, after three decades of playing catch-up, Québec increased its spending substantially, but still stood 9 percent behind Ontario! Hence, we must conclude either that this relatively low level of spending satisfied public demand, or that it reflected the limit of government intentions to improve the literacy of the people. Reader's choice. In any event, making up for Québec's century-long underfunding in this area will require substantial extra spending on public libraries for several decades. And, there isn't much sign of that on the horizon. Now, on to Québec's schools.

Table 6-3: Public Libraries		
Expenditures-$ / Capita		
	1962	1992
NFLD	0.38	10.71
PEI	0.36	12.50
Nova Scotia	0.37	10.89
NB	0.17	10.56
Québec	0.09	4.06
Ontario	0.33	4.46
Manitoba	0.14	3.91
Sask.	0.28	7.97
Alberta	0.14	5.29
BC	0.24	3.31
Canada	0.23	5.04
Sources: StatCan 81-205, 1962 87-206 1991/92		

The Quiet Revolution: Public School Curricula

Here again, the historical record is not kind to Québec. To begin with, as argued earlier, one has the right to be suspicious of the curricula in Québec's public schools. Moreover, judging by what is promoted at some meetings of *Québécois* teachers, it would appear that very doubtful pedagogy permeates French schools in Québec. For instance, *Le Devoir* claimed that those hawking services at teachers' conventions in Québec seemed to be more interested in the questionable *touchy-feely* aspects of pedagogy than in anything of value to students.[6] In addition, there is the negative impact on the learning environment in Québec's schools brought about by an obvious resistance to modernity, a condition described so tellingly by Jean Blouin.

In the December 1982 issue of the magazine *L'Actualité* there appeared an article entitled "*The New Illiterates*" where Blouin reported on the pitifully low level of computer literacy in Québec's French schools. To Blouin, the advent of the personal computer signalled the end of the old economy in Québec just as much as the invention of Gutenberg's printing press had signalled the end of the Middle Ages in Europe. However much one may wish to temper this strong comparative imagery, no one should doubt that computer literacy is a *sine qua non* in modern economies. Blouin argued that one of the tests of the quality of Québec's public school system was the extent to which it used personal computers as teaching aids in the classroom. He reported that:

1.   Where there were computers in the classrooms of 72 percent of Ontario's schools and in 30 percent of Alberta's, Québec's elementary and secondary schools were running at about 11 percent![7] Not good, said Blouin.

2.   New Brunswick, with less than one-quarter of Québec's population, had 25 percent more classroom computers. Really not good!

3.   With less than 10 percent of the total student population, Québec's English schools had 67 percent of the computers. In Montreal, English schools had over 80 percent of the computers. This was worse than awful, it was humiliating!

Blouin noted that, where the governments of Ontario, Alberta and New Brunswick were well on the way to installing many more classroom computers, Québec was still at the discussion stage, appointing committees of every description to study the issue and recommend the obvious. This, said Blouin, was classic stalling on the part of a government more concerned with restructuring school administrations than with what was being taught in the schools. I might also add that this government was also more concerned at that time with keeping immigrant children out of English schools. To put this government inattention into proper focus, Blouin quoted a computer teacher from an English school who mocked his *Québécois* colleagues at a meeting, saying: "*Continue to discuss and do nothing, my students will have all the jobs.*"

In addition, Blouin took a poke at culpably innocent parents and Luddite teachers afraid of losing their jobs to machines! For instance, where teachers in Ontario had recommended the accelerated integration of computers into the curricula, teachers in Montreal's French schools had just timidly given their approval to the introduction of computers to the classroom.

Moreover, when the government of Québec finally became interested in this subject, it was to see if the computers needed in the schools could be designed and manufactured in Québec! Here Blouin almost lost his composure. He pointed out, with scarcely disguised scorn, that it was more important to the Québec economy to train students to use computers, anyone's computers, than to worry about where they were manufactured. Blouin noted,

Table 6-4: Classroom Computers, 1996

	Students per Computer		
BC	8	Alberta	11
Manitoba	8	PEI	13
Ontario	9	NB-English	14
NScotia	10		
NB-French	10	Québec	21

Source: "Computer Literacy"
Education Quarterly Review
1996, StatCan 81-003

and he was subsequently proven correct, that 80 percent of jobs in the near future would be computer-related. Therefore, said Blouin, why worry about a few manufacturing jobs when the spinoff benefits were so much more valuable?

Blouin's article embarrassed everyone in the Québec education establishment. It would seem, without wishing to be unfair, that the embarrassment arose, not so much from the pitiful state of computer literacy in French schools, but from the fact that anglophone parents and educators had risen to the occasion when their *Québécois* counterparts, as well as the provincial bureaucracy, had fallen on their collective face. Where anglophone parents and educators saw the need for computers in the classroom, *Québécois* parents were either oblivious to that need or suspicious of it; where anglophone parents sold cookies and chocolate bars to finance the purchase of these teaching aids, their *Québécois* parents, by and large, waited in classical feudal fashion for direction from their political masters. As a result of Blouin's article, the embarrassed Minister of Education rushed off in all directions, appointed several new committees to study the situation and promised to supplement local cookie drives with new funding from the provincial treasury.

Now, consider the situation in 1996 (Table 6-4), fourteen years after Blouin: Although the situation had improved *absolutely*, Québec's *relative* position had not improved at all. Whereas there was one classroom computer for every 3,000 students in Québec in 1982, there was one for every 21 students in 1996. But, Québec still stood in last place, 50 percent behind second-to-last place New Brunswick and light years behind BC, Manitoba and Ontario.

The Quiet Revolution: School Drop-Outs

Obviously, there is reason to be suspicious of what goes on in Québec's schools. It should come as no surprise then that poor academic achievement confirmed these suspicions (Table 6-5). Québec performed poorly relative to Ontario in two critical areas: Enrolments and drop-outs. Where the enrolment of school-age children reflects the ability of the system to get children into school in the first place, the drop-out rate measures its ability to keep them there. In the first area, to equal Québec's 1991 enrolments per 1,000 people, 17 percent less than Ontario's, we would have to go all the way back to about 1910. But then again, let's pause and reflect for a moment: These statistics may be misleading.

Since it now takes 13 years to get through Ontario's elementary/secondary school system versus 11 in Québec, Ontario would

Table 6-5: Public Schools

	1961		1991	
Enrolments Per 1,000 People				
Qué vs Ont	- 6	%	- 17	%
Adults With Less Than Grade Nine				
Québec	61	%	21	%
Ontario	47	%	12	%

Sources: Statcan Censuses
1961/91

naturally have more students enrolled. Therefore, I would conclude only that Québec's performance here is unclear.

But, when we consider the second area, the ability of the system to keep the kids in school until grade nine, we see that Québec clearly did not do well. In 1961, about 30 percent more adult Quebecers than Ontarians fell into this unfortunate category (61/47). By 1991, although both provinces had improved absolutely, Québec's relative position deteriorated seriously to a 75 percent deficit with Ontario (21/12).

Although the reasons for Québec's relative inability to get students past grade nine are no doubt numerous and complex, I can identify two key suspects. The first is that some kids simply never showed up for school. The second, and more probable, is that, once having started elementary school, they simply dropped out before completing grade nine. How many dropped out at the end of elementary school (grade seven), or after having commenced their high school studies in grade eight, is arguable: The only firm data I have are first, that 21 percent of adults did not complete grade nine (Table 6-5), and second, that 43 percent of those who started high school did not graduate (Table 6-6). I will argue later that the true drop-out rate for Québec was likely in excess of 50 percent in 1991.

To get a flavour of the difficulty getting kids through elementary school, and to introduce a linguistic dimension, note that about 21 percent of those entering high school had spent more than the minimum time getting through elementary school.[8] In other words, they had repeated at least one year of elementary school. Whether 21 percent is good or bad, I have no way of knowing. The data also show that schools in rural areas and in the inner city performed relatively badly (about 30 percent of students in both were late starters in high school); on the other hand, only 17 percent of kids in the suburbs were similarly afflicted. Now, here is the kicker.

Since those living in rural areas and in Montreal's inner city are mostly *Québécois*, they would thus have figured more prominently than non-*Québécois* among the late starters to high school. That is, it would appear that English schools did a better job than French schools in getting kids through elementary school on time. And, when we zero-in on high schools, we see the same pattern: Québec did not do as well as Ontario in keeping kids in school. In Ontario, determination of the number of drop-outs is not complicated: Subtract the number of high school graduates from the number of 18-year-olds in the total population. This calculation yielded a drop-out rate of 22 percent in Ontario for the 1992-93 school year.[9]

Figure 6-6: High School Dropouts - %	5-Year Rate	7-Year Rate
Montreal Inner City		
French	54	39
English	43	25
Mtl West Island Suburbs		
French	36	21
English	13	9
All Québec	43	31

Source: Diplomation, T 17

But, Québec took a different approach, starting from an already discounted level, those who started the first year of high school. This meant that, whereas Ontario included all potential students in its calculation, Québec ignored those who (a) had never attended school, or (b) had dropped out before getting to the first year of high school. Whether this represented a lot or a little, I know not. But, if this number had been included in Québec's official numbers, the number of *bona fide* drop-outs would have been higher.

At any rate, carrying on with its unique definition, the Québec Ministry of education calculated two (very sensible) drop-out rates, one at the end of the normal five-year high school study period, the other after allowing an additional two years for the earlier drop-outs to make up their missing credits. Thus, the five-year drop-out rate in Québec was 43 percent in 1993, the seven-year rate 31 percent *of those who had started high school* with them (Table 6-6). Although one can only guess what these rates would have been using the Ontario methodology, I estimate that the five year rate could have been as high as 64 percent, three times the Ontario rate.

That is, if you assume that there were no drop-outs in elementary school, it follows that the 21 percent of the adult population that did not complete grade nine must have been included in the 43 in Table 6-6. Hence, under this assumption, Québec would have had a total drop-out rate in 1991 of 43 percent. On the other hand, if you assume that the 21 dropped out before getting to high school, it follows that the overall drop-out rate must have been 64 percent, again apart from the uncounted no-shows. Since the truth probably lies somewhere in between, it is easy to see that Québec's true drop-out rate was likely in excess of 50 percent in 1991. Clearly, there are no bragging points here for Québec. And what about other linguistic implications?

Unfortunately, the specific data required to answer this question directly are not available to me. But, I have reasonable surrogates, the two data sets shown in Table 6-6 for Montreal's inner city and its West Island suburbs. The two school boards within each data set occupy the same territory, provide the same course of instruction, one in French, the other in English, and are subject to the directives of the same Ministry of Education. Hence, we might conclude that differences in their performance were probably due to variations in (a) the socio-economic status of their students, and/or (b) the competence of those providing the instruction, and/or (c) ..... what? Look closely at Table 6-6 and weep ... or scream with rage! Although one may draw many conclusions from these data, four leap from the page:

1.   Drop-out rates were much lower in the relatively more affluent suburbs than in the inner city.

2.   Drop-out rates were much lower in English schools.

3.   The drop-out rate in Montreal inner city French schools was substantially greater than the rate in French rural schools (With the French inner city drop-out rate at 54 percent, and the overall Québec average at 43, the rural average must have been less than 43 percent, probably around 30).

4.   English schools did a better job reducing the drop-out rate in the two years following the normal graduation year.

Advantage suburbs over inner city, English schools over French schools, and French rural over French inner city. What explains these hard facts?

    Not wishing to spend too much time proving the obvious, let me declare that relative affluence was probably the single most important factor accounting for the lower drop-out rate in the suburbs. That is, since the more affluent can afford to keep their children in school, they usually do. Not so simple for the variation between English and French schools, or between French inner city and rural schools. Was the English-French variation due to cultural and historical differences in their respective student populations, differences that were better addressed in English schools? If so, what were these differences, and what did English schools do that French schools did not do, or at least not do well enough? The same questions can be repeated for the French urban-rural comparison. When I deal later with the tests administered by the Minister of Education, I will address these questions again and suggest an explanation.

    Although I am quite able to pose these important questions, I am unable to answer them completely. But the Québec Minister of Education not only had an obligation to ask the questions, he/she also had the ability to answer them and then to provide the resources required to resolve them. But, from the data cited above, it is clear that the problems implicit in the questions, whatever they were, went unresolved. Were the questions even asked? If asked, were solutions identified? If identified, why were they not implemented? I am not aware of anyone really pursuing this issue effectively. I would argue that, as a direct consequence of this delinquent behaviour on the part of the educational establishment, the *Québécois* drop-out rate in 1991 was at a level that bordered on the criminal. Let me explain.

    In an economy that increasingly demands skilled workers, these drop-outs will almost certainly end up as society's rejects at the bottom of the economic heap. Moreover, such a high drop-out rate may very well create an economically deprived social class so large that serious social unrest may become inevitable. That is, if one-percent of the population feels deprived, the remaining 99-percent can always be taxed a little for the money required to calm the stormy waters. But, you cannot do this if half the population feels maligned: Taxes levied on the unmaligned would have to be so high as to introduce social unrest there as well. If you think this far fetched, take a peek at your history books: What do you think caused the French Revolution of 1789, the Russian Revolution of 1917, and the overthrow of many bumbling governments in this century? If you want to avoid this predictable cataclysm you know what to do: Do not get into this mess in the first place. Unfortunately, Québec is sliding down hill fast, and its leaders are doing nothing about it, except to seek scapegoats. In fact, as will be shown later, this deprived and potentially revolutionary *Québécois* social class already exists ... in Montréal.

But, why is this necessarily near criminal? Why can't it be a case of routine incompetence? First, because education is the constitutional responsibility of the government of Québec, a responsibility it proclaims aggressively whenever provoked; second, because Québec has the resources required to resolve these problems but chooses instead to invest in other less important areas, some profligate and wasteful, others simply frivolous, and a few clearly destructive of the well being of *Québécois*. That is why the drop-out rate is near criminal. More on this later. But, first, back to the classroom.

The Quiet Revolution: Secondary School Performance

What about those who did not drop out, those who stayed in school, how did they fare? To answer this question, the Québec Ministry of Education subjects all students in their final year of high school to standard tests in history, geography, economics, French and English. Why they do not also test mathematics, for instance, is puzzling. It seems as if the interests of the educational establishment have not changed since the Church was dislodged in 1964: The subjects tested here are the same ones that dominated the curriculum in the now-abandoned Church-controlled classical system.

The reader may also recall my reference to some of these subjects in a previous chapter. For instance, one of the high school texts in economics contained a monstrous lie, that Québec paid more in taxes to Ottawa than it received in services in return. Other texts also contained absurdities-- French and English were taught within a program extolling the virtues of astrology, numerology and UFOs! Moreover, the English translations of the original French versions of the standard province-wide exams were so bad that some honour students in English schools were failing the tests because they could not understand the questions! When administrators in English schools recommended that their students be given the exams in French rather than have to use the execrable English translations, they were turned down by Ministry officials. Too embarrassed, I suppose. So, with this in mind let us examine the results of these standard tests.

First, the only really clear difference in 1993 was between

Table 6-7: Québec High School Tests		
	% of Students Passing Tests	Index
	1993 1989	93/89
Boys	83.9 79.5	1.055
Girls	83.7 77.5	1.080
Public	81.4 75.5	1.078
Private	94.7 89.6	1.057
French	83.9 77.9	1.077
English	82.5 83.6	0.986
Québec	83.8 78.4	1.069

Source: Diplomation, p. 44

private and public schools (Table 6-7): Pass rates were much higher in the former (94.7 percent) than in the latter (81.4 percent). No surprise there. Pass rates in the other five categories were roughly mirror images of one another. In fact, the slightly higher pass rate for French over English schools in 1993 (83.9 to 82.5) was what I had originally expected ... for two reasons.

First, the relatively greater drop-out rate in French schools would have had the effect of cleansing French schools of underachievers, thereby intellectually enriching the remaining student body. That is, all other things being equal, the average student in French schools would have been more motivated than his opposite number in English schools. Second, the miserable translations cited above should have had a depressing effect on English scores. Now, it gets sticky.

In 1989, the English pass rate exceeded the French by a substantial margin, 83.6 to 77.9. By 1991, their relative positions had reversed. Was the reversal reasonable? Was it the result of the translations or drop-outs described above?

Consider the trend from 1989 to 1993 for all six categories in Table 6-7. If we use as reference the 1989-93 trend for private schools, we see that the pass rate in private schools in 1993 was 1.057 times the 1989 rate. Public schools did even better: the 1993 rate was 1.078 times the 1989 value. Students in French schools did equally well: 1993 was 1.077 times the 1989 rate. On the other hand, students in English schools did very poorly: Their pass rate *dropped*--1993 was only 0.986 times the 1989 value. If pass rates at English schools had instead grown at the private school rate, increasing 1.057 times between 1989 and 1993, the English pass rate in 1993 would have been 88.4, not 82.5. This would have maintained English schools in second place in 1993, right behind private schools, the same position they occupied in 1989. To explain the puzzling drop in pass rate in English schools from 1989, in addition to the large shortfall from the theoretical 88.5 in 1993, are we to believe (a) that students and/or teachers in English schools became delinquent after 1989, or (b) that the negative effect of the poor translations of the Ministry's standard tests was more pronounced than expected, or (c) ..... what? Smell a rat?

Also revealing are the actual scores in these tests. Have a good look at Table 6-8 where in column "A" are scores for the test in French, "B" in English, "C" in Economics, "D" in Geography, and "E" in History. If the reader will take the time to do some rough averaging of the Montreal data and

Table 6-8: Individual Tests in 1993					
% Of Students Who Passed Tests In:					
All	A	B	C	D	E
Montreal Inner City					
French	78	78	81	79	73	75
English	75	72	76	79	66	65
Montreal Suburbs					
French	79	78	81	78	74	76
English	86	82	86	84	80	77
All Québec					
French	84					
English	82					
All	84	82	80	83	82	78

Source: Diplomation

compare the results with the overall Québec averages, you will find, *mirabile dictu*, that the schools outside the Island of Montreal (not shown but deducible), most of which are French, were the clear winners. Yes, rural had bettered urban in the pass rate, as it had in drop-outs! In second place were the English schools on the Island of Montreal followed by French schools in the same territory.

Of particular interest was the superiority in all subjects--including French--of English over French schools in the suburbs. This is somewhat baffling since the higher drop-out rate in French schools should theoretically have produced a generally more motivated student body in French schools. Was it because English schools did a better job teaching French? Not likely. Were their students better able to benefit from the instruction provided? Stay tuned. Equally baffling was the superiority in the teaching of French in French rural schools over *both* urban and suburban French schools. Was this because the overpowering presence of English in Montreal made the teaching of French that much more difficult? Not improbable, but this did not appear to be an obstacle for the English suburban schools whose students did rather well in French. Were French rural teachers more competent than their urban counterparts? Can't imagine why they would be. Could variations in student-mix be a factor? Perhaps.

Where anglophones and allophones formed a tiny part of the student bodies in francophone-dominated rural French schools, anglophones formed a significant share of suburban French schools (anglophone parents recognized the linguistic imperatives of the time), and, allophones came to dominate inner city French schools. Why? Simple. As inner city *Québécois* migrated toward the suburbs, or shifted to private schools, they were replaced in inner city French public schools by allophones directed there by the commands of Québec's language laws. And, since the *Québécois* role model was disappearing from these schools, the remaining allophone students would have had more difficulty learning French. Mystery solved. Solution? Read on.

Whether extra pedagogical effort could ever resolve this *problem* in Montreal is arguable. I believe that it would help. But, doing something really effective would take more political courage than is evident to the naked eye. For instance, it would take massive new public investments in libraries and French language teachers. Also potentially effective, but politically impractical, would be to encourage *Québécois* to remain in the inner city, to not move to the suburbs as their financial situations improved. Since this would be like trying to make water flow uphill, it is an obvious non-starter. Voluntary decisions by *Québécois* parents to keep their kids in public schools, to stop bleeding the public sector to feed private schools, would also be helpful. This could be done by making it more expensive to attend private schools by reducing the level of government grants to private schools. This, of course, would be political suicide for any politician silly enough to even contemplate such a notion. If not that, then what? By really improving the quality of public education! Although all governments in Québec profess that this is exactly what their never-ending educational reforms are supposed to do, the results are always the same: More mediocrity. And parental response is also the same: Accelerated abandonment of the public school system.

So, unwilling or unable to implement effective solutions, to what do the *Québécois* intelligentsia resort? You guessed it, they tend to solemnly proclaim the imminent demise of French unless further restrictions are placed on the public use of English. For instance, consider the antics of these *patriots* at the national meeting of the PQ in early November 1996.

Where moderates in the party wanted to soft-pedal language issues, the extremists (apparently about one-quarter of the delegates) insisted on draconian changes to Québec's sign laws. At that time, English was legally *permitted* on public signs as long as French also appeared in bigger letters and was otherwise more prominent than the English text. However, this was not enough for party extremists who wanted English banned altogether. That these anglophobes were, with great difficulty, defeated is of little relevance here. But what is relevant was the purpose of the proposed ban on English signs.

That it could not have addressed the real issues is clear. For instance, that it could help teachers to better impart French to allophones is absurd. But, that it would gratify anglophobes is certain. That it would make Québec in general, and Montreal in particular, any more French, other than on the surface, is nonsense. Unless ..., unless this obvious provocation had the effect of convincing a few more anglophones and allophones to leave Québec. That is, although linguistic provocations such as this make no social or pedagogical sense, they are politically brilliant if they succeed in reducing the political influence of the opposition. Some call this process ethnic cleansing ... about which more later.

The Quiet Revolution: Private Schools

Before moving on to Québec's post-secondary educational system, let us return to its controversial network of private elementary and secondary schools. These schools are noteworthy because: (1) they receive substantial grants from the Québec Ministry of Education thereby subsidizing the fees paid by their students, and (2) people think, erroneously, that they are the exclusive domain

Table 6-9: Private Schools (PS)

Enrolments in PS as % of all
Enrolments in Elementary
and Secondary Schools

	1920	1961	1991
NFLD		0.4	0.2
PEI	3.7	2.4	0.5
NScotia	2.7	3.3	1.1
NB	3.4	1.6	0.7
Québec		7.7	9.0
Ontario	1.5	1.9	3.2
Manitoba	2.3	5.3	4.8
Sask.	0.8	2.1	1.5
Alberta	1.6	2.0	3.2
BC	3.4	6.1	7.6

Source: StatCan, Historical
1983, W94-149
81-229 XPB 1995, T7

of the rich.   Speaking from personal experience, I can refute the second point. Most kids attending private schools, were/are there as a result of the financial sacrifices of their parents. And why do they make these sacrifices, you wonder?   The reasons are numerous, but near the top of the list is parental loss of confidence in public schools.

Although Québec is not unique in its ardor for private schools, the evidence confirms first, that it is Canada's leader, and second, that the Quiet Revolution did nothing to dampen this ardor (Table 6-9). *Au contraire*, so unhappy were Quebecers with their public school system that, *during* the Quiet Revolution, they rushed to private schools in ever increasing numbers.   For instance, in 1961, private schools accounted for 7.7 percent of all enrolments in Québec's elementary and secondary schools.   By 1991, after 30 years of reforms to education in Québec, the private school share had increased to 9.0 percent! On the Island of Montreal, about 20 percent of students studying in English were in private schools in 1993 versus about 35 percent of those studying in French.[10] If private school share can be taken as an indicator of the quality of public education, these data suggest that the perceived quality of education in Québec declined during the fabled Quiet Revolution.

The reader should note that, in the mid-1960s, the Parent Commission investigated the state of Québec education, found it wanting, recommended many changes and went down in *Québec* history revered for its wisdom. However, in 1996, about thirty years after Parent, another government-appointed group bearing the pretentious title "*The Commission of the Estates General*," declared (my translation):

> *Montreal schools are in such a state of decay and devastation that, if left uncorrected, they will adversely affect the whole of Québec society.[11]*

It would appear that this warning went essentially unheeded by the authorities. No wonder then that *Québécois* are abandoning Montreal's public schools as fast as they can.   And, with *Québécois* absent, who is supposed to act as role models and integrators of immigrant allophones in the French public schools, immigrants who would much rather be in English schools? The tooth fairy? No kudos here for the Quiet Revolution.

The Quiet Revolution: Colleges

Based on the evidence advanced to this point, there is nothing to suggest that the *Québécois* élite have done very much in the field of education to help the people, notwithstanding the fact, I would argue, that the institutional reforms they enacted were theoretically sound. For instance, having grade eleven as the last year of high school makes sense to me: Grade thirteen in Ontario is defended only by teachers' unions concerned about jobs. However, neither province seems to be doing a particularly good job by the looks of it. Clearly, a good educational system requires more than the proper institutional structure. The same applies at the next level, the post-secondary, pre-university colleges.

In my view, Québec colleges, commonly called *Cégeps* (*Collèges d'enseignement général et professionel*), make pedagogical sense. In one instructional path are found various three-year professional programs (nursing and law enforcement, for example) that produce graduates ready for the workforce; in the other are two-year programs that prepare students for university. To calibrate your compass, note that it takes 16 years of schooling to get a BA in both Québec and Ontario. Without offering any proof whatever, I will claim here that the Québec path is pedagogically more effective ... in theory. Whether it in fact produces a better product is of course another matter.

To put these *Cégeps* into some perspective, consider their overall relationship to the high schools that feed them: In 1988, 77,208 students graduated from Québec high schools; three years later 54 percent of them graduated from *Cégep*, 41 percent going into the work force, 59 percent into universities.[12] Whether these splits are good, bad or indifferent, I am unable to say. But I do know that those who set up the original *Cégep* system were planning on a smaller proportion going on to university, the assumption being that Québec's economy needed the *Cégeps'* professional graduates more than it needed university graduates. Recognizing the political correctness of such an assumption, I nevertheless cannot imagine where they dredged up such a silly idea. As I showed earlier, modern economies are driven more by the highly educated than by the lesser educated, more by university graduates than by lesser mortals. This is even more evident today: The brain industries are crying for skilled workers while their brawny predecessors no longer employ the unskilled ... because they are either closing down or moving to the Third World.

But, oblivious to the obvious, Québec soldiers on, emphasizing the production of clerks when the economy is crying for engineers. Fortunate are those who followed their own informed instincts rather than the assumptions of those who set up the *Cégep* system. Unfortunately, the majority of *Québécois* seem to have been more influenced by their leaders' wonky assumptions than by their own informed self-interest.

Whereas French schools house about 90 percent of all students in elementary schools, their share of high school graduates drops slightly to 89. Only at the *Cégep* level are students free of the strictures of Québec's language

Table 6-10: French Schools	
Students in French Schools As a % of all Students	
Enrolments	
Primary School	90
Graduates	
High School	89
Cégep - 3 Yr Pgm	93
- 2 Yr Pgm	78
University - BA	72
- MA	72
- PhD	66
Québécois Share of Provincial Population	82
Source: Statistiques de l'éducation	

laws: Where the law does not allow *Québécois* and allophones to attend English elementary and secondary schools, it makes no restrictions at the post-secondary level. Already having freedom of choice, anglophones attend French *Cégeps* at the same rate that they attend French elementary and secondary schools: About 5 percent of all anglophone students. Going the other way, about 5 percent of francophones and 60 percent of allophones attend English *Cégeps*.[13] Given a choice, allophones would obviously prefer English schools.   Since this abandonment of the French *Cégeps* by these *Québécois* and allophones really annoys some nationalists, you can bet the mortgage that they will be howling for restrictions here in the near future.

As mentioned earlier, *Cégep* students can choose between a three-year professional program and a two-year pre-university program: In 1992, 48 percent chose the pre-university program in French *Cégeps* versus 69 percent in English colleges. The French share of graduates went from 89 percent in high school to 93 percent of *professional* graduates in *Cégep* and 78 percent in the pre-university program.[14] As a result, you can see two trends developing here: First, where French schools, assisted by language laws, dominate the early years, their dominance fades in later years as students start to exercise their freedom of choice; second, where French *Cégeps* tend to push their graduates directly into the workforce, English *Cégeps* move them into universities. Advantage Québec anglophones and allophones.

The Quiet Revolution: Universities

The declining influence of French schools in Québec continues into university. In 1961, 3.4 percent of the relevant adult population of Québec had university degrees versus 3.9 percent in Ontario. By 1991, these figures had risen to 11.5 and 14.6 respectively. Stated another way, Québec was about 13 percent behind Ontario in university graduates in 1961, 21 percent behind in 1991. To put it plainly, despite the fact that Québec improved its performance absolutely (3.4 to 11.5 percent), it lost ground to Ontario during this 30-year period, the period during which educational reforms were supposed to be rescuing the people from the educational humiliation of the Church-run system. Some rescue!

So much for not producing enough university graduates, but what about the distribution of those enrolled in Québec's universities, how did Québec compare with Ontario? If, for instance, Québec universities were

Table 6-11: Universities, 1988/89		
Enrolments Per 100,000 People		
Québec	Ontario	Rest of Canada
Economists	41	69	33
Teachers	172	114	201
Engineers	344	389	290
Admin.	270	186	160
Lawyers	46	43	29
Social Workers	26	15	18
Doctors	106	84	94

Source: ASDEQ, 1990

dominated by musicians while those in Ontario trained engineers, I would conclude that, unless Québec's was a musical economy, its student-mix was out of line with its economic needs. This issue drew the attention of *L'Association des économistes québécois, ASDEQ* (The Association of Québec Economists). It studied 1988-89 enrolments and published its findings in 1990.[15]

After crunching a few dozen numbers from their report, I determined the ratios in Table 6-11. The reader should note that I have listed the categories in more or less chronological sequence: Economists plan the economy, teachers instruct those who must eventually participate in it, engineers help to implement the economists' plans, administrators and lawyers administer everything while social workers and doctors care for our souls and bodies. Relative to Ontario, Québec is obviously short on economists and engineers and long on everything else. Is that good or bad? It depends, I suppose.

If your concern is with the economy, you would have to be worried about the relative disinterest of *Québécois* in economics (41 per 100,000 people versus 69 in Ontario, or 40 percent behind Ontario) and engineering (12 percent behind Ontario). On the other hand, if you think that a healthy economy depends first of all on an effective teaching corps, you would have to be very happy with the fact that there are proportionately 51 percent more prospective teachers in Québec (172 versus 114). On the other hand, when you harken back to some of the evidence advanced earlier concerning the lamentable record of Québec's public school system, the system that would eventually employ these prospective teachers, you might wish to pause and reflect a moment before allowing your emotions to overcome your informed judgement: Will more teachers solve Québec's deplorable performance in its public schools, or does the solution lie elsewhere? I would argue that, until the Québec Ministry of Education does something to reduce the high drop-out rate, correct faulty curricula and segregate its political agenda from the pedagogical needs of students, throwing in more teachers is akin to throwing good money after bad.

If, on the other hand, you, along with the Quiet Revolutionaries, are concerned with breaking with the past, you would have to be disappointed with Québec's relative superiority in Administrators (45 percent more than Ontario), Lawyers (7 percent more), Health Care Workers (26 percent more) and Social Workers (73 percent more). Why? Because these data suggest that the preferences of the Church's discredited classical system are with us still. Of course, there is nothing wrong with that ...if that is what you need.

But, is the health of *Québécois* so bad that Québec needs 26 percent more health care workers? I doubt it. Is Québec so litigious that it needs 7 percent more lawyers? Perhaps. Are *Québécois* so screwed up that they need 73 percent more social workers? I hope not. Is the Québec economy so complicated that it requires 45 percent more administrators? Not likely: Its economy is a mirror image of Ontario's. Does it need more public administrators? Perhaps: Québec does, after all, act more like a complex independent state than a simple province. Are relatively more *Québécois* attracted to teaching, social work and administration because these disciplines are more prestigious than economics, for instance? Plausible. Or is it because, let us not be cute, the academic requirements for these three disciplines are simply less demanding than for economics, science or literature? I assume that no one in his/her right mind would dispute the perfectly reasonable conclusion that the study of teaching or social work is less demanding than the study of literature, biology or computer science. On the other hand, since some may resent my dumping on administrative studies, let me explain.

I would argue that, in general, subject matter is intellectually more demanding than procedure. Thus, physics is more demanding than cooking because, where the study of physics demands a reasonable level of literacy and some prior knowledge of mathematics, geometry and chemistry, learning to cook requires not much more than the ability to follow the instructions on a recipe ... with all due respect to cooks. Let me suggest then that, as a discipline, administrative studies is closer to cooking than to physics. That said, let me differentiate between the study of administration at the graduate level (MBA) and at the undergraduate level (BBA).

In my professional experience I found that some of the most motivated and accomplished students were following MBA programs. And the reason is clear: The MBA mystique tends to attract the best and the brightest undergraduates. Thus, when the most motivated engineers, lawyers, biologists and literature majors interact in a prestigious MBA program, they feed off each other to their mutual benefit. Not the same, alas, with undergraduates in a business program pursuing a BBA. Where the engineer, for instance, entered MBA school with a reasonably strong scientific background, or where the literature major had learned the difference between Shakespeare and Molière, what accompanied the young man or woman commencing BBA studies was a high school diploma which may not have demanded anything more difficult than grade nine mathematics! Without wishing to be unkind, let me declare my colours: As a professional administrator looking for management trainees, I found better prospects among improbable literature graduates than among those sporting a BBA. And, of course, although BBA-type studies are not unique to Québec, they appear to be particularly popular there.

Therefore, Québec seems deficient not only in the number of university students, but also in the mix: Too few being trained to help the economy grow and generate jobs, too many destined to live off the avails of the

Table: 6-12: Québec University Enrolments		
	1962 % Dist'n	Absolute Growth %	1992 % Dist'n
Health	9.2	470	11.3
Engineering	16.5	400	17.8
Education	5.3	1350	16.6
Gen'l Arts	50.5	50	16.0
Law	2.6	530	3.5
Admin.	15.9	920	34.8
Total		361	
Provincial Pop'n		40	

Source: Statistiques de l'éducation, 1994
Annuaire du Québec, 1962

economy and the taxes of the few. Now, the question is: Did the Quiet Revolution alleviate or exacerbate a situation that was already in disarray when the revolutionaries knocked the Church from atop the social roost?

First of all, it did a great job increasing university enrolments: From 1962 to 1992, when the provincial population was increasing by about 40 percent, university enrolments (in the disciplines shown) in Québec universities were increasing by 361 percent (Table 6-12). Good work, it seems ... but not good enough: Ontario did even better without benefit of a revolution. Moreover, in this 30-year period, we can see that study preferences changed a great deal: Where the general arts curricula were dominant in 1962 (50.5 percent of all enrolments), they seem to have fallen out of favour, accounting for only 16 percent of enrolments in 1992. Although all of the remaining disciplines increased their shares of enrolments, the biggest winners were Education and Administrative Studies; engineering was second to last. Since these three disciplines were adequately described above, there is no need to say more than that the Quiet Revolution seems to have fostered the growth of the least demanding, and economically least useful disciplines.

Finally, there is, as always, the linguistic dimension. First, as described earlier, English *Cégeps* tended to send proportionately more students to university than did French *Cégeps*; second, as we progressed through university, from BA to MA to PhD, the *Québécois* share continued to decline. That is, although over 90 percent of all elementary school students in Québec attended French schools, only 67 percent of those studying for a PhD did so at French universities. Expressing this another way, for every 100,000 people of French mother tongue in Québec in 1992, about 3,300 attended university versus 6,100 for Québec anglophones and 3,500 for Québec allophones. Moreover, about 92 percent of anglophones studied at English universities as did 5 percent of *Québécois* and 53 percent of allophones.[16] To complete this sorry tale, have a close look at Table 6-13.

Consider Québec's two university systems--one dispensing instruction in English, the other in French--and ask how well each satisfied the needs of its constituents. Although there are several ways of making this comparison, consider the production of graduates with respect to their relevant provincial populations: All anglophones plus 53 percent of allophones (derived from data cited previously) for English universities, and all *Québécois* plus 47

Table 6-13: Québec	
University Graduates Per 100,000 People	
English	French
BA 780	325
MA 165	70
PhD 31	10
Source: Statistiques T 3.4.1, 3.4.2	

percent of allophones for French universities. These data suggest fairly strongly that the English universities out-performed their French counterparts by a very wide margin, in fact by 2 or 3 to 1. Note that, since Québec's English universities attract a significant number of students from other Canadian provinces as well as from foreign countries, the production of graduates relative to their respective linguistic communities in Québec should be tempered a little. On the other hand, the relatively greater foreign presence probably provides students at Québec's English universities with an intellectually more enriching pluralist environment.

What, you may wonder, explains this sorry state of university education in Québec ... among *Québécois*? It cannot be the cost to the user: There are no pre-university fees in Québec, and university fees there are the lowest in Canada (23 percent below Ontario in 1993/94),[17] and have been lower since the late 1960s! They are so low that Québec's universities attract a significant number of students, not only from other provinces, but from other countries as well (Table 6-14). For instance, I know of a professor at Cornell, a prestigious Ivy League university in New York state, who sent his daughter to McGill in Montreal instead of to Cornell! Not only does McGill have an outstanding international reputation, it's tuition fees are a lot lower than Cornell's--lower even than the fees available to the children of its professors. However, lest anyone conclude that Québec's universities are being over-run by rapacious Americans, let it be noted that our southern cousins account for only 2 percent of foreign students at French universities, 18 percent at English universities in Québec. Overall, 55 percent of foreign students in Québec attend French universities. So, if high fees are a deterrent to education, low fees should encourage attendance-- as they surely did for foreign and out-of-province students! Since low fees did not encourage greater university enrolments among *Québécois*, there must be another factor at play.

Table 6-14: Sources of Students Québec Universities			
	French		English
Québec	90 %		60 %
Rest of Canada	2 %		22 %
Foreign	8 %		18 %
Source: Statistiques, 1994 Tables 2.4.6, 2.4.7			

Could the historic poverty of *Québécois* be a factor? Perhaps, but not very convincing since allophones, whose parents were poor immigrants, attend university in relatively greater numbers than do *Québécois*. Or what about the historic resistance to modernity by the Church? When, for generations, you hear from the pulpit that "*On est né pour un petit pain*" (We are born to live on crumbs), it doesn't do much to enhance one's self-esteem or promote the need to improve one's lot in life. Moreover, if, with the advent of the Quiet Revolution in 1960, all you ever heard was that the mighty Québec state was going to right all wrongs, real or imagined, why would you break your neck going to school and have to extend yourself intellectually? Whether for these reasons or others, there is some evidence to support the notion that *Québécois* do not harbour great educational expectations for themselves. When surveyed in 1991, 33 percent of anglophones, 20 percent of allophones and 16 percent of *Québécois* said they expected to get a university degree.[18] The record shows, of course, that life did indeed reflect these expectations. And, as a result, *Québécois* continue to come out on the short end of the stick.

Whether *Québécois* leaders did enough during the Quiet Revolution to overcome this historic antipathy toward education is a matter for legitimate debate. But, I have never even heard the issue broached in public! If it was, it certainly did not make great waves. In any event, nothing came of it: *Québécois* attendance and performance in school was, and remains deplorable. If Québec's Quiet Revolutionaries had paid more attention to the legitimate needs of the people instead of to the posturing of anglophobic nationalists, they might have been able to do something about this problem. I would argue that if they had, *Québécois* would be competitive today with their fellow citizens. But they didn't, and they aren't. What the Quiet Revolutionaries did instead was to seek scapegoats: Anglophones in Québec and the federal government in Ottawa. Language laws were enacted to deal with the former, threats of secession to repulse the latter. And, in the fine traditions of Roman circuses and emperors without clothes, the scapegoat strategy has been successful ... so far.

The Quiet Revolution: Language Laws

First, some historical perspective.

Until about the 16th-century, Latin was the universal language of European scholars and diplomats. That is why a German could study at an Italian university: The texts studied, as well as the language of instructors, were the product of the Church's Latin-based scholarship. Thus, the great literature of Europe was written first in Latin and then translated into the national language of the author. Sir Thomas More's "*Utopia*," for instance, was written in Latin and then translated into the author's native English. But, with the growth of national languages, the need for Latin declined. With this evolution, some countries defended their national languages with great vigour, others did not.

In France, for instance, Cardinal Richelieu established *L'Academie Française* in 1635 as the final arbiter of linguistic orthodoxy. Proper French was defined by *l'Academie* as that used by the most accomplished writers. And, in the event of disputes between scholars, *l'Academie* was the ultimate authority. It was with this authority that it recently turned down the recommendations of French teachers to abolish the use of some useless accents.

Moreover, *l'Academie* has been vigilant trying to keep foreign words out of the language. That does not mean that the people necessarily follow all of its admonitions. For instance, it must irritate them to hear even the educated French say things like "J'ai eu du *fun* noir ce *week-end* avec mon *chum*."

The British, on the other hand, took a different approach. First of all, they appointed no official body to administer their language; second, they assumed that orthodoxy would be determined by common usage. Not surprisingly, therefore, there was some chaos in English until the first dictionaries appeared in the 17th-century. Although these dictionaries helped stabilize the language for a while, the post-revolutionary Americans threw a few spanners into the works to distance themselves from Britain. This included changing British spelling (of labour, for instance) to the American variant (labor). Finally, where *l'Académie* resisted the invasion of French by foreign words, English grew by accepting them. Consider how poor English would be without foreign words such as, *hors d'oeuvre, oboe, chutzpa, putz, sombrero, toreador, leitmotif, schlochmeister* and *apartheid*.

All that said, what explains the undeniable fact that some languages are more popular than others? In the old Soviet Union, Russian dominated all other languages because Russia was the dominant republic in the Union; in Britain, English displaced Gaelic in Scotland, Wales and Ireland because of the overwhelming influence of the English economy--not to mention the compelling impact of the British bayonet; in India, where each state has its own unique official language, English, the language imposed by its then colonial masters, appears to be the language of national administration. In the international arena, French was once accepted as the language of diplomacy and culture because of the dominant position of France in both areas. Then, French gradually gave way to English as the British Empire spread across the world. When the United States eventually displaced Britain as the world's dominant power, the continued international dominance of English was guaranteed. Not that English had necessarily been imposed on everyone, most simply saw it in their economic interests to adopt it as their national second language and as their principal international language. As a result, English is the most widely used second language in the world. While most countries have adapted to this fact of life with relative ease, France pouts. And so does Québec.

As mentioned earlier, the various language laws adopted by *l'Assemblée Nationale du Québec* were intended to protect an allegedly fragile French culture in Québec from the corrosive influence of English. But when you strip away the glitter, you soon realize that this protection took the form of simply restricting the public use of English. Thus, most allophones, and some *Québécois*, who had previously chosen to send their children to English rather than to French schools, saw this choice prohibited by law. And to make non-*Québécois* residents of Québec really feel at home, the government of Québec decided to only provide administrative services in French unless the law obliged them to also provide them in English. That English language services had been provided in Québec for over two-hundred years was considered as no more than an historical anomaly, a mere privilege that was being withdrawn since it was not justified! However, in a sensible gesture to the practical, the law did permit the government of Québec and its equally money-hungry agencies to publish their financial reports in English. This was no doubt much appreciated by the money lenders on Wall Street. Moreover, the legal use of English on public signs was severely restricted. Where it *was* permitted, it had to be accompanied by the French version in larger print in a predominant position on the sign. Finally, companies larger than a certain size had to demonstrate their ability to carry on their business in French whether they needed to or not. This found an echo in Montréal's small Chinese Hospital in 1998 when it attempted to hire a new head nurse. Although its patients are unilingual Chinese speakers, very few of whom even understand English or French, Québec's language law required them to hire a French speaker whether he/she could speak Chinese or not![19]

Before 1974, language laws in Québec were not restrictive of English.[20] But, as described earlier, the anglophobes gradually won the day in the early days of the Quiet Revolution and constraints on English have escalated ever since. These restrictions on individual freedoms were of course rebranded to read "*protection of fragile French culture.*" Without this protection, it was argued that the francophone share of the population of Québec would decline precipitously. And this is where the argument starts to crumble. That is, it is not obvious that the francophone share of Québec's population was or is at risk: It climbed steadily in the 20th-century before the first restrictive language law was enacted.[21] It, in fact, had increased by 0.6 percent between 1901 and 1971, or, about 0.009 percent per year. Therefore, justifying these restrictions by resorting to share-protection is an obvious crock. By the same token, the same francophone share increased by 1.9 percent between 1971 and 1991, or, about 0.095 percent per year--in the period during which these restrictive language laws *were* in effect. These data suggest two major conclusions:

1.   If the justification for the adoption of Québec's language laws is that they were needed to arrest a decline in, or a threat to, the francophone share of Québec's population, the evidence shows that, since there had not been a decline in share, the laws could not have been justified by that argument.

2.   Since the annual increase in the francophone share after 1971 was about 10-times that of the pre-1971 annual increase, might we not conclude that the language laws were in fact meant to increase the francophone share, not to arrest its alleged decline?

But, to be precise, what the proponents of these laws were really concerned about was the francophone population share on the Island of Montreal. Note that Montreal and the rest of Québec are not linguistic twins: Francophones account for less than 60 percent of the population of the former, over 90 percent of the latter. Now, consider the reactions of the Quiet Revolutionaries in the 1960s as they attempted to come to terms with some fairly disquieting facts:

1.   Montreal, the economic engine of Québec was not as francophone as the rest of Québec.

2.   This was so because Montreal was obviously less attractive to francophones than to non-francophones (less than 20 percent of the province's francophones lived on the Island of Montreal as opposed to over 85 percent of its anglophones and 95 percent of its allophones).

3.   Allophones, and some francophones, preferred to send their children to English rather than to French schools.

Conclusion?

Québec's economy would continue to be dominated by non-*Québécois* and that was bad according to the most strident nationalists. Moreover, what could not have been foreseen at the time was that increased immigration and a declining *Québécois* birth rate would exacerbate the *problem*.

In any event, making Montreal more French became the goal of the 1960s' language*meisters*. Somehow the notion of providing economic incentives to encourage *Québécois* to move into Montreal from the Québec hinterland seemed not to interest them. If they had paid attention to their own history, they would have noted that many of their ancestors had migrated from rural to urban areas in both Québec and New England in search of work. Thus, if they could have found a way to increase job-creating business investment in Montreal and concurrently to improve the educational level of *Québécois* to permit them to fill those jobs, wouldn't *Québécois* outside of Montreal have migrated to Montreal? And wouldn't this have been the best long-term solution to the problem of francophone under-representation in Montréal?

Unfortunately, there is no evidence to suggest that this market-oriented solution was ever considered. More attractive apparently was legislation that could command compliance: Legislated Joy. Thus, their solution was to force the conversion of allophones into francophones rather than allow them to voluntarily convert themselves into anglophones; and for that to take place, allophones would have to send their children to French schools rather than to the English institutions they generally preferred. Thus, legislation would be required to force them into French schools. That in a nutshell was the focus of the first restrictive language law in 1974. Subsequent versions went on to outlaw English on public signs, to reduce the level of public services in English, and to force French as a language of work on the business community.

And what was produced by these legislative initiatives? If I can jump first to the second group of laws, those affecting the public use of English, I would argue that, other than irritating over one million Quebecers, many businessmen and who knows how many potential investors, not very much. What possible benefit can one imagine accruing to *Québécois* by reducing English language services to anglophones? How does prohibiting English signs advance legitimate *Québécois* interests? How does imposing French on major corporations encourage them to expand or to even stay in Québec? In what way are francophone interests advanced by imposing French on hospitals that cater only to Chinese speakers? The answer of course is not at all, other than to give the false impression that Montreal is more francophone than it really is, to give a warm fuzzy feeling to insecure nationalists. But is offending fellow citizens and turning off potential job-creating investors a fair trade-off for false advertizing and the warming of a few immature egos? I think not ... unless other goals were being pursued, about which more later.

And if we return to the main thrust of the first restrictive language law and its successors--to get allophones into French schools--we would have to conclude that they were both successful and unsuccessful. That is, allophones eventually obeyed the law and sent their children to French schools. But this success was chimeric: Although they learned French in school, they also picked up English in the school yard, on the street and in front of their television sets. In fact, there is ample evidence to suggest that English remained their normal second language, French their third! As mentioned earlier, this failure to integrate allophones into the *Québécois* community was exacerbated by *Québécois* abandonment of the public schools in favour of private schools. Moreover, this abandonment was made worse by the growing exodus of relatively affluent and better educated *Québécois* to the suburbs. When your integrating role models are absent, who is supposed to do the integrating, francophone tooth fairies?

Language Laws and Secessionists

Now this is where the issue really becomes political.

Before the Lesage Liberals ushered in the Quiet Revolution in 1960, you would not have been far off the mark describing Québec-Ottawa relations as the continuous fight by Québec to exclude Ottawa from areas of provincial jurisdiction. But, during the Quiet Revolution, Québec started to demand expansion of its powers ... with complete independence a clear goal. It started down this road with programs to make Québec more French. Some of the more significant political dates on this journey are listed below.

1960   Election of the Lesage Liberals who ushered in the Quiet Revolution.

1968   Birth of the secessionist Parti Québécois (PQ).

1969   Bill 63, Québec's first language law enacted by the conservative Union Nationale government; it provided for continued freedom of choice in schooling but encouraged the use of more French in the workplace. This confirmed the status quo thus angering nationalists.

1974   Bill 22, Québec's first restrictive language law passed by Robert Bourassa's Liberal government. It prohibited all francophones and most allophones from attending English schools; many businesses were required to demonstrate their ability to carry out their operations in French; public signs, with some exceptions, were to be in French only; English public institutions were required to offer services in French.

1976   The PQ came to power in Québec, the first officially secessionist political party to do so.

1977   Bill 101, a more restrictive version of Bill 22, was adopted by the PQ; access to English schools was limited to children whose parents were educated in English in Québec; public signs were to be in French only.

1980   Québec's first PQ-inspired Referendum on secession was lost by secessionists by a wide margin.

1983   PQ's Bill 57 eased up on French tests for professionals; it agreed that it is possible for English social agencies to provide services in French without everyone at the agency having to be competent in French.

1988   Bill 178 passed by Bourassa Liberals; it maintained French-only status for outdoor signs but allowed indoor signs to be bilingual as long as French was predominant--with the exception of large department stores where only French was permitted on indoor signs.

1993   Bill 86 allowed new Québec residents from other parts of Canada to send their children to English schools; bilingual signs were allowed as long as French was predominant.

1995   Québec's second Referendum on secession was lost narrowly by secessionists; Jacques Parizeau resigned as premier of Québec, replaced by Lucien Bouchard.

1996   Bouchard is suspected by PQ anglophobes, a minority within the party, of wanting to soften provisions of Québec's language laws; militants wanted to make them even more restrictive. Bouchard's compromise: No new restrictions in the law in return for more vigilant policing of the existing restrictions on anglophones and allophones.

Some of the conclusions that leap from this list are:

1.   Language legislation was passed in Québec by all political parties.

2.   The legislation was essentially negative, focussing on restricting the public use of English and/or access to English institutions.

3.   Each time this legislation was amended, it became more restrictive.

4.   Legislation was passed or amended in response to the demands of an anglophobic minority in Québec.

The significance of the fourth point should not be under-estimated. For instance, access to English schools was denied to *Québécois* despite the fact that public opinion polls had showed for a long time that *Québécois* generally preferred freedom of choice in this matter. Moreover, even though public opinion polls showed that people were prepared to accept bilingual outdoor signs, and even though Robert Bourassa promised, if elected, to amend the PQ French-only policy to reflect this public preference, once elected, he nevertheless chose to retain the PQ's French-only policy on outdoor signs. Why? He said it was to preserve social peace among *Québécois*, most of whom felt insecure about their language. What this means in translation is that he did not have the courage to tell this anglophobic minority to grow up or get lost. The influence of this minority was particularly evident in 1996 when Premier Bouchard had to deal with a fringe group within his own party at PQ policy conventions. Read on.

In September 1995, just before the October 31 referendum on sovereignty, the PQ government of Jacques Parizeau asked two academics, Josée Legault (remember her?) and Michel Plourde, to report on the status of French in Québec. Plourde is a past-President of *Le Conseil de la langue française*, one of several bodies charged with monitoring the implementation of Québec's language laws. They were called upon to establish the facts, after which Parizeau and company would evaluate the need, if any, to amend the language law. Bill 101 had been promulgated in 1977 by the first PQ government of René Lévesque, so a review was probably timely.

But Legault and Plourde smelled a rat: They felt (probably correctly) that Parizeau's successor, Lucien Bouchard, in attempting to build post-referendum bridges to Montreal's non-*Québécois* communities, would probably moderate those sections of the language law that most irritated anglophones and allophones. Since Legault and Plourde are considered language hardliners, the mere hint of such heresy would of course horrify them. They wanted the language law to become more, not less, restrictive of English in general and anglophones in particular.

In their report, they announced that, although French had made some progress, it was running out of steam because of the lack of political will to enforce the spirit and letter of the law, which was to put a French face on Québec. They felt that French was especially in danger in Montréal because allophones still seemed to prefer speaking English rather than French. Thus, by going beyond their strict fact-finding mandate, they limited the policy options open to the PQ government. For example, how could the government relax any dispositions of Bill 101 when its own blue ribbon consultants recommended more severe measures? If they nevertheless still wished to relax some provisions of the law, they would have to first repudiate the report's main conclusion: That the French language was still at risk, especially on the Island of Montréal. And, how could they do that when the fragility of French was, and remains, the basis on which Québec social, economic and political policies have been built since 1960? Moreover, recent history has shown that it does not take much to spook governments in Québec on language matters. They usually cave in after seeing a letter to the editor in *Le Devoir* from any obscure, but suitably outraged, nationalist xenophobe. And Legault and Plourde knew this.

Thus, when a copy of their preliminary report was leaked to the media in the week of Feb. 20, 1996, the government's goose was cooked: Language policy was to be discussed at an important policy meeting of the PQ National Council during the week-end immediately following the leak. As it turned out, Premier Bouchard, though hard pressed, eventually got his way: He convinced the Council to postpone discussion on this divisive issue until April, thus avoiding, albeit only temporarily, having to commit political suicide by refusing to make the language law more restrictive. In the past, Québec Premiers, though personally dovish on language issues, generally gave in to cabinet colleagues who were attentive to hawks such as Legault and Plourde.

Indeed, at the April meeting, Bouchard reached a compromise with the party's extremists: Bill 101 would be made neither more nor less restrictive; but the existing language regulations would be policed more vigilantly. Indeed, funds were provided to increase the number of language police whose job it is to sniff out offensive English on public signs and food packages.[23] More later on some of the more ignoble consequences of this compromise. Thus, although Legault-Plourde were not able to make the language law more restrictive, they prevented new concessions to non-*Québécois*. Advantage Legault-Plourde and the anglophobic minority in Québec.

Interesting was the attitude of the *Québécois* press toward this issue. On the day preceding the PQ Council meeting, *Le Devoir* waded in on the side of the anglophobes by running an OpEd article favouring tougher measures in the language law. And it used heavy artillery: The article was written by the popular novelist and ardent secessionist Yves Beauchemin. However, after the meeting, no *Québécois* commentator of any status "*cheered the tone, content or result of this language debate.*"[24] Alain Dubuc of *La Presse* warned:

> *The city (Montréal) cannot afford the luxury of linguistic battles with their various excesses. That, incidentally, is the wish of a majority of Québecers and, we suspect, of Bouchard himself.*

It should be noted that *La Presse* in general, and Dubuc in particular, have generally been anti-secessionist. Michel C. Auger, whose nationalist credentials are not in doubt, wrote in *Le Journal de Montréal*:

> *The government should refuse to fall into the logic of a linguistic crisis that some would like to impose on it. Apart from those who have built a profession on this type of debate, there is no linguistic crisis in Montréal.*

Given this journalist attitude, what evidence did Legault-Plourde advance to make a case so convincing that Lucien Bouchard, the messianic Premier of Québec, was prevented from even considering the slightest moderation of the language law? Especially since Bouchard knew that, if he was unable to moderate the law, non-*Québécois* would never accept his attempts to reconcile them with the *Québécois* majority. Since Bouchard did not get his way, we must assume, notwithstanding the comments of Dubuc and Auger, that the Legault-Plourde evidence was so convincing that he had, in effect, to concede defeat. Read on and be prepared to weep.[25]

In their report, Legault-Plourde claimed that Bill 101's main objective, to make French the normal language of all public activity in Québec, "*is still far from having been achieved.*" Moreover, because of concessions to the anglophone and allophone communities, they charged that Québec's institutions had become progressively bilingual instead of unilingually French. Just in case anyone has forgotten, Bill 101 rejected bilingualism and insisted on a unilingual French Québec. Legault-Plourde assumed that the original objective was valid and that the legislative means chosen to pursue that objective were equally valid. I would argue that, even if the original objective had been valid (an assumption I dispute), there was no evidence in the report to suggest that the means selected to pursue that objective have been, or can ever be, effective.

For example, even with laws *encouraging* the use of French in the workplace, 55 percent of anglophones and 37 percent of allophones and francophones still work mostly in English. And it is not because of any inability to speak French: In 1991, 59 percent of anglophones and 69 percent of allophones spoke French competently, according to the report. This also represented a substantial improvement since 1971. Nor was it due to a lack of francophone corporate power: Most companies were controlled by francophones. These data might have suggested to a discriminating observer that the use of English in the workplace might perhaps be a condition driven by imperatives beyond the influence of language laws; and that, horror of horrors, it was thus impractical to expect a much greater penetration of French! Of course, hell will freeze over before this is ever admitted by nationalists of the stature of Legault and Plourde. So convinced are they in the efficacy of laws proclaimed by *l'Assemblée nationale* that one has the impression that repealing the law of gravity might also be within its power. It is Legislated Joy all over again.

Legault-Plourde also found fault with the fact that only 87 percent of commercial signs on the Island of Montréal were in French. Since *Québécois* make up less than 60 percent of the population of the Island, fair minded observers might thus conclude that the commercial needs of francophones had been reasonably well met. Not according to Legault-Plourde. In addition, they claimed that, in 95 percent of cases, *Québécois* obtain consumer services in French. Since *Québécois* commercial and consumer interests appear to have been, for all practical purposes, satisfied, why would they still insist that the law be made more restrictive? I would argue, first, that it is because their mischievous anglophobic ideology had triumphed over the obviously inconvenient implications that derived from their own data; second, because they harboured the absurd notion that legislation can resolve all problems, even those that do not exist.

But the report was particularly tough on allophones. According to the provisions of Québec's language law, children of immigrants, the so-called allophones, must attend French elementary and secondary schools. The report's complaint? Despite the fact that all allophones in fact attend French elementary and secondary schools, when they are at play, between 40 and 60 percent of them still converse in a language other than French. This presumably means in English or in their own mother tongues. Since Bill 101 is concerned only with the public use of language, private conversations being beyond the practical purview of legislators everywhere on this planet, it is clearly not the business of Legault-Plourde what language people use in private! But they nevertheless converted a private matter into a public issue. What is so objectionable about immigrant children conversing with one another in their own mother tongues? Moreover, when they talk to children from other language groups, they will use the common language that they find most useful, no matter what legislators proclaim. And, despite the fact that they all attend French schools, and consequently probably speak French reasonably well, the common public language for these '*immigrant*' groups appears to be English. And how can a law force people to use one language over another in private? Why should it?

And if Legault-Plourde wish to know why these *immigrants* prefer to use English rather than French, they need go no further than the rationale used to justify Québec's restrictive language legislation in the first place: Given a choice, almost all allophones and many *Québécois* would choose to attend English schools. How Legault-Plourde expect language legislation to convince people to change their private lives escapes me! It is scary that they and their ilk think language legislation should intrude into private life.

While still in the private sphere, their report noted that

allophones prefer English (American) video cassettes 67 percent of the time; 60 percent prefer to watch English television; the great majority prefer to read English newspapers. The report would have helped by putting these figures into some context by citing the related figures for *Québécois* who patronize the English media. Clearly, and not surprisingly, when given a choice, English will beat French every time, even in Québec.

But back to the public sphere where discussion on the impact of language legislation is more appropriate. Legault-Plourde claimed that one reason explaining the naughty practices in the private lives of non-*Québécois* is the fact that *Québécois* no longer constitute the majority in French public schools on the Island of Montréal. Thus, the critical mass required to effect integration is absent. This is a logical conclusion, especially since history has shown that only a massive francophone presence has a chance of holding back the English tide in North America. After all, water does not run uphill without a helping hand. The report claimed that the *Québécois* share of the population of the Island of Montréal declined from 61 percent in 1971 to 57 percent in 1995. *Québécois* migration to the off-Island suburbs apparently explained this worrisome trend, said Legault-Plourde ... in partial error. This helps explain why, in about 59 percent of French schools, more than half the students have neither French nor English as their mother tongue. The same might be said, by the way, of many inner city schools in Toronto, Vancouver and Ottawa. Also relevant, but tellingly not mentioned in the report, is the fact that a growing proportion of *Québécois* students has abandoned the public school system in favour of private schools. This transfer has been so great that Québec's, mostly French, private school system is Canada's largest. That is the major reason there are so few *Québécois* role models in Montreal's public schools. That Legault-Plourde made no reference to this testifies not so much to their analytical incompetence but to their political astuteness. No fools these two.

But, undeterred by these analytical lacuna, Legault-Plourde pressed on. Once allophones have completed their obligatory stay in French elementary and secondary schools, 36 percent had the temerity in 1994 to continue their studies at English *Cégeps*, while more than 50 percent attended English universities. What the report did not mention was the attendance of *Québécois* at McGill, the English university par excellence: Of all the Québecers studying at McGill in 1995/96, about one-third were *Québécois*.[26]

The report urged the government to direct its attention to this *problem*. Imagine the possibilities here for stand-up comedians! All future immigrants to Québec would be forced to settle only in areas where *Québécois* predominate--in the Gaspé region, perhaps, where they could live on welfare instead of in Montreal where they might find work!. Allophones wishing to move from one part of Québec to another would require permits, following traditional practice in totalitarian states. If they insisted on moving without a permit, it would have to be out of Québec. Or perhaps *Québécois* migration to the suburbs could be forbidden. Better still, why not offer financial incentives to *Québécois* to eschew suburban life. The costs of such a program could be recovered by levying a special tax on all suburbanites, most of whom would probably be anglophones. Allophones would not, of course, be permitted to live in the suburbs. To be sure, all those allophones and *Québécois* attending English *Cégeps* and universities would be dragged, kicking and screaming, to appropriate French institutions. Imagine how happy this would make those *Québécois* who, for some strange reason, chose McGill instead of, say, the internationally obscure UQAM. And on and on.

What the government could possibly do to *rectify* this *problem* is beyond my ability even to imagine. As I inferred earlier, if Legault-Plourde had really wished to recommend legislation that might have had a chance of addressing the *problem*, they would have recommended making it more difficult for *Québécois* to abandon the public school system. Since they did not, one can only assume that they were not really interested in solving that *problem*.

And then of course there are the anglophones. Despite the fact that, according to Legault-Plourde, 59 percent are competent in French, 39 percent cannot speak French at all. They cited this as evidence of laxity in the implementation of Bill 101. Another crock! What has the linguistic capability of anglophones to do with the ability of *Québécois* to live and work in French? Nothing, nada, zip! But, to repeat the obvious, it might interest Legault-Plourde to know that Bill 101 is only concerned with the use of language in public places; that some of these unilingual anglophones may be home-bodies and hence have little need to learn French; that others may work for small businesses that are exempt from Bill 101's dicta. But, I am sure that this duo would argue that these anglophones remain unilingual because institutions, such as some provincial government departments and many commercial enterprises, provide bilingual services despite Bill 101's command to provide services only in French. In fact, these delinquent institutions probably provide bilingual services for two reasons: First, they probably find it easier to do so than to abide strictly by the unilingual strictures of Bill 101; second, some may be guided by a simple desire to treat their clients courteously.

Even after allowing for a small measure of sarcasm in my analysis, I think it reasonable to conclude that the evidence offered by Legault-Plourde would not have passed muster at a freshman seminar. But they were sufficient to cow a *Québécois* hero like Lucien Bouchard. Moreover, so mean have language laws in Québec become that late in the summer of 1996, when anglophone militants insisted that stores post legal bilingual signs (French-only signs had become the common practice), the PQ government threatened to change the law to make these legal English signs illegal. Something like the constitution of the Soviet Union: Very democratic in theory until someone tries to live by its provisions. Clearly, evidence, logic and legality have little standing in discussions on culture and language in Québec; mythology and ethnically motivated patriotism are far more saleable and politically profitable.

All this to conclude that, when *Québécois* nationalists wrap themselves in the flag and proclaim that legislation to protect French is an unassailable imperative needed to protect their culture, their argument is clearly built on unstable sand. But then again, perhaps their true objective is not cultural protection after all, that it is instead political. That is, by playing the scapegoat game, by wrapping themselves in the cultural flag and by appealing to people's baser instincts, nationalists know that history is on their side, that the credulous masses would flock to their banner. But, this cannot be sustained for too long: Sooner or later, even the most credulous will see through this smoke and realize that the emperor indeed has no clothes. Therefore, nationalists have to attain their true objective before the people wake up. And the true objective of these language laws is, I would argue, to drive enough non-*Québécois* from Québec to reduce the remaining anti-secessionist votes to insignificance. That is, since the anglophone exodus from Québec has increased substantially since the passage of these language laws, and since the authors of these laws benefit from this exodus, I draw a cause-effect relationship between the two.

My argument, in summary, goes something like this. Secession is the primary objective of *Québécois* ultra-nationalists. To obtain a majority vote in favour of secession, they must minimize the massively negative vote of anglophones and allophones. This they could accomplish either by legislation to deprive these people of the vote, or by encouraging them to leave Québec. Although some nationalists have already urged non-*Québécois* to voluntarily refrain from voting in secession-oriented referenda in order to allow *Québécois* alone to determine the political future of Québec (and Canada), legislation to deprive these inconvenient voters of their rights is not yet under consideration in Québec. Therefore, nationalists are left with the second option: To encourage anglophones and allophones to leave Québec, in effect to ethnically cleanse Québec of the politically inconvenient. Coincident with this expulsion strategy, is another, to sell hokum to the masses using smoke and mirrors.

Secessionists and Hokum

When I say that the *Québécois* élite tend to blame anglophones in general and the federal government in particular for everything from bad breath to inclement weather, I am obviously using hyperbole to make a point. Moreover, as I demonstrated earlier, the record shows that the *Québécois* élite have also resorted to lies and half-truths to advance their agenda. So effective were they with this strategy of aggressive mendacity that they carried it to breath-taking levels in the referenda of 1980 and 1995 ... where they added cheating and electoral fraud to their portfolio.

For those not familiar with referenda in Québec, they are political instruments used by *Québécois* politicians to periodically determine whether Québecers wish to secede from Canada. They are peculiar, however, in that the Referendum questions have not, so far, asked Québecers if they wished to secede! In fact, they have been vague enough to mean one thing to some voters and something else to others. That is, while some voters interpreted the Referendum questions as clear questions about secession, others were equally certain that they had nothing to do with secession. No surprise then that confusion reigned before, during and following the 1980 and 1995 referenda.

Moreover, practice has shown that, in Québec, a clear Referendum question is an oxymoron. However, and this is the beauty of referenda in Québec, that is not a problem: Whatever the question, secessionist politicians have said they would interpret an affirmative response as a vote to secede. Thus, a clear question like "*Do you wish Québec to secede from Canada?*" is not only not necessary, it could even prove to be counter-productive: Most analysts agree that a clear question would tend to minimize the number of votes favouring secession. Unhappy élites. The same analysts also feel that a vague question would tend to maximize the level of the affirmative vote. Happy élites. Thus, even if the question was "*Do you like gravy on your roast beef?*" an affirmative vote would be considered by the secessionists as approval of the implicit question: "*Do you wish Québec to secede from Canada?*" Excuse the sarcasm, but I kid you not. This correlation is taken for granted among secessionist politicians and the news media where breaking up Canada is not a matter of substance but of procedure. Whether this is *chutzpa* or breath taking hypocrisy, Macchiavelli would have been impressed.

The first Referendum was held in 1980 when 40 percent voted to secede, the second in 1995 when the secessionists raised their vote to just under 50 percent. It is probable that the next will be held around the turn of the century and every few years thereafter until secession is approved or until *Québécois* tire of it. As a democrat, I am prepared to accept the informed will of the people of Québec to remain or go even though I may grind my teeth just a little if they choose to go. But the evidence suggests that secession is not what *Québécois* want. Public opinion polls consistently tell us that between a quarter and a third of *Québécois*, say 30 percent, are convinced secessionists and will vote to secede knowing full well what secession means: Cleavage of Québec from Canada to form an independent country. The remaining 70 percent range from indifferent to militantly anti-secessionist.

In polls conducted just before the 1995 Referendum many of those who said they intended to vote "Yes" (to secede) thought that their vote would merely give Québec's provincial politicians a mandate to seek better terms for Québec within the Canadian Confederation; others thought secession meant independence within Canada (whatever that means); many harboured the absurd notion that, in an independent Québec, they would still retain their Canadian passports, receive pensions and unemployment benefits from the government of Canada and send representatives to the Canadian parliament in Ottawa!

When clear polling questions determine consistently that something like 30 percent of the respondents favour secession, how does one explain the results of referenda where the secessionist vote was 40 percent in

1980 and 50 percent in 1995? The only difference between the polls and the referenda was the wording of the questions asked. Whereas the polls asked questions like *"Do you want Québec to separate from Canada, Yes or No?"* the Referendum questions represented obfuscation at its best. For example, in the 1980 Referendum there was a one-paragraph preamble followed by the question:

> *The government of Québec has made public its proposal to negotiate a new agreement with the rest of Canada based on the equality of nations. This agreement would enable Québec to acquire exclusive power to make its laws, levy its taxes and establish relations abroad--in other words, sovereignty--and at the same time to maintain with Canada an economic association including a common currency. No change in political status resulting from these negotiations will be effected without approval by the people through another referendum.*
>
> *On these terms, do you give the government of Québec the mandate to negotiate the proposed agreement between Québec and Canada.*

Clear enough? No explicit mention of secession as such in these words. However, it was generally conceded that an affirmative vote would be considered a vote favouring secession. If you accept the accuracy of public opinion polls, this question seems to have tricked about 10 percent of the voters (40-30) into voting for secession. Now consider the 1995 question:

> *Do you agree that Québec should become sovereign, after having made a formal offer to Canada for a new Economic and Political Partnership, within the scope of the Bill respecting the future of Québec and of the agreement signed on June 12, 1995?*

In 1995 there was no preamble and the question was qualified by two items, neither of which was appended to the Referendum ballot. In fact, the two items were detailed in a 24-page pamphlet that was apparently mailed to all Quebecers: 24 pages of poetry and dense legal prose! How many recipients do you imagine would have read the pamphlet and understood it before casting their votes? How many do you think would have treated it as junk mail? Methinks more of the latter than of the former. In this case, about 20 percent of the electorate (50-30) seem to have been tricked into voting for secession. On the assumption (a) that you have not seen this pamphlet, and (b) that you are interested in *chutzpa*, herewith my summary, with my apologies to the poets who prepared the original text.

Bill number one (of the Québec National Assembly) declares that, since Québec is a distinct society, and since Québec has been very badly treated within the Canadian Confederation, Québec needs to become an independent country. Thus, Québécers will be asked in a referendum to approve the next step toward independence. After an affirmative referendum vote on Oct. 30, 1995, Québec will open negotiations with Canada to form a new economic and political union. If, by Oct. 30, 1996, a new union with Canada is not concluded, the National Assembly will unilaterally declare Québec independent.

The June 12, 1995 tripartite agreement referred to in the Referendum question was between Jacques Parizeau, Premier of Québec, Lucien Bouchard, head of the *Bloc Québécois* and Leader of Her Majesty's Loyal Opposition in the Parliament of Canada, and Mario Dumont, head of *l'Action démocratique* in the Québec National Assembly. In this agreement were spelled out the procedural details of the post-Referendum negotiations with Canada. The new political union sought would include a parliamentary Assembly where Québec would have 25 percent of the seats, not unlike the current distribution in the Parliament of Canada. Overseeing this assembly would be a Council where Canada and Québec would have equal representation. Since each side would have veto rights, decisions of the Council would have to be unanimous.

I usually develop a great headache reading this piece of sanctimonious, nay hypocritical trash. Clearly, hell would freeze over before the proposed political process would ever work. Except for the most mundane issues, such as deciding when the sun would rise, the proposed Council would be in continuous deadlock. If you need proof of this, simply look around. You will not find anywhere a functioning democratic system where unanimity is required. So why should it work here? Who would want to propose a political arrangement that was guaranteed to fail? Those who wanted it to fail, of course: The secessionist leaders, Messrs. Parizeau, Bouchard and Dumont.[27] But that is the nature of Referendum politics in Québec: The people are asked to vote for secession by wolves garbed as angels.

That the voters were confused was confirmed when the referendum results were compared with a poll carried out by the magazine *L'Actualité* in the spring of 1996, a few months after 49.4 percent of the Québec electorate had apparently voted to secede from Canada.[28] In its poll, *L'Actualité* asked a clear question: "*Are you in favour of the sovereignty of Québec?*" About 49 percent responded in the affirmative, almost mirroring the previous Referendum result. However, the same poll also reported that 17 of this 49 said that, despite their affirmative vote, they did not favour Québec's secession from Canada. By sovereignty they obviously meant something other than secession. Thus, only 32 percent of those polled supported secession, a figure confirmed in many previous opinion polls. And how did the secessionist *Parti Québécois* interpret this poll?   Read the following sentence very carefully.

> *If 49 percent of those polled supported secession, the PQ claimed that only one percent more (plus one vote) is thus required to obtain approval for secession!*[29]

And they said this shamelessly ... with straight faces. Thus, the PQ strategy is clear: Ask any question as long as it obtains a "Yes" vote, even though they know that only about 30 percent would in fact favour pure secession. Moreover, the same poll reported that the majority thought that an affirmative vote in excess of 60 percent was required to justify secession, not the 50 percent plus one vote trumpeted by the PQ. This is clear proof of deceit being used to advance a political agenda not supported by the people.

Moreover, in addition to deliberately misleading the people, the secessionist government of Québec also resorted to cheating during both referenda. This came to prominence in the months immediately following the 1995 Referendum when the English language Montreal Gazette commented on the fact that there was an unusual number of rejected ballots in some polling stations, all of which had anti-secessionist majorities. Cheating by polling station officers was alleged. I am not sure how the *Québécois* press handled this suspicious anomaly. To dimension the potential consequence of these rejected ballots, note that the secessionists would have won a majority if only three more anti-secessionist votes per poll had been rejected! It was that close.

The vote was so tight that I've often wondered why the secessionist side did not demand a recount. In normal elections, recounts are routinely demanded by the losing side when the losing margin is often much greater than what the secessionists experienced in the 1995 Referendum. Could it have been because the Referendum legislation did not permit it? If so, why? Could it have been because the secessionist side knew that a recount would have embarrassed them by exposing their chicanery? Although the first option may apply, the second is more likely. Let me explain.

In Québec referenda on secession, the law requires that those campaigning in favour of a vote to secede be grouped into a 'Yes Committee,' those opposing it into a 'No Committee.' It also requires that each poll have three polling officers, one nominated by each committee and one by the government of Québec. Thus, secessionist sympathizers necessarily occupy two of the three positions. Their function is, *inter alia*, to rule on the validity of the ballots cast. Let me give you an example of how this function was fulfilled at one poll during the 1980 Referendum, a precursor to the 1995 imbroglio.

My wife was the representative of the 'No Committee' at a polling station in a largely anglophone district during the 1980 Referendum. When the polls closed she expected to routinely complete her administrative duties and leave for home without delay. No such luck. Her two fellow polling officers decided that ballots marked with an 'X' with one side of the 'X' longer than the other were invalid; so also were those with one side darker than the other; and on and on! No surprise then that she spent several fruitless hours arguing with these two thugs only to be outvoted by them every time. Since the anti-secessionists won by a healthy 60-40 margin, nothing much was made of this objectively disgraceful behaviour by the 'Yes Committee' and by extension the secessionist government of Québec. That might explain why these patriots returned with a vengeance in the 1995 Referendum.

But, since the winning margin was so slim in 1995, the anti-secessionists could no longer ignore these incidents. They raised hell, charges were laid and the justice system was set in motion. As I write, the representative of the 'Yes Committee' at one polling station has been found guilty of some minor misdemeanour and given a slap on the wrist. After all, said the judge, he was only following the instructions of his superiors on the 'Yes Committee'! As I understand it, it is the intention of the prosecutors to pursue this matter into the hierarchy of the 'Yes Committee' organization and presumably into the leadership of the secessionist government of Québec, the people who controlled the 'Yes Committees.' Although I do not wish to second-guess the final results of this judicial process, I would conclude from the evidence before us that the 'Yes Committee' and their political masters in the secessionist government of Québec are guilty of cheating the voters.

Five clear conclusions leap at us from these two referenda:

1.   The secessionist objective pursued by *Québécois* provincial politicians was not supported by a majority of *Québécois*.

2.   A substantial number of *Québécois* was obviously misled by complicated, unclear and misleading referendum questions.

3.   The misleading of the people by their politicians was deliberate.

4.   If you can convince people to vote against their best interests, your influence over them must indeed be impressive.

5.   If regular measures do not work, *Québécois* secessionists are prepared to cheat to attain their goal, the secession of Québec from Canada.

But, some may argue, the second and third conclusions, although true, may be relatively meaningless. After all, don't all politicians lie? Perhaps, but the lies advanced by the politicians cited here are of a more dangerous order. First, they tend to be motivated, not by the simple desire to get elected, but by anglophobia and ethnic imperatives. These are social evils that lead inevitably to unwarranted hatred of our fellow man and hence must be avoided like the plague. Second, if successful, these lies will produce secession, not just a change of government. If you err in the selection of a government, you can rectify matters in a few years; but if you are tricked in a vote for secession, it is forever. Clearly, there are lies and then there are real lies.

Others might argue that it is not lying at all, that purveyors of this nonsense are simply incompetent. Plausible if you are dealing with the uneducated, but not in this case: One of the prominent blarney slingers was the Premier of Québec, a graduate of the London School of Economics, a man backed up by a horde of economists (some with Harvard PhDs) in the largest provincial public service in the land. Nay, we are left with the most probable explanation: They clearly intended to play loose with the facts. Why, you ask?

Obviously to further their own interests, interests that are better supported by slight of hand than by the truth. But how, you may ask, do they get away with such obvious whoppers? First, some might argue; it has to do with the subservience and credulity common to the masses in all societies with strong feudal traditions. And, Québec's antecedents are definitely feudal. Second, since *Québécois* have been, and remain, relatively poorly educated, it is not reasonable to expect that they would be able to defend themselves against better educated leaders who are intent on misleading them. Third, you might seek the counsel of that great American snake oil salesman, P.T. Barnum. He, it was who said something like *"There is a sucker born every minute."* Clearly, *Québécois* politicians know their Barnum well and follow his implicit advice with great devotion. Fourth, as described earlier, many in the *Québécois* media have become willing conduits for secessionist propaganda. Federal anti-secessionist propaganda, on the other hand, is usually given short shrift.

The Québécois Media and Hokum

That the *Québécois* media practice selective and biased journalism is clear from the evidence. For example, consider how *Le Devoir*, *La Presse* and the English language *Montreal Gazette* reported an important pre-Referendum event in Montreal on Feb. 15, 1995. It was one of a series of public hearings concocted by the PQ government to consult the people on what they, the people, expected from a post-secession Québec. Although these hearings sounded very noble and democratic, they were considered to be PQ propaganda instruments and were hence boycotted by almost all parties opposed to secession. One of the exceptions was B'nai Brith, the Jewish organization dedicated to fighting antisemitism. It made a presentation at the Feb. 15, 1995 hearing.

On Feb. 16, the *Gazette* dedicated about 12 column-inches to the hearing, *La Presse* about 16, and *Le Devoir* 25. If we divide the reporting between the portion dedicated to B'nai Brith and that dedicated to all other participants, we can see biases, good and bad, revealing themselves.

The *Gazette* dedicated about 40 percent of its coverage to B'nai

Brith, *La Presse* about 3, *Le Devoir* less than 1. Clearly, this suggests that the *Gazette* considered the B'nai Brith brief newsworthy, that *La Presse* thought it was not newsworthy and that *Le Devoir* considered it so inconsequential that it effectively ignored it. Which one had it right? Let's consider what happened at the hearing, starting with a *verbatim* extract from the *Gazette* news report.

> *B'nai Brith Canada argued that Québec could gain nothing in terms of human-rights protection, economic benefit or protection for French by leaving Canada. "There is no compelling reason to support sovereignty," B'nai Brith's Greg Bordan said. He said most Quebecers are fair minded and tolerant, but economic instability after separation could give extremists room to "empower themselves and prosper." Bordan, who was accompanied by former Equality Party leader Robert Libman, who is B'nai Brith's Québec regional director, and other B'nai Brith officials, was (sic) heckled repeatedly during his presentation. When he argued that a small country like a sovereign Québec would have trouble flourishing, several audience members shouted: "What about Israel?" He also took some tough questions from commissioners, including one from lawyer Jacques Bellemare who asked "By what perversion, what genetic malady" Quebecers would be more oppressive after secession than before. Answered Bordan: "To bring us here to make us say what we didn't say is a bit regrettable." Libman said: "Don't put words in our mouths."*

La Presse reported (my translation):

> *B'nai Brith Canada feels there is no justification for sovereignty.*

Le Devoir reported (my translation):

> *While the vast majority of those presenting briefs were convinced sovereigntists, or were at least leaning toward sovereignty, B'nai Brith and the Metropolitan Montréal Chamber of Commerce departed from this sovereigntist consensus.*

Did *the readers of La Presse* and *Le Devoir* miss out on useful news? It depends of course on how important you consider the opinions of the Jewish community, a community that has suffered greatly at the hands of nationalists throughout history, a community that has thus earned the right to be heard respectfully on matters it perceives to be troublesome. It also depends on whether the heckling of Jews at public hearings is considered contemptible and hence newsworthy, or simply of no consequence and hence not newsworthy. Clearly, the officials and audience at the hearing, as well as *La Presse* and *Le Devoir*, were unimpressed by, and arguably disinterested in, what the Jewish community had to say. *La Presse* and *Le Devoir* also evidently considered the heckling of Jews to be of no importance and hence ignored it. Thus, those who read the French language press in Montréal got quite a different version of presentations at the hearing than did readers of the English language *Gazette*. If we are to be guided by the evidence, we must conclude that the *Gazette's* readers were properly informed, those of the French-language press misinformed.

Consider another case where *Le Devoir* again failed the test of journalistic integrity by ignoring the inconvenient. During the summer of 1996, Normand Lester, a TV journalist with the French-language section of the Canadian Broadcasting Corporation (*Société Radio Canada* or SRC) entered the Jewish General Hospital in Montreal to undergo heart surgery. As an anglophone institution, the Jewish General obviously provides medical services in English. *L'Office de la langue française* also attested to the competence of its services in French. It also provides services in something like 42 foreign languages.

Nevertheless, Lester made headlines by accusing an anglophone nurse of screaming at him because he, Lester, insisted on speaking to her in French, not in English. This made headlines in Québec: One more example of lack of respect for French intoned the *Québécois* media. The more strident nationalists protested this *outrage* by demonstrating in front of the hospital. It seemed to matter not at all that *L'Office* declared that it was an isolated incident that merited no further action. However, it did say that the hospital should ensure that all francophone patients were served in French. Why this admonition was required after finding no cause for complaint seems to have escaped the attention of the *Québécois* media, especially *Le Devoir*.[30] But, let us consult the English Montreal Gazette for the whole story.[31]

Since Lester had conversed with the nursing staff in flawless English, they assumed he was an anglophone and hence spoke to him in English. This included two *Québécoise* nurses who later confronted Lester on an English-language open-line radio program where they accused him of not only talking to them in English, but of insisting that they answer in English. This, they said, required them to respond in tortured English when they could have conversed more easily in their common French mother tongue! One has the impression that Lester had used his dominant position as a patient to amuse himself at the expense of these vulnerable *Québécoise* nurses. He also had fun with an anglophone nurse by demanding to be spoken to in French after having spoken to her until then in his flawless English thereby giving her the impression that he was an anglophone. When she became flustered and asked him to continue speaking English, he of course leapt atop his high horse and cried rape. The rest you know from the reporting in *Le Devoir*.

Here again I would argue that, where the Gazette's readers were well served, *Le Devoir*'s were short-changed. Where the *Gazette* in effect suggested that Lester was a jerk who had fomented the misunderstanding to amuse himself, *Le Devoir* inferred that he was the innocent victim of a minor linguistic infraction: After all, the anglophone nurse did apologize to Lester!

These examples help explain how the *Québécois* news media shape public perceptions on important social, political and economic matters: They trumpet their biases and ignore the inconvenient. As a result, I would argue that the *Québécois* media have become shills for secessionists.

For example, in mid-January 1996, the federal government of Jean Chrétien declared that, in future referenda in Québec, secessionists would require much more than 50-percent plus one vote to win, perhaps as much as 67 percent. After all, one does not break up a country on a simple majority. Seems reasonable: Criteria current in the international arena suggest minimum break-up rates in excess of 60 percent. This higher hurdle rate is also supported by public opinion polls ... in Québec! But why did the higher break-up rates not apply to the referenda of 1980 and 1995 as well? Fair question, and the answer is simple: The feds assumed that the secessionists had no chance of winning and hence could be ignored. Well, the 1995 Referendum showed that those who harbour stupid assumptions sometimes get burned. And Chrétien was torched! In fact, we all had the living hell scared out of us. In any event, Chrétien's new break-up rate aroused more than a little interest among the secessionists. Denunciation, of course, was visited upon poor M. Chrétien from on high, low and other quarters, especially but not exclusively from the media in Québec.

Among the commentators was the *Québécois* journalist Michèl C. Auger who was asked on CBC English radio for his reaction to Chrétien's trial balloon.[32] His negative response was par for the course and entirely reasonable for a member of the PQ, even for the most fair minded of journalists. In fact, more than a few anglophone journalists dumped on Chrétien for wanting to change the rules part way through the game. But that is not surprising since many earnest bleeding hearts are unable to distinguish between the insignificant and the lethal. However, the logic behind Auger's negative response was not soft-headed, it was mischievous, hardly what one expects from a distinguished member of the *Québécois* media. He said that, if 52 percent was sufficient in the 1949 Newfoundland referendum to legitimate its entry to the Canadian Confederation, why wouldn't the same percentage be acceptable for Québec if it decided to leave Confederation? Seductively plausible but misleading since it was irrelevant, as Auger must have known.

Clearly, joining a country is not the same as leaving it. If you want a familiar analogy, getting married is less complicated than obtaining a divorce. In both cases, the first is joyous and to be celebrated, the second disruptive and to be avoided; the first is relatively straight forward, the second a psychological and legal nightmare. Hence, I see no problem with lower hurdle rates for friendly entrants than for disagreeable secessionists. Then, I would draw to Auger's attention the fact that Newfoundland's hurdle rate was set by Newfoundland and its colonial masters in Great Britain, not by Canada. It is difficult to imagine that Auger did not know that.

Clearly, Auger's misleading response was either the product of incompetence, his unfamiliarity with the subject matter, or his political biases. Since he is not incompetent, he must be either misinformed or biased. If he is as badly informed on other subjects on which he comments, pity his poor readers; if his response was politically motivated, shouldn't we expect his commentary on other political issues to be similarly biased? Small wonder then that Auger tends to ridicule evidence and argument advanced by federalists.

I should add here that this equation of the Newfoundland and Québec referenda appears to be a mantra with other *Québécois* journalists. For example, Michel Vastel, a journalist with impeccable secessionist credentials, looked so very serious on national television as he intoned solemnly that *Québécois* had as much right to leave the Canadian Confederation via referendum as Newfoundlanders had to enter it.[33] That there is a market in Québec for such intellectual bilge is breath-taking. Let me hasten to add that I have no problem with either Auger or Vastel shilling for any political party that meets their fancy. But I object when the partisan portray themselves as balanced journalists. The least they can do is concede the facts when they trip over them and be guided by an elementary sense of reasonably disciplined logic and fair play. Unfortunately, for their readers, they are more likely to be guided by ideology than by logic, and to distort inconvenient facts, assuming they do not ignore them altogether. And to add insult to injury, anglophone journalists who interview these people on radio and TV seem unable to see through this puffery or are unwilling to challenge them. Political correctness, I suppose.

Auger was also innocently involved in an incident that exemplified shoddy *Québécois* journalism. On Monday Feb. 5, 1996 Auger and Don Macpherson of *The Montreal Gazette* were guest commentators on *Morningside*, the popular English language national radio program. The subject of their comments was Pierre Trudeau's article that had appeared the previous Saturday in two Montreal newspapers, *The Gazette* and *La Presse*. In the article, the former Prime Minister of Canada accused the current Premier of Québec, Lucien Bouchard, of having

> betrayed the population of Québec in the sovereignty referendum (Oct. 30, 1995) by distorting history and unfairly blaming English Canada for thwarting Québec's constitutional evolution.[34]

Trudeau went on to contrast Bouchard's claims with the facts as Trudeau saw them. His denunciation of Bouchard's demagoguery was scathing. In a news report by Paul Gessel, the president of a polling firm said that "*Quebecers will be affected by any intervention Trudeau makes, but for the effect to be substantial, the attack has got to be sustained.*" However said Gesssel,

> *This means other politicians will have to prolong the debate and the news media, especially television, will have to provide continuing prominent play to stories that question Bouchard's truthfulness.*[35]

And there's the rub. What if the *Québécois* news media simply ignored Trudeau? In this day and age, if the media ignores something, it will have no political effect. And that is what is happening in Québec. Both Auger and MacPherson said that Trudeau's article would likely have no effect, that it would be an event of the moment and then be quickly forgotten. What was left unsaid was, no matter how much the anglophone media reported Trudeau's article, it would go unnoticed among *Québécois* as long as it was ignored by the francophone media. Auger said mockingly that cartoonists were having a field day with Trudeau's intervention. Indeed, the Tuesday Feb. 6 editorial cartoon in *Le Devoir* depicted a tiresome Trudeau rising once more from the dead.

Trudeau's article was published on Saturday Feb. 3, 1996 not in *Le Devoir*, but in two competing Montreal dailies. Not surprisingly, *Le Devoir* carried no mention of the article on the day it was published. But on Monday Feb. 6 it did mention it--buried on page 2--and only in passing in a Canadian Press report on the meeting of the youth wing of the Québec Liberal Party. By so doing, *Le Devoir* in effect ignored Trudeau's arguments, as if the opinions of the man they hated and feared did not merit their attention; as if Trudeau was some unimportant hick; as if he wasn't one of Canada's most eminent ex-Prime Ministers; as if the facts he described might challenge their ideologically-driven and ethnically-based editorial policy. However, what *was* worthy of comment in this most influential of *Québécois* newspapers was the remote possibility of changing something like a comma to a semi-colon in the Charter of the French Language. This most sacred of sacred cows merited an OpEd article in *Le Devoir* on that day. Priorities, in Québec![36]

But Trudeau's comments were important enough to merit a reply from the offended Lucien Bouchard. *Le Devoir* of course accorded Bouchard's response star treatment. On Saturday, Feb. 10, one week after Trudeau's article, Bouchard's reply appeared simultaneously in *La Presse, The Gazette* and *Le Devoir*. This time *Le Devoir* commented on Bouchard's reply on the same day it was published, and on page one. It would be unfair to reproach them for having ignored Trudeau's article on the day it was published: They were unofficially unaware of it until they saw it on competitive OpEd pages. But it is fair to compare their next-day reporting of Trudeau's accusations with its same-day reporting of Bouchard's response.

As mentioned earlier, *Le Devoir* all but ignored Trudeau by submerging his comments within another story on page two. Bouchard's response, on the other hand, received star treatment on page one from Pierre O'Neill, one of that paper's more experienced journalists. O'Neill quoted extensively from Bouchard's text. In its limited reporting on Trudeau a few days earlier, Trudeau was not quoted at all! Since this otherwise important political event is not relevant to the further evolution of this study, I have consigned to Appendix II my comments on the substance of the Bouchard-Trudeau exchange.

But there are no real surprises here, *Québécois* journalists, like biased journalists everywhere, tend to be selective not only in what they report but in how they report. For example, the attentive reader may well have noticed that federalists generally fare badly in the *Québécois* media while secessionists are accorded some deference. Commenting from inside the profession, Don Macpherson of the *Montreal Gazette* noted that, where the *Québécois* media savaged Liberal Premier Daniel Johnson, a federalist, for not having condemned illegal English signs in his riding during the 1993 provincial election, they ignored similar inactivity by the PQ and secessionist Premier Lucien Bouchard in 1996. This is the balanced journalism that informs the people of Québec.

All this to conclude that, by its actions, *Le Devoir* has proved itself unwilling to provide balanced coverage to political commentary at variance with its secessionist ideology. And if this is typical of Québec's most influential newspaper, and it is, imagine how well informed are its readers, and, by extension, the movers and shakers of Québec who are guided by its dicta.

The same happened on French television. Trudeau's article received attention only as an adjunct to Bouchard's reply. Moreover, shortly after the Trudeau episode, French television displayed its bias once again. The Federal Minister of Indian Affairs, Ron Irwin, had the temerity to state that, in the event of the secession of Québec, aboriginal lands in Québec would remain in Canada since over 95 percent of the aboriginal people on these lands had declared their intention via their own referendum to remain in Canada. Aboriginal land accounts for most of mineral-rich northern Québec. The secessionist government of Québec of course huffed and puffed and cried rape, the usual offended virgin stuff. On English TV, Irwin was shown making his statement followed by an interview with Matthiew Coon Come, Grand Chief of the Cree, the Indians who claim treaty rights to this land. Coon Come agreed with Irwin. This was followed by a clip showing a displeased Lucien Bouchard, Premier of Québec, and some of his cabinet ministers who were suitably outraged and humiliated.

When I switched to French TV I saw the same news item, but with a mischievous twist. Sandwiched between Irwin's statement and lengthy denunciations by Bouchard and company was, not the Chief of the Cree agreeing with Irwin, but some minor Cree official criticizing Irwin for his provocation! This gave the impression that Irwin did not enjoy the support of the people he purported to be defending. This was, of course, intended to mislead the program's *Québécois* viewers. About as dishonest as dredging up a Jew willing to deny the Holocaust, or a black South African ready to say that Apartheid was really pretty neat. Journalism at its lowest with its biases flying high.[37]

Le Devoir: A History

Clearly, *Le Devoir* is a newspaper like few others. It sees itself, and is seen by others, as the interpreter of Québec's soul and guardian of its culture. Nationalists use its pages to disseminate the most current orthodoxy; politicians take its editorial pronouncements seriously; when it finds itself in financial trouble, all *Québécois* of consequence rally to rescue it. First published by the legendary Henri Bourassa in 1910, it had a very special mission. Where newspapers such as the New York Times might boast that its pages contained "*All the news that's fit to print*," Bourassa had a more lofty vision.

> *The first item in the social program of Le Devoir affirms the need to teach patriotism to French-Canadians in such a way that they, French Canadians, will accept and carry out their national responsibilities: Conservation of the Catholic faith and its traditions; aggressive protection of their constitutional rights; respect for the legitimate rights of others; personal development; attachment to the soil; active, informed and patriotic participation in the life of the nation.[38]*

This was clearly an agenda more suited to a social or political movement than to a mere newspaper. And, all those who followed Bourassa in the director's chair officially reaffirmed their faithful adherence to his vision, which included promotion of rural life and "*respect for the authority of the Church in public education.*"[39] In fact, when the paper's retiring director, Gérard Fillion, went looking for his successor in 1964, "*he was looking for a replacement who would be acceptable to the (Catholic) Archbishop (of Montreal) and whose thinking would be consistent with that of Le Devoir. He described his successor, Claude Ryan, as one of the lay people closest to Cardinal Léger.*"[40]

How they could still ally themselves with two areas rejected by the people escapes me: First, the people had never accepted their Church-proclaimed vocations on the farm; second, starting as a trickle in the 1960s, the abandonment of the Church by the people turned into a flood in the 1970s. As a result, Québec today is neither rural nor more than nominally Catholic.

But, notwithstanding official allegiance to the founder's dicta, *Le Devoir* did evolve. In 1964, it was critical of the formation of the first Ministry of Education because too many concessions had been made to the Church, the previous master of Québec's educational system.[41] Moreover, although *Le Devoir* did provide the Church with a good press outlet at one time, Jean-Pierre Proulx argued in <u>Le Devoir: Reflet</u> that, after the 1960s, *Le Devoir's* attention to the Church declined significantly.[42]

Therefore, if the current (1998) occupant of Bourassa's chair is to be taken seriously as a faithful apostle of the master, as she (Lise Bissonnette) insists, she should start writing editorials promoting the return of modern Québec to its rural Catholic roots. But, since Bissonnette is not stupid, she obviously recognizes that these two items in Bourassa's agenda are no longer relevant. Hence, when she says that Bourassa is still her guide, she presumably means that she is guided by those elements of Bourassa's vision that have not already been rejected by the people--or by *Le Devoir* itself.

For instance, when Bourassa dumped on Québec nationalism in 1935, *Le Devoir* distanced itself from the master.[43] One wonders which of Bourassa's remaining dicta will be rejected next by the people or by *Le Devoir*. I must point out that adjusting principles is not new to this august paper: Where it tended to be relatively dovish on matters linguistic when Bill 101 was enacted in 1977, its pages now abound with articles and editorials urging increased restrictions on English. At any rate, *Le Devoir* saw itself leading Québec's cultural vanguard. Lise Bissonnette claimed that, were it not for *Le Devoir*, it is likely that Québec's Quiet Revolution would have left Québec's culture relatively unchanged.[44] Whether this was true or not is, of course, arguable. Nevertheless, its extensive coverage of *Québécois* culture was indeed impressive.

To obtain an appreciation of what was considered important by *Le Devoir* and its admirers in the evolution of the paper, consider its more-or-less official history, Le Devoir: Reflet du Québec au 20e siècle. Since the preface was provided by Lise Bissonnette, we can presume that the paper's management approved of it. Published in 1994, this book revealed more than was probably intended. For instance, when it sub-titled the book "*A reflection of Québec in the 20th century,*" did it mean that it reflected one among many interpretations of Québec or that it reflected *the correct* interpretation? The text does not leave much doubt: *Le Devoir* reflected *the correct* interpretation.

And, what was the essence of this interpretation? Some clues can be gleaned by analyzing the book's table of contents. That is, since the book's contributors wrote about *Le Devoir's* greatest reflections, we can assume that the number of pages in each chapter reflected, in a general way, that paper's assessment of the most important elements in Québec in the 20th-century.

In Table 6-15 the major topics are listed in order of the space accorded to them. Although I do not intend to claim a direct correlation between the amount of space accorded each topic and the actual importance accorded by *Le Devoir*, I would nevertheless argue that some directional conclusions are possible. For instance, since politics received the most attention and the economy the least, I think it reasonable to conclude that these two subjects were ranked properly.

Table 6-15: Le Devoir: Reflet	
% of Sspace Dedicated to:	
Politics	30
Art, Lit., Mus.	22
Unions	11
Feminism	10
Education	8
Science	7
Religion	7
The Economy	5

However, I am not prepared to argue that, in the eyes of the management of *Le Devoir*, politics was thus 6-times as important as the economy (30/5): These data simply do not permit that precise a determination.   Another reasonable conclusion would be that *Le Devoir* was most interested in social matters, followed by politics, with the economy a very poor last.

In fact, it was only in the 1950s that *Le Devoir* even became interested in economic debates, or so claimed Michel Nadeau, author of the chapter on the economy.[45] Nadeau had been the financial pages editor of *Le Devoir* from 1974 to 1984. So unimportant was economics that the paper's editorialists were sceptical of business, especially of the anglophone-dominated business sector of the Québec economy. In fact, when Claude Ryan retired as its editor in January 1978, in his final editorial "*he spoke of the evolution of Québec and his paper without once mentioning economics.*" During the 1980s, the paper was more interested in constitutional matters and in opposing Pierre Trudeau than in economics.[46] And, there were consequences, said Nadeau, who, after leaving *Le Devoir*, became the first vice-president of *La Caisse de dépôt et placement du Québec*, the institution that manages Québec's huge public pension fund. He said:

> What would Québec be today if an institution such as Le Devoir, so influential with the Québécois élites, had chosen as one of its priorities the development of the economy, research and technology (instead of culture and politics)?

Had *Le Devoir* acted as Nadeau had wished, I would argue that *Québécois* would be more affluent today than they are in fact. Nadeau concluded that, if *Québécois* had been more affluent in 1980, they might well have approved the Referendum on secession rather than rejecting it.[47] Arguable, but a fair point.

Before leaving this section of <u>Le Devoir: Reflet</u>, note that the chapter on education dealt only with the period ending in 1964, the year which marked the formation of Québec's first Ministry of Education and the completion of the work of the Parent Commission whose recommendations would lead to a host of educational reforms. Does this absence of apparent interest in the post-1964 period suggest that it was assumed that the educational reforms that emanated from the Parent Commission were successful? But we know from evidence advanced earlier that these reforms were only in part successful. Therefore, wouldn't you expect Québec's cultural leader to have been interested? Those who wrote *Le Devoir's* history did not seem to think so.

This type of anomaly was repeated in the section that analyzed *Le Devoir's* history in time-periods. For instance, in the part dealing with the 1930s, one might have expected a significant reference to the Depression and unemployment, to Hitler and antisemitism, especially to its own antisemitic activities. Of the 10 pages dedicated to the 1930s, about a half page dealt with these items: About 5 percent of the total. The remaining 95 percent dealt with

Québec-related politics. Below is my translation of this half-page.[48]

> *Le Devoir often bemoaned the "deserters from rural areas"*
> *that make Montreal "the Mecca of the unemployed" with its*
> *240,000 people without work. Those responsible? On the one*
> *hand, the trusts--demonstrating "their contempt toward the*
> *government officials they controlled," wrote (editor) Georges*
> *Pelletier on August 20, 1934--and on the other hand, to be*
> *consistent with the times, the Jews! If anti-Jewish jokes*
> *characterized earlier times--"If you are not Jewish, pack your*
> *bags; Canada's Jews will deport you to Russia and replace*
> *you with their kin"--anti-semitism characterized the 1930s. Le*
> *Devoir quoted Hitler admiringly in 1933 when he said: "My*
> *generation has suffered too much from the horrors of war to*
> *inflict it on others." It also applauded the Montreal Bar for*
> *having refused Jews the title of "Councillor". It also wanted*
> *to prevent entry of German Jews to Canada because Germany*
> *considered them to be marxist and communist, ... and*
> *because, by the nature of their religion, customs and*
> *unassimilatable character, they would be a source of division,*
> *dispute and trouble for Canadians.*

And in the same vein, from 1933 to 1935, *Le Devoir* often commended the efforts of a new youth movement headed by Father Lionel Groulx: Young Canada, whose members--André Laurendeau and Pierre Dansereau, to mention only the better known--expressed their antisemitism in *Le Devoir*. This was not unusual, said Laurendeau, since "*antisemitism is international, as are the Jews.*"

Thus, although tomes have been written on the Depression, it apparently figured so little in the preoccupations of this paper that it merited but a couple of sentences in its official history. Sadder still was how it sullied its honourable *mea culpa* concerning its antisemitism with the Laurendeau comment: After all, everyone was antisemitic then! Moreover, although this citation correctly associated the sainted Lionel Groulx with some of Québec's leading antisemites, Groulx's name appears in fourteen other places in the book, not as an antisemite but as an honourable Québec nationalist!

There are, of course, other interpretations of *Le Devoir's* record during the 1930s. One of these is contained in Esther Delisle's The Traitor and the Jew. According to Delisle, between 1929 and 1939, *Le Devoir* was closely associated with the antisemite Lionel Groulx. For instance, during this period, it published 101 articles, speeches and advertisements by Groulx. In 1935, it carried two of Groulx's racist novels in comic-book form, supplementing them with 27 articles or editorials on Groulx's writings.[49]

Among *Le Devoir's* concerns was the propensity of Jews in Montréal to change their names. Why the concern, you ask? Well, if someone was called Rosenberg, the faithful could protect themselves from him because they could identify him by his Jewish name. But, what if Rosenberg changed his name to McTavish or Latulippe, how then could the Jew be identified and the necessary protective measures taken? *Le Devoir* apparently considered this to be so serious that it organized a public campaign in 1933 to stop people from changing their names![50] This followed its rejection in 1932 of *"The Jew Einstein (who) has convinced us to accept the theory of relativity on trust."*[51] And, to complete this overview, the reader should note that *Le Devoir* proclaimed in an editorial in 1936 that *"in many federal government departments, typists, clerks and inspectors are hired because of their Yiddish fluency."*[52]

If antisemitism was not so heinous, these citations are so ridiculous as to invite laughter. But, *Le Devoir* and its apologists seem to take refuge behind the claim that everyone was antisemitic in the 1930s. This of course was true and untrue but irrelevant. First, there is the matter of personal responsibility that makes us accountable for our acts no matter what those around us are doing. Since this is a central tenet of Catholic social doctrine, it must have been known and understood at *Le Devoir*. Moreover, this notion of personal responsibility was confirmed by the War Crimes Tribunal at Nuremberg after WW II when it rejected *"obeying orders"* as a defence for committing war crimes. Second, if *Le Devoir* had really been in the vanguard of cultural change, as it insisted, you would think that, as the self-proclaimed teacher of the people of Québec, it would have used its considerable influence to promote civilized tolerance rather than hateful antisemitism. Unless, of course, it saw the antisemitism of the 1930s as the wave of the future ... and approved it!

So, behold *Le Devoir*, the undisputed intellectual leader of *Québécois* nationalists. Whether it reflects or leads nationalist thought is an open question; but that it portrays nationalist ideology with theological certainty is clear. Also clear is the reason for its great influence: Those who exercise influence tend to read it, finding support for their ideologies within its pages. This suggests that *Le Devoir* reflects the thinking of those who read it. And who reads this paper?

Some claim that, given its messianic mission, *Le Devoir* has always been read by the *Québécois* élite, first by Church officials and more recently by their secular successors. With a daily circulation of 31,000 in 1995 it was not exactly a world beater. In fact, the most widely read newspaper in Québec in that year was *Le Journal de Montréal* (279,000), followed by *La Presse* (176,000), the English language Montreal Gazette (148,000), *Le Journal de Québec* (100,000), *Le Soleil de Québec* (92,000), *La Nouvelliste de Trois Rivières* (46,000), *La Tribune de Sherbrooke* (34,000), and then *Le Quotidien de Chicoutimi* and *Le Devoir* at 31,000. Next on the list is the mighty *Voix de l'Est de Granby* (15,000). Even *Le Droit d'Ottawa* (34,000) outsold *Le Devoir*.

To put this paper into further perspective, some claim that fewer *Québécois* read it than read the English Montreal Gazette. Moreover, its circulation puts it into the same league as the Brantford Expositer (25,000),

Kingston Whig Standard (28,000), Peterborough Examiner (26,000), Sudbury Star (26,000) and Thunder Bay Chronicle-Journal (35,000). Canada's 'national' newspaper, the Toronto Globe and Mail has a national circulation of 313,000 (200,000 in Ontario, 18,000 in Québec). Canada's largest paper, the Toronto Star has a daily circulation of 478,000.[53] Without wishing to be unkind, I would argue first, that it is clear that Le Devoir's influence cannot derive from its pitifully small circulation and, second, that Le Devoir (31,000) exercises more influence in Québec than does the Globe and Mail (200,000) in Ontario. Its influence must derive from the influential people who read it, people whose opinions and ideologies are reflected in the pages of this unique newspaper.

And what type of message is it propounding today? Consider, for example, its analysis of the report of the FTQ (Fédération des travailleurs et travailleuses du Québec) pension fund. By way of comparison, note that L'Actualité, the French-language sister of the English-language McLean's magazine, provided an in-depth analysis of the financial performance of this fund in its November 1, 1996 edition. It reported that, although most contributors to the fund, Québécois workers, believed that their contributions were earning returns in the order of 20 percent per year, the fund had in fact only earned about 5 percent per year since its inception, not much better than an ordinary bank-account rate of return. L'Actualité concluded that this was unsatisfactory and that managers of the fund were guilty of questionable public relations tactics to cover up this lacuna.

I would argue that at least three conclusions can be derived from this article in L'Actualité: First, the financial performance of the fund was objectively unsatisfactory; second, this unsatisfactory performance must have been known, or at least suspected in the media; third, the clearly exaggerated claims by the fund's managers should have whetted the appetites of discriminating journalists. That probably explains why L'Actualité became interested in the story. Now consider what happens when ideology triumphs over professional integrity in the media.

On January 4, 1996 the front-page headline in Le Devoir read: Record Profit for the FTQ Fund; the sub-heading read: 11.6 percent return on $122 million invested. Although 11.6 percent is not bad, it is hardly worth a headline. Within the text, the Fund is referred to in politically correct terms as the workers' solidarity fund. The reporter, Robert Dutrisac, noted that the Fund's profit was derived from investments in Québec-based enterprises (4 percent return) as well as from stock market investments (18 percent return). He also noted without comment that 53 percent of the Fund's investments were in (much less profitable) Québec-based enterprises. Also noted was the intent of the Fund to carry out its promise to the government of Québec to set up locally managed solidarity funds in each of Québec's sixteen regions ... for returns of 4 percent! Not once in the article was any comment made concerning the Fund's curious investment mix. Wouldn't you expect an orthodox financial reporter to ask why the lion's share of workers' pension funds was being invested at a 4 percent return when 18 percent returns were available? And, shouldn't an attentive and inquisitive reporter have wondered about the ethics of government intervention that forced the Fund to invest even more money in these marginally profitable Québec enterprises? Why is it salutary that workers invest at 4 percent instead of 18 percent? If it was in the public interest that money be invested at marginal returns, why did the government require the workers' pension fund instead of the provincial treasury to carry the load? If there were good reasons for this unorthodox behaviour, Dutrisac failed to raise them. He in fact insisted that this curious financial behaviour was normal and laudable.

Or, consider its reporting of the assembly of concerned Canadians that took place in Montreal on October 28, 1995, three days before the Referendum on secession where *Le Devoir* supported the secessionists. This assembly was essentially a last gasp grass-roots attempt by ordinary Canadians to make up for both the incompetent management of the anti-secession campaign by the so-called federalist forces in Québec, and the arrogant *laissez-faire* attitude of the federal government of Jean Chrétien. People could read the polls and they reacted in predictable horror at the prospect of losing the country because their leaders had taken leave of their senses. Since I am not much of a flag waver I paid little attention to the event ... until it occurred. Although I do not think it made much of a difference to the final outcome (non-secessionists won a squeaker), I was thrilled to see those thousands of unabashed flag wavers milling about in Montreal on that cold windy day, proclaiming their patriotism and urging *Québécois* to reject the secessionists on October 31. It was a wholesome gesture and deserved more respectful treatment from *Le Devoir* than Lise Bissonnette and her colleagues provided.

On the day after this assembly, *Le Devoir's* front page headline read (my translation) *"Supporters of the No Side Unfurl Themselves"* By No Side it meant the anti-secessionists, and the headline referred to the flag waving of the people. The sub-headline read *"Federalism's Tourists"* because the reporter treated these flag wavers as tourists with nothing better to do. In the editorial, Lise Bissonnette decried this assembly essentially as too little too late. In her last sentence she referred to the assembly as *"An unhealthy affair that it was pathetic to see unfold in this confused and ignorant way, on the eve of a major decision (to be taken by the people of Québec)."* About as dismissive as one can get. In an accompanying article, Daniel Latouche was equally contemptuous, saying *"Oh, the English love us, they love us to death, but only if their travel costs are paid, if their vacation is paid for, and if the whole episode commits them to nothing."*[53] Pretty anglophobic! Almost as hateful as Josée Legault's column in the same paper about eight months later.

Commenting upon the hyper-patriotic festivities in Ottawa on Canada Day (July 1, 1996), Josée Legault disgraced herself once again (July 10, 1996) with a diatribe in *Le Devoir*, a rant usually associated with rags published by scum, not with responsible mainstream newspapers among which *Le Devoir* claims membership. Her headline read:

EIN VOLK, EIN REICH ..... EIN FLAG

For those with a limited appreciation of recent history, let me just say that this is a parody of part of Hitler's racist speech at the Nuremberg rally of 1938, the meeting of the Nazi party that preceded Hitler's famous meeting with Neville Chamberlain at Munich. At that rally, the thousands of flag wavers cheered when Hitler promised them a purified Germany for their master race, one free of Jews, gypsies and other undesirables. As everyone knows, the Nazis then went on to exterminate some 6 million Jews. Clearly, one does not associate nice people with these vermin. In her column Legault wrote:

> *The combative character that was evident among anglophones on their Canada Day ..... was also evident by the use of the Canadian flag as a (primitive) fetish.*

> *In fact, flying the Canadian flag is becoming increasingly the thing to do in areas that are heavily anglophone. In what Ottawa calls the "National Capital Region" this has attained quasi-psychotic proportions.*

> *With this type of disagreeable and primitive patriotism, we can feel the general aggression emanating from all this red (on the flags).*

> *All along Confederation Boulevard, a ring-road that encompasses Ottawa and Hull .... (there are so many flags) that it reminds one of Munich (sic) in 1938.*

> *In francophone areas of Hull, we see few Canadian flags, and only the occasional Québec flag, proving that francophones are (mentally) healthier and more mature (than anglophones).*

Got that?

I suppose that the best way to deal with such trash is to dismiss it as yellow journalism. Fairly easily done if you are dealing with a tabloid rag; not so easy with *Le Devoir*, which, although objectively a rag, is nevertheless an influential rag. Therefore, let me make a few points in rebuttal.

First, the comparison of Canadians waving flags to a similar gathering of Nazis in Hitler's Germany is wildly inaccurate and clearly inappropriate. The Nazis were celebrating laws and policies that would rid

Germany of Jews--ethnic cleansing. If Legault knows of any similar laws or policies in Canada--outside of Québec--she would do us all a great favour by identifying them forthwith. But she won't because there aren't any. However, if she had compared Canada Day activities to those seen at any secessionist political rally in Québec, she would have found a great similarity between the two: Lots of flags. On the other hand, there was one great difference: Where Canada Day celebrants embrace everyone, secessionist rallies are usually marked by the racist chant "*Le Québec aux Québécois,*" an invitation for the ethnically impure to leave Québec. Thus, when Legault states that the absence of flags in Hull is a sign of maturity, she was obviously being preposterous or mischievous, or both. A more accurate conclusion would have been that the absence of Québec flags was probably due, not to maturity, but to old fashioned intimidation. Although I have not seen many Québec flags at Canada Day celebrations, I have seen some--in the hands of those making a valid point: Québec is and will remain part of Canada. And, who but a fool or an invincibly impolite *Québécois* nationalist would introduce the Québec flag as a secessionist symbol to a gathering celebrating Canada!

Clearly, *Le Devoir* has deviated considerably from Henri Bourassa's guidelines. Where Bourassa proclaimed the supremacy of rural life and the authority of the Church, *Le Devoir* has obviously abandoned both; where Bourassa dumped on nationalism, *Le Devoir* is the organ of *Québécois* nationalist orthodoxy; where Bourassa was a reasonably orthodox *Canadien*, *Le Devoir* appears to be unreservedly secessionist; where *Le Devoir* was once antisemitic, it is now clearly anglophobic; where *Le Devoir* reporters once ignored the financial, they now interpret it in terms of politically correct, but objectively incompetent socialist ideology. But, there is one constant: It remains as confident as ever about its mission in life, to teach *Québécois* to do their duty. That this duty is now described in the words of anglophobes and secessionists is yet another departure from the founder's message.

The Masses: Hokumed

To the extent that the *Québécois* media influence public opinion, their influence will obviously tend to have a secessionist bias. Thus, if secessionist propaganda goes unchallenged in the media, and if the media ignore inconvenient facts, how can the people inform themselves within this information environment? With great difficulty, obviously! I would argue that the people have little choice but to rely on their leaders to provide competent and truthful interpretations of complex issues. And if their leaders say one thing when someone less august claims or argues the opposite, whom will the masses believe?

It depends on many things, of course, not the least of which is the amount and quality of information made available to them. It was relatively simple, for instance, for nomads navigating the Sahara to evaluate the quality of information concerning the location of oases. If the oases were where they were supposed to be, the nomads lived; if they were elsewhere, they died. Since word gets around, purveyors of inaccurate information no doubt received appropriate gestures of displeasure in due course. Although the potential consequences of bad information are not so drastic in Québec, the same principal applies. Historians will look back some day and wonder why, in the 1990s, *Québécois* made such peculiar political choices.

They will find, I will argue, that the masses were greatly influenced by their political leaders, and that these leaders pursued objectives inimical to the best interests of the people. In fact, *Québécois* seem to have accepted as gospel the pronouncements of their leaders, especially as regards criticisms of anglophones and the federal government. Moreover, historians will find that the federal government did precious little either to promote its interests within Québec or to dispute secessionist misinformation. Ever since about 1960, Ottawa in effect has left the field free to secessionist-minded interests. As a result, the only political messages heard consistently in Québec have been those with a secessionist bias. Thus, as routine psychological association with Canada withered, devotion to Québec naturally moved in to replace it. Small wonder then that, at international conferences, delegates from Québec tend to wear name tags identifying their country as Québec while their colleagues from other Canadian provinces routinely identify themselves as Canadians. Moreover, I am told that immigrants arriving in Canada at Québec ports of entry are welcomed, not to Canada, but to Québec. And, the federal government pays for these immigration services and international conferences!

So, what have the feds been doing to promote national interests in Québec? To counter secessionist propaganda? So far, nada, zip, nothing! Well, who speaks for Canada in Québec? Certainly not the so-called federalist provincial parties: They make too fine a living dumping on Ottawa. Consequently, the tendency of *Québécois* to identify with Québec rather than with Canada was, alas, predictable and inevitable.

So how is the federal government to promulgate a pro-Canada message to the people of Québec? Certainly not through secessionist-minded news channels. To be fair, however, not all *Québécois* news channels are unreservedly secessionist-minded. But, common to them all is the propensity to accept and propound the *Poor-Québec-Syndrome* that permeates political discourse in Québec. Same effect in either case, an anti-Canada bias. But, since necessity is the mother of invention, the feds have finally started to fight back. Whenever the secessionists resort to fibs and the occasional whopper, the feds now apparently intend to challenge them aggressively. Given the communications impediments described above, this is no small challenge.

That is the misleading information environment in which *Québécois* have been immersed since about 1960. Even the best intentioned and most resourceful would have difficulty resisting such an overwhelming tide. As one who grew up in Catholic communities in Québec that harboured traditional Catholic biases, I swear (half in jest but all in earnest) that I was 27 before I realized that Protestants did not have horns! Catholics of my youth harboured few doubts about who was going to heaven--Catholics--and who was going to hell--everybody else. Misinformation is a heavy burden that can produce terrible consequences when imposed upon the naive and credulous.

Compounding the effect of misinformation is the gullibility of the people as described earlier. In some societies, people are very distrustful of their leaders, in others they treat them with great deference and respect. In the former, if a politician, for example, stated that the earth was round, you can bet that some of his constituents would be suspicious. In the latter, if a leading holy man declared that the earth was flat, we all know where this absurdity would find widespread acceptance among the faithful. As I said earlier, it depends. In Québec, the élite have a proven track record selling hokum to the masses.

For example, during the 1995 Québec Referendum campaign, three *Québécoise* law students from the University of Ottawa were interviewed on CBC English Radio concerning their decisions to vote "Yes", to vote for secession. Their decision, they said, was driven by the bleak employment prospects awaiting them upon graduation. Their concern was obviously not misplaced: The current surplus of lawyers makes job prospects for new lawyers everywhere very problematic. But having been told that job prospects for lawyers would be much better in an independent Québec, they decided to vote "Yes". It was the only way to guarantee a job! Some guaranty! And what are the facts? A family friend completing her law degree told us that where, in the past, about 15 percent of applicants failed at least one of their Québec Bar exams, the failure rate soared to about 75 percent in 1996. It seems that the exams were made more demanding to control the entry of surplus lawyers to the profession. So how did these three law students arrive at their wonky conclusion? Were they gullible? Is the Pope Catholic? They had to be either gullible or thick. Remember that these were university students, people you expect to be able to discriminate between fact and fiction. Can you imagine being represented by lawyers such as these?

Another prize for breathtaking gullibility can be awarded to the members of *L'Union des producteurs de lait du Québec*. The leaders of this association convinced its dairy farmer members that their interests would be well served if they voted to secede from Canada. Sound advice? Consider the facts. With about 25 percent of Canada's population, Québec supplies about 50 percent of Canada's subsidized demand for industrial milk (for cheese production *inter alia*). Although neighbouring Canadian and American dairy farmers are lusting after, and could easily supply Québec's share of this market--with reduced subsidies--this association's leaders preached an obviously misleading fairy tale: That dairy farmers in an independent Québec would continue to be Canada's dominant supplier of industrial milk, and with the same subsidies! And Québec's dairy farmers appear to have believed them. Pigs would of course fly before this preposterous fairy tale ever became fact.

But the all time winners in the gullibility sweepstakes must be *Québécois* voters during the 1995 Referendum campaign. That an otherwise sophisticated electorate could be so credulous astonished journalist Jeffrey Simpson of the Toronto *Globe and Mail*.[55] He described how, during the campaign, federalists became increasingly frustrated by the success of the secessionist leader, Lucien Bouchard. People were flocking to the secessionist side because of Bouchard's charisma despite that fact that some of Bouchard's claims were--according to the federalists--factually wrong, outrageous or both. How, they asked, could *Québécois* be fooled by such nonsense?

To answer the question, they convened focus groups of secessionists and asked them *"Do you believe that Lucien Bouchard made this outrageous statement?"* Not surprisingly, the responses generally were *"Of course not, Lucien Bouchard would never say such a thing!"* Then, when the focus groups were shown videos of Bouchard actually making *this outrageous statement*, they responded that Bouchard must have meant something else, or that there must have been legitimate reasons for him having made *that outrageous statement*. The faithful were clearly not prepared to question or doubt Saint Lucien. They went on to vote for the Messiah, he who promised that secession would solve Québec's problems *"like the wave of a magic wand."*

Sellers of hokum can reap handsome short term rewards. In the longer term, however, they should prepare for the less agreeable whirlwind.

Québec Inc: A Perspective

Some claim that close cooperation between government and business in Japan was largely responsible for the spectacular success of the Japanese economy since 1945. Although historians disagree about the degree of importance of this partnership, they all agree that it was effective. In fact, so business-minded did Japanese governments become that the country came to be called Japan Inc. We have been hearing the same acronym applied to Québec since the mid-1980s.

The term Québec Inc. was not invented by outsiders to describe what they observed in Québec--as was the case with the perceptive Americans who saw the effects of the marriage of business and government in Japan and called the union Japan Inc. The term Québec Inc. was invented within the province by those seeking a greater role for their government in the management of the provincial economy. Nothing wrong with this in my view since government is ultimately responsible for what goes on in any economy. However, how the government should fulfil this role is arguable. But, whatever school you belong to, you should not ignore one of history's imperatives: Business investment generally creates jobs, public investment generally does not. Thus, if the creation of jobs is a priority, government policies and practices should at least not discourage business investment. If you belong to the practical school, you might argue that government should set the rules but leave job-creating investment to the private sector. However, if you belong on the left of the political spectrum, you will tend to argue for greater government investment in the economy despite its poor record in job creation. On the other hand, if you feel more comfortable on the right, you would tend to diminish the importance of government investment, even investment that belongs in the public sector: Public schools, for instance. Public policy in Québec since 1960 has not only been driven from the left, but from that portion of the left that feels that government investment or policies can make up for business shortfalls. That there is no historical evidence to support this silly notion seems to have cut no ice with those *Québécois* policy makers from the loony left.

Moreover, at the outset of the Quiet Revolution, the government of Québec decided that putting economic power in the hands of *Québécois* was a high priority. Thus, privately owned producers and distributors of hydro-electric power were nationalized to augment the publicly owned Hydro-Québec ... about half a century after similar action was taken in Ontario. In the election campaign where nationalization was the issue, the anglophobic slogan was *"Maîtres chez nous."* It was anglophobic since many of the nationalized companies were owned by anglophone Québecers and hence, by definition, *deserving* of expropriation. Hydro-Québec then launched a host of gigantic hydro-electric construction projects in northern Québec which required it to borrow huge sums on Wall Street. Eventually, this public utility became Québec's largest company as well as the pride of all *Québécois*.

Although thought to be very profitable, evidence that came to light in the 1990s shows that it was not overly so. For instance, when it became apparent that most, if not all of Hydro-Québec's profits derived from the very advantageous purchase of surplus power from the province of Newfoundland's Churchill Falls power plant in Labrador, and not from its own Québec operations, the financial weakness of Hydro-Québec became clear. Even at the technical level, Hydro-Québec's vaunted superiority has come under critical review. This criticism reached its peak in January 1998 when freezing rain caused power lines to fail all over eastern Ontario and southern Québec. As a result, up to 3 million people in Québec, and 0.5 million in Ontario, were without power for weeks ... in the middle of winter; about 30 people died for reasons attributed to this power-outage, 25 in Québec. And though Québec received only half the freezing rain that fell on Ontario, damage to its hydro-electric distribution system was greater.[56] Although there are several reasons to explain this relatively greater disaster in Québec, one must be that Hydro-Québec was technologically delinquent. For example, to de-ice its major power transmission line supplying the Island of Montréal, it had to resort to dropping logs from helicopters onto the ice-covered cables! Although more effective modern technology is available to de-ice power cables, Hydro-Québec drops wood from helicopters! Clearly, Hydro-Québec has been profligate, inefficient and technologically delinquent, and thus does not deserve the hero status that *Québécois* nationalists have thrust upon it. More later on this public utility.

But the notion of Québec Inc. received a real boost with the formation of the *Caisse de dépots et de placements du Québec*, hereafter called the *Caisse*. The *Caisse* was formed in Québec to manage and invest the huge sums of money that would become available with the establishment of the public pension plan in the 1960s. Outside of Québec, this pension plan, the Canada Pension Plan (CPP), was to be a pay-as-you-go plan: Benefits were to be paid out of current contributions with any surpluses loaned to the provinces at preferred interest rates. The government of Québec said, correctly in my view, that this was not the way to do it. Better to invest the contributions of those paying into the plan and pay the beneficiaries from the profits generated by the plan. The *Caisse* was formed to manage this huge pool of investment capital; the notion of Québec Inc. was on the rise.

Although the *Caisse* invested in all sorts of companies, it obviously favoured Québec enterprises. Some claim that it used its influence to foster the advancement of *Québécois* in the companies in which it invested. Moreover, with this large pool of investment funds at its disposal, it was only a matter of time before the government of Québec discarded its arms-length relationship with the *Caisse* and intervened directly in its management. For instance, when the province's asbestos industry fell on hard times, the government directed the *Caisse* to bail it out with an injection of new capital. That is, the *Caisse* was directed to make unprofitable investments with the workers' pension fund to support the government's political objectives. As most people know, the demand for asbestos has been dropping like a stone for years, ever since it was found to be carcinogenic!

In a similar vein, the *Caisse* invested heavily in Québec's troubled pulp and paper industry. I will show later that the future of Québec's pulp and paper industry is not encouraging. Hence, why would a prudent shepherd of a public pension fund invest in a declining industry? Obviously not to satisfy the workers' financial objectives. To satisfy the boss' political objectives? Do vultures eat meat?

Moreover, during the 1995 Referendum on sovereignty, the secessionist government of Jacques Parizeau used the *Caisse* again for purely political purposes. In the days immediately prior to the Referendum, it was thought by many, including Parizeau, that uncertainty over the outcome of the vote might cause the value of the Canadian dollar to fall on international money markets. If this happened, some secessionist-minded voters might find it difficult to vote for secession. Hence, Parizeau directed the *Caisse* to prop up the Canadian dollar with large purchases of Canadian dollars in international markets. He also planned to use the *Caisse* to spend huge sums doing the same thing after the Referendum if his secessionists won the day: He expected the value of the Canadian dollar to fall following a secessionist victory. This was divulged by Parizeau himself after the Referendum. So what happened?

Because the secessionists lost the Referendum vote, the value of the Canadian dollar rose slightly, and the *Caisse* made a profit! But, had the vote gone the other way, the value of the *Caisse's* purchases would obviously have declined as Parizeau expected and the public pension fund would have taken a billion dollar beating. As a result, people's pensions would have been much lower than expected. This was Québec Inc. at the service of politicians instead of the public. And, to make matters worse, the government of Québec could not even get onside with Québec's businessmen, the people who could make Québec Inc. work, if it was to work at all.

In the fall of 1996, Québec's Premier Bouchard met with representatives of labour, business and community groups to arrive at a consensus about how to balance the province's books and reduce its very high rate of unemployment. Not surprisingly, everyone thought that those were two fine objectives. Equally unsurprising, no one agreed on how to accomplish them: Labour and community groups recommended that the books be balanced by raising taxes on the rich, not by cutting programs; business recommended that programs be cut. Moreover, although they all agreed that creating new jobs was the right thing to do, they differed on how to create them: Labour and community groups wanted massive infusions of public investment (which do not create many jobs); the government quite correctly thought business would do a better job creating jobs by increasing its level of investment. Businessmen also thought so but said that they would continue to minimize their investments until the language laws were relaxed and the secessionist threat was erased from the political agenda. The government refused to ease up on either one.

Clearly, the notion of Québec Inc. was an interesting invention, but one that existed more in people's imaginations than in fact. Moreover, to the extent that it did function at all, it was to pursue the political and social interests of the *Québécois* élite, not the economic interests of the people of Québec.

Summary

During the Quiet Revolution, secular nationalists displaced the Church from atop the socio-political totem pole in Québec. Moreover, these nationalists, the modern *Québécois* élite, seem to be driven by the same secessionist imperatives that inspired the rebellious Patriots of 1837. Also, their secessionist zeal seems to be fuelled by anglophobia, the ulra-nationalist daily newspaper *Le Devoir*, and the Marxist-inspired ideologies that drove various anti-colonial revolutions in Africa and Asia after WW II. In addition, they feel the Québec economy should be driven more by state economic power than by private sector investment. These nationalists can be found in any of the many nationalist groups that abound in Québec. The most influential, of course, is *La Société Saint-Jean Baptiste*. Nurtured within these chauvinistic organizations is an anglophobic ideology that has come to dominate Québec politics and poison social discourse.

Central to this ideology is the notion of Québec as the victim of anglophones in general and of the federal government in particular. To rectify the situation, these nationalists prescribe a three-step process. The first step is to marginalize English influence in Québec via restrictive legislation; the second, to ethnically cleanse Québec of non-secessionist anglophones and allophones; the third, to have Québec secede from Canada.

Although this ideological culture is common to all political parties in Québec, its natural home is within the secessionist *Parti Québécois* (PQ). However, it would be a mistake to assume that there is any political party in Québec that is truly non-secessionist. For instance, the allegedly pro-Canada provincial Liberal Party has adopted so many secession-related positions that it must be called effectively secessionist.

Cheering on these true-blue nationalists are fellow travellers whose careers have flourished within this xenophobic culture. I refer here to intellectuals such as journalists, public school teachers, university academics and artists. Also included are various unions, especially those in the public sector, as well as those *Québécois* employed within the bloated provincial bureaucracy.

It was these nationalists who directed the Quiet Revolution, concerning which the historical record is clear: Relative to Ontarians, *Québécois* remained as uneducated in 1991 as they had been in 1961; they were also relatively poorer in 1991 than in 1961. One sign of Québec's inferior educational environment is its very high rate of illiteracy. Specifically,

1.   Québec anglophones are much more literate than *Québécois*.

2.   Québec anglophones are more literate than anglophones elsewhere in Canada.

3.   *Québécois* are less literate than any language group anywhere in Canada outside of Newfoundland.

Québec's pitiful public library system must be held partly responsible for this high rate of illiteracy. Also to be condemned is the province's public school system which simply has not measured up to expectations. To begin with, its curriculum has been found wanting. Also deficient is the school system's use of modern teaching aids. This includes the use of classroom computers where Québec is shamefully behind the rest of Canada. And to make matters worse, the overall drop-out rate in Québec's public schools is over 50 percent, about twice the Ontario rate. And when we dig below the surface, we find:

1.   Drop-out rates were much lower in English schools.

2.   The drop-out rate in Montreal inner city French schools was substantially higher than the rate in French rural schools.

These very high drop-out rates among *Québécois* could have tragic social consequences in the years ahead.

Proof of the deteriorating quality of education in French schools can be found in the report of "*The Commission of the Estates General*" which declared:

> *Montreal schools are in such a state of decay and devastation*
> *that, if left uncorrected, they will adversely affect the whole of*
> *Québec society.*

Of course, this was old news to many discriminating *Québécois* parents. Long ago recognizing the poor state of Québec's public schools, they reacted predictably by abandoning them. As a result, enrolments in Québec's mostly French private schools became the largest in Canada. In addition, students in Québec's English schools were hobbled by the incomprehensible exams they were required to write by the Minister of Education. Translated from the French originals, they were so bad that, where the marks of students in French schools improved between 1989 and 1993, those in English schools actually declined.

Moreover, where French schools, assisted by language laws, dominated the early school years, their dominance waned as post-secondary students started to exercise their freedom of choice. For instance, where French *Cégeps* tended to push their graduates directly into the workforce, their English equivalents tended to direct them instead into universities. And, within the university sector, English universities out-performed their French counterparts by a very wide margin: In per capita terms, enrolments in English universities were 2 to 3 times those in French universities. This was a reflection of differing attitudes seen in polls where 33 percent of anglophones, 20 percent of allophones, and 16 percent of *Québécois* said they expected to get a university degree. Moreover, students in French universities favoured the soft social sciences instead of the demanding disciplines of engineering and economics.

But, *Québécois* poverty was only in part caused by a faulty education system. Also responsible was the lack of job-creating business investment. And this can be attributed first to the strategic decision of the early Quiet Revolutionaries not to court business investment, but to count instead on the economic power of the Québec state. But since this public investment model has not worked very well elsewhere, it is not surprising that it has not worked so far in Québec. Second, the abrasive language laws enacted to protect French culture also had the effect of discouraging job-creating business investment. Third, the threat of secession acted as a deterring sword of Damocles over the heads of potential investors.

The various language laws adopted in Québec were intended to protect an allegedly fragile French culture from the corrosive influence of English. But when you dig below the fine print, you soon realize that this protection took the form of simply restricting the public appearance of English. In fact, the data suggest that:

1.   If the justification for the adoption of Québec's language laws was that they were needed to arrest a decline in the francophone share of Québec's population, the evidence shows that, since there never was a decline prior to adoption of these laws, the laws could not have been logically justified by that argument.

2.   Since the annual increase in the francophone share after adoption of the first restrictive language law was about 10-times the rate before its adoption, might we not conclude that the language laws were in fact meant to increase the francophone share, not to arrest its decline?

In addition,

1.   Language legislation was passed in Québec by political parties of every political stripe.

2.   Each time this legislation was amended, it was to make it more restrictive of English.

3.   Legislation was passed or amended in response to the demands of an anglophobic minority.

Moreover, the evidence suggests that these language laws will fail to assimilate the allophones who have been forced into French schools. For example, it would appear that allophones, even those who attend French schools, still prefer to speak English rather than French! And what is the reason for this failure? Among other reasons, the assimilating *Québécois*, having abandoned Montreal's inner city where allophones live, are not available to assimilate them!

All this to conclude that, when *Québécois* nationalists wrap themselves in the flag to proclaim that protection of French is an unassailable imperative needed to protect their culture, their argument is clearly built on unstable sand. But then again, perhaps their true objective is not cultural protection after all, that it is simply political: To rid Québec of anglophones.

And then there are Québec's famous referenda.

The *Québécois* élite have resorted to lies, half-truths, cheating and electoral fraud to further their interests. So effective were they with this strategy that they carried it to breath-taking levels in the referenda of 1980 and 1995 from which five clear conclusions can be derived:

1.   The secessionist objective pursued by *Québécois* provincial politicians was not supported by a majority of *Québécois*.

2.   A substantial number of *Québécois* were obviously misled by complicated, unclear and misleading questions.

3.   The misleading of the people by their politicians was deliberate.

4.   If you can convince people to vote against their best interests, your influence over them must indeed be impressive.

5.   If regular measures do not work, *Québécois* secessionists are prepared to cheat to attain their goal, the secession of Québec from Canada.

And this brings up the role of the media.

That the *Québécois* media practice selective journalism is well supported by the evidence.   For instance, Québec's most influential newspaper, *Le Devoir*, is clearly anglophobic and secessionist, promoting nationalist ideology with theological certitude.   Although its mission has been adapted to suit the imperatives of the moment, it remains faithful to the original mission set by its founder Henri Bourassa in 1910: To teach *Québécois* to do their duty.   That this duty is now described in the words of anglophobes and secessionists is a major departure from Bourassa's intentions.

Thus, if secessionist propaganda goes unchallenged in the media, and if the media ignore the inconvenient, how can the people be other than misinformed?   Consequently, within this environment of misinformation, the people are vulnerable to the self-serving hokum served up by the hucksters among their leaders.   Although these retailers of baloney seem to be reaping short term rewards, let us hope they are eventually hoist by their own pétards.

As regards the seductive notion of Québec Inc., the evidence shows that it was an interesting invention that existed more in people's fertile imaginations than in fact.   Moreover, to the extent that Québec Inc. functioned at all, it was to pursue political objectives, not the economic interests of the people.

Moreover, Québec's business leaders told the Premier of Québec that they would continue to minimize their job-creating investments in Québec until the language laws were relaxed and the threat of secession was removed from the political agenda.   Not surprisingly, the Premier refused to give ground on either point.

Notes

1.   The *Bloc Québécois* (BQ) is a secessionist party from Québec allied with the Parti Québécois (PQ). It sits in the federal Parliament in Ottawa.

2.   Ottawa Citizen, Sept. 30, 1996, A-3

3.   When Duplessis' body was being transported from Québec City, where it had been lying in state, to his home town of Trois Rivières for burial, it was said that the body was lying on its side. The reason? So that the citizens of Québec could kiss his backside for the last time.

4.   1931 Census, Table 63.

5.   Adult Literacy in Canada: Results of a National Study, Science and Technology Canada, 1991.

6.   Le Devoir, February 10/11, 1996, p. A4.

7.   Blouin actually reported that there were only 388 computers in 19 of Québec's 273 school commissions. In 1982 there were in the order of 3,500 elementary schools in Québec.

8.   Diplomation Par Commission Scolaire, juin 1993, Ministère de l'Éducation du Québec, 1994 Table 18.

9.   Letter from D. Cook, Minister of Education of Ontario, March 30, 1995.

10.   Diplomation, Table 18.

11.   Le Devoir, pp. A1, A8; 31 janvier 1996.

12.   Statistiques de l'éducation, 1994, Ministère de l'Éducation du Québec, Table 3.1.1.

13.   Statistiques de l'éducation, Table 2.3.11

14.   Statistiques de l'éducation, Table 2.3.9, 3.3.2

15.   L'Éducation au Québec: La formation de base, C. Lemelin, département des sciences économiques, UQAM, in Éducation et formation à l'heure de la compétitivité internationale, Association des économistes québécois, 1990.

16.   Statistiques de l'éducation, Table 2.4.5.

17.   StatCan 81-219, 1993/94

18.   Diplomes et accès aux diplomes dans les universités québécoises, 1976-80 (Québec: Ministère de l'Éducation du Québec, 1991), T-8.

19.   Gretta Chambers, Montréal Gazette, Aug. 7, 1998.

20.   There was a non-restrictive language law passed in 1968.

21.   According to the various censuses, the francophone share of Québec's population
      was: 1991   82.7 %   1951   82.5 %   1911   80.0 %
             1981   82.5 %   1941   81.6 %   1901   80.2 %
             1971   80.8 %   1931   79.8 %
             1961   81.2 %   1921   80.0 %

22.   Those who watch American TV might have seen this aspect of Québec's language
      law ridiculed on or about February 2, 1998 on "60 Minutes".

23.   As reported by Irwin Block, p. A13, *Ottawa Citizen*, May 3, 1996.

24.   Montreal Gazette, La Presse, Le Devoir, Feb. 22, 1996

25.   McGill Fund Council: Report on Private Giving, 1994-95

26.   In the Sept. 3, 1998 edition of *Le Devoir*, Jacques Parizeau claimed that he had
      proposed, and was in favour of, a clear Referendum question such as suggested
      by the author. He was apparently over-ruled in 1995 by Lucien Bouchard who saw
      certain defeat resulting from a clear question.   Bouchard replaced Parizeau.
      Hence, obfuscation won the day.

27.   L'Actualité, 1 nov. 1995 (Montréal).

28.   *L'Actualité, 1 nov. 1995*

29.   *Le Devoir*, August 15, 1996, p. A-2.

30.   *Montreal Gazette*, August 16, 1996, p. A-1, Katherine Witton.

31.   Morningside, CBC radio, Jan 1996.

32.   CBC National News, May 13, 1996.

33.   Paul Gessell in the Ottawa Citizen, p. A3, Tues Feb 6, 1996.

34.   Gessel in the Ottawa Citizen Tues Feb 6, 1996, p. A3.   Pollster was Conrad Winn
      of Compas Inc of Ottawa.

35.   Le Devoir Feb 4/5 OP-Ed p. A9.

36.   I saw Bernard Dérome report this on RDI about 2115 hours on Feb. 14/96.

37.   Le Devoir: Reflet du Québec au 20e siècle, sous la direction de Robert Lahaise,
      Éditions Hurtubise HMH, La Salle, Qué., 1994: p.257.

38.   Le Devoir: Reflet, pp. 276, 406.

39.   Le Devoir: Reflet, p. 408.

40.   Le Devoir: Reflet, pp. 275-6.

41.   Le Devoir: Reflet, pp. 275-6.

42.   Le Devoir: Reflet, p. 418.

43.   Le Devoir: Reflet, p. 44.

44.   Le Devoir: Reflet, pp. 11, 12.

45.   Le Devoir: Reflet, p. 390.

46.   Le Devoir: Reflet, pp. 391, 398, 399.

47.   Le Devoir: Reflet, p. 401.

48.   Le Devoir: Reflet, p. 41

49.   Esther Delisle, The Traitor and the Jew, (Montréal: Robert Davies, 1993), p.115.

50.   Delisle, p. 129, notes 40-44.

51.   Delisle, p. 137, note 33.

52.   Delisle, p. 169, note 44.

53.   Canadian Advertising Rates and Data, Sept., 1996.

54.   Le Devoir, Oct. 28/29, 1995.

55.   Toronto Globe and Mail, editorial page, Thurs. Dec. 28, 1995.

56.   According to a report in the Ottawa Citizen, Feb. 11, 1998, Montreal received about 41 mm of freezing rain accumulations during this storm versus from 70 to 90 mm in Eastern Ontario.

7

CONSEQUENCES: THE PEOPLE LOSE

Overview

Sir Isaac Newton informed us long ago that to every action there is an equal and opposite reaction. Since clever use of this universal law eventually permitted us to put men on the moon, I guess we can conclude that Newton knew what he was talking about. So also did my mother who claimed that chickens always come home to roost. She was of course paraphrasing the biblical dictum that we reap what we sow. Consequently, Québec is reaping the unfortunate consequences of over two centuries of misguided leadership. And, at the head of this harvest is the deplorable state of public civility toward those targeted by the racist taunt, "*Le Québec aux Québécois.*"

Politically Correct Anglophobia

By helping to temper social friction, civility helps societies function efficiently. That is, if we are polite toward one another, if we understand and are prepared to accommodate our differences, social harmony will normally prevail, the right things will get done and we can call ourselves civilized. Although this is important in all societies, it is more difficult to attain in some than in others. For instance, in ethnically, racially or religiously monolithic societies, social harmony is relatively easily attained since there exists an important common thread binding everyone. However, if this monolithic society lives in crowded conditions, such as in Japan, civility is more difficult to attain. The same difficulty exists in modern pluralistic societies where various ethnic, religious and language groups struggle to live together in some measure of harmony. That is, although respectful of one another, they still cherish and celebrate their unique identities. If civility prevails when they attempt to find common ground, then peace reigns. But, where one group seeks instead to impose its will on others, civility is the first victim and social strife the inevitable result.

In Québec, where the *Québécois* élite are attempting to inflict an ethnically-based state on the people, public incivility is never very far below the surface. In fact, this lack of civility manifests itself in a seemingly unending series of events where *Québécois* notables with axes to grind seem driven by the anglophobic Poor-Québec-Syndrome. As a result, normal social intercourse becomes a deplorable tirade of us-versus-them. And since these mean spirited gestures are almost never criticized in the *Québécois* press, it should come as no surprise that this lack of civility has become a characteristic of Québec society.

Some of the most distressing examples of this tirade appear in the form of comments from the lips of *Québécois* politicians. The first example that comes to mind surfaced during the 1980 Québec Referendum on sovereignty when the Prime Minister of Canada, Pierre Elliot Trudeau, was campaigning against the secessionists. "*No surprise there,*" sniffed René Lévesque, the secessionist Premier of Québec, "*it is the Elliot side of his family speaking.*" Then, following the secessionist defeat in the 1995 Referendum, another Premier of Québec, Jacques Parizeau, shamed himself in a similar fashion when he attributed the secessionist defeat to money and the large ethnic vote that had opposed secession. During the 1997 federal election, secessionist Suzanne Tremblay of the *Bloc Québécois* told a large TV audience in Québec that, before they made the mistake of voting for Jean Charest, leader of the federal Conservative Party, they should take note that the name on his birth certificate was John, not Jean. Less than a year later, when Charest was considering the leadership of the provincial Liberals, the secessionist-dominated *Québécois* media were full of contemptuous references to this Jean Charest whose baptismal certificate read John James Charest. In other words, he is not really one of us: "*Le Québec aux Québécois!*" Although these are examples of despicable behaviour by *Québécois* leaders and the media, it was not always this bad. I would argue that it took a turn for the worse with the rise to power of secessionists during the post-1960 Quiet Revolution.

In 1976, there was a dispute between federal Air Traffic Controllers and some *Québécois* pilots that, some have argued, propelled the *Parti Québécois* to power in Québec later that year. As I recall, the controllers wanted all pilots to follow international practice and communicate with them in English. But some *Québécois* pilots insisted on speaking French. Since the controllers refused, a wide-ranging and vigorous public debate ensued. At about the same time, when some Boy Scouts from Toronto lost their lives in a drowning accident, it made headlines as well. This prompted one *Québécois* radio commentator to say something like: "*There may be no French in the air, but there certainly is lots of English in the water.*" That this tasteless comment was generally deplored in the *Québécois* press testified to a sense of common decency at that time. But public civility, and media reaction to it, went downhill from there.

Contrast the 'English in the water joke' to one of the jokes on the French CBC TV program "Bye Bye 95" in 1995. This end-of-year program traditionally pokes fun at some of the year's significant events. Since the Referendum had taken place but a few months earlier, it was fair game for the program's comedians. The opening scene portrayed Canadians in a plane heading for the pre-Referendum rally in Montreal. As William Johnson reported, "*It (Bye Bye 95) portrayed these Canadians as drunks, ignoramuses, racists, hypocrites who really despise francophone Quebecers and who planned to stuff ballot boxes. The scene ended with the Canadians being directed off the plane in mid-air.*" One *Québécoise* commentator, Lysianne Gagnon, said that "*if the CBC had allowed the same kind of jokes to be broadcast against francophones, Quebec would be up in arms.*" However, other commentators in *La Presse* and *Le Devoir* thought that that particular joke was pretty neat.[1] Obviously, the *Québécois* media's sense of common decency had deteriorated since 1976. During that 19-year interval, anglophobia became politically correct.

After the passage of Bill 101 in 1977, the more mean spirited started to emerge from their intellectual sewers. One woman made headlines by charging that her mother had not died in French in an English hospital in Montreal ... two years earlier! The event received a lot of press. St. Mary's Hospital, the target of this attack, had to prove that the deceased had indeed been cared for by francophone medical staff before the bloodhounds in the *Québécois* media let up. No one asked about the quality of medical care afforded this poor woman, or if she had died in peace. Publicly sanctioned anglophobia was on the rise.

The St. Mary's incident was substantially repeated at the Jewish General Hospital in Montreal in 1996 when a *Québécois* patient, Radio Canada reporter Normand Lester, decided to pick a language fight with a couple of defenceless nurses. This predictably drew other jerks out of hiding to cry rape, even though *L'Office de la langue française* said that Lester had no case. You can bet your boots that, if *L'Office* could have found a way to side with Lester, it would have, a fact it proved about a year later.

In July 1997, *L'Office* announced that it was about to carry out a special investigation to ensure that all English health establishments were providing services in French. It suspected that they were delinquent. English-rights groups called this measure an unnecessary and gratuitous provocation. But, *L'Office* justified the investigation on the basis that it had received a number of complaints *"similar to that lodged by Lester at the Jewish General Hospital!"*[2] It was obvious to all but the obtuse that this investigation had nothing to do with health services in French and everything to do with annoying Québec anglophones: The Québec version of the Chinese water torture.

Sometime in the 1980s, two *Québécois* academics claimed that *Québécois* were being discriminated against in the National Hockey League. They arrived at this conclusion by noting that, where *Québécois* made up about a quarter of Canada's population, they accounted for less than a quarter of the players in the NHL. Moreover, they found that *Québécois* tended to earn less than other players. It apparently had not occurred to them that relative ability may have played a part in this situation. For example, in the last fifteen years, an increasing number of players in the NHL, especially the more skilled, have come from Europe, Russia and the United States. Fewer are now coming from Canada, fewer still from Québec, except for goal tenders where *Québécois* seem to excel.

I am told that Europeans and Russians tend to dominate among the highly skilled because they grew up in systems where the game is played on large rinks that promote skill development, and where officials discourage rough play. (Item: At the 1998 Nagano Olympics, the men's hockey medals went to the Czech Republic, Russia and Finland; Canada and the United States were shut out!) In Canada, smaller rinks tend to stunt skill development, and officials exacerbate this phenomenon by encouraging rough and tumble hockey. In Québec, the problem is also one of development strategy.

That is, Québec hockey officials decided long ago to foster the development of *elite* players. This meant that the more skilled among the very young (eight year olds, for instance!) would be given more attention than the less skilled. Since smaller players in their earlier years tend to be more skilled-- or at least less awkward--than bigger players, this policy tended to favour smaller players. Hence, the big kid who developed late was out of luck in Québec. Consequently, the skilled *Québécois* players tended to be relatively small. This was not a problem in the lower leagues where *Québécois* did reasonably well. But remember, kids' leagues ain't the majors. For instance, Taiwan very often wins the Little League World Series in baseball but has not yet sent a single player to the major leagues.

In hockey, when a good big man opposes a good little man, the big guy wins most of the time. This becomes evident in Junior Hockey, the last stepping stone to the NHL. If you look at the winners of the Memorial Cup, the champions of Junior Hockey in Canada, you will find that Québec teams went 24 years without winning before emerging on top in 1996 and 1997. The remaining winners have been split between the Ontario and Western Junior leagues. Moreover, in the last 78 years, Québec has won the Memorial Cup 9 percent of the time, Ontario 51 percent and Western Canada 40 percent. And if you look at the NHL today, you will find that the distribution of Canadian players in the league resembles these splits. From this evidence, I would conclude that, if Québec supplied more than 9 percent of the Canadian players in the NHL, it would be doing well, its 25 percent population share notwithstanding. Thus, the study by these particular academics was, to put it squarely, an incompetent and mischievous crock.

To conclude this particular case, the apparent *Québécois* dominance among goalers is also explained by the structure of Québec minor hockey. If your skaters are highly skilled, and hence more likely to favour offence over defence, they will probably make life miserable for those in goal. Thus, goal tenders from Québec's minor leagues are likely to be well tested and that explains why they do well professionally. This simple analysis was apparently too complex for these *Québécois* academics.

Or how about the Eaton's syndrome. That is, how many times have we heard in the last 25 years of some *Québécois* claiming to have been insulted at Eaton's department store in Montreal because a unilingual anglophone clerk was unable or unwilling to speak French? This *humiliation* is identified not only as the reason for the general rise of separatism in Québec, but also as the cause of sunspots, pimples, anorexia and migraine headaches. It appears that anyone who is anyone in Québec claims this experience: To have been humiliated at Eaton's is a mark of prestige among many nationalists! That it is now possible to be insulted at Eaton's by *Québécois* unable or unwilling to speak English is of course beside the point, it being politically correct to dump on anglos.

Although I do not doubt that some *Québécois* may indeed have had difficulty obtaining service in French at Eaton's, the evidence shows that, on balance, *Québécois* nevertheless preferred to shop at Eaton's instead of at a nearby *Québécois*-owned and operated major department store: Dupuis Frères. In fact, Dupuis closed its doors many years ago because it could not compete with the likes of Eaton's, even though its clerks were presumably not given to insulting their *Québécois* customers .. in English or French!

Many might say that the most odious tasks in Québec are those assigned to the so-called language police of the *Commission de la langue française:* They are required to investigate alleged violations of the province's language laws and to recommend appropriate corrective action. To assist in this endeavour, the public is encouraged to advise the language police of any infractions, such as public signs with English on them. The record shows that most *Québécois* are not interested in demeaning themselves by snitching on their neighbours. I know some *Québécois*, ardent supporters of the language laws who do not approve of signs in English, who would nevertheless consider it quite improper to complain to the *Commission*. But not all *Québécois* are so noble. For example, between January and May, 1993 the *Commission* received 1,855 complaints, 90 percent of which had been submitted by only four people. In 1992, one person submitted 1,000 complaints.[3] It was common practice, apparently, for these stalwarts to crawl through anglophone Montreal with their cameras looking for illegal signs in English. But then, crawling is what vermin do best.

Then, in 1996, the officials of the *Commission* really outdid themselves: They directed the language police to get matzos off the shelves of Montreal's stores just before Passover! For those unfamiliar with matzo, it is unleavened bread that figures prominently in Jewish religious practice, especially at Passover. Since Montreal's matzo supply comes from New York, it is labelled in English and Hebrew. Although the language law requires French labels, these matzos must have been exempted since they had been sold in Montreal for years without incident. Until 1996, that is.

That this attack on matzos was a stupid, vindictive and arbitrary act is obvious. Even the *Québécois* press, usually tolerant of other similar idiocies by the language police, thought this was too much. And of course the cartoonists had a field day depicting the dangerous unilingual matzo attacking poor defenceless *Québécois*. The issue was finally and mercifully resolved via an old fashioned, face-saving retreat by the *Commission*. Consequences? Any potential investor wishing to avoid unnecessary hassles is likely to steer clear of Québec. But what is the loss of a few jobs to language zealots? Keeping English off store shelves is apparently worth the candle. Besides, the zealots know whose jobs are at risk: Not theirs!

But that was not the end of the involvement of Québec's language police with things Jewish. In December 1997, they decided that a sign at a Montreal manufacturer of tombstones for Jews was illegal.[4] This sign had been in place outside this business establishment for about 50 years. During the past 20 years or so, it was subject to the restrictions imposed on signs by

Québec's various language laws. And, during this period, no one told this establishment that its sign was illegal .... until Dec. 1997. The language police then declared that the sign which bore no English, only the French message "*L. Berson & Fils, Monuments*" and an equivalent message in Hebrew, was not French enough: Sandwiched between the French words "Fils" and "Monuments" were Hebrew symbols meaning tombstone *that were bigger than any French word on the sign.* Verboten! When this was made public, all hell broke loose: The laughter and derision could be heard from coast to coast, the government of Québec was very embarrassed and declared that, even though the language police had acted legally, they were directed to back off. The police obeyed their political masters and backed off. Conclusions? First, that such silly and vexatious harassment is in fact legal in Québec, second, that its application is arbitrary and subject to political direction. This was made all too clear when Howard Galganov insisted on legal signs in English in Montréal.

In 1996 Galganov manifested his concern with how the sign law was being implemented. That is, although the law permitted the use of bilingual indoor signs, most stores had simply adopted the habit of posting unilingual French signs. Galganov objected to this and recommended that concerned consumers boycott stores that did not post legal bilingual signs. The threat of the boycott worked: Stores started to post legal signs in English. But the nationalists were outraged; the Vice-Premier of Québec was apoplectic, threatening to have the law changed to counteract Galganov's legal manoeuvre; extremists at a PQ policy convention insisted that the sign law be changed to insist on French-only signs (they were defeated); the *Québécois* media tut-tutted Galganov for disrupting the *social consensus* on this issue although they admitted that he was acting legally.

But some *Québécois* politicians really went off the deep end. The leader of the *Bloc Québécois*, Her Majesty's Loyal Opposition in the Parliament of Canada, called upon the Jewish National Congress to dissociate itself from Galganov's legal manoeuvre. This was echoed in the *Québécois* press by other notables. What Galganov's Jewishness had to do with his actions is beyond me. These offended virgins didn't call upon the Cardinal Archbishop of Montreal to dissociate the Catholic Church from Prime Minister Jean Chrétien's anti-secessionist policies! In any event, Galganov was acting legally to promote anglophone not Jewish interests. Isn't it interesting how the cretins of the world slide so easily into antisemitism when hoist by their own pétard.

In the run-up to the 1995 Referendum, it was suggested by more than one *Québécois* notable that non-*Québécois* should refrain from voting in it: After all, it was not up to non-*Québécois* to decide the destiny of *Québécois*. So much for the democratic notion of the equality of citizens before the law, especially during elections. Among these notables were Pierre Bourgault, then a senior counsellor to the governing *Parti Québécois*, and Jean-Marc Léger, a former senior official in the earlier secessionist government of René Lévesque.[5] Since non-*Québécois* tended to vote against secession, it would only be fair, according to these two, if non-*Québécois* stood aside while *Québécois* alone decided the fate of the whole country. Bernard Landry, the Vice-Premier of Québec, made much the same point on Montréal radio station CKAC on August 31, 1998!

By the way, this arrogant attitude was not unusual. What else is meant by the hymn, "*Le Québec aux Québécois*," the racist taunt brayed by the faithful whenever they meet in numbers sufficient to disguise their individual identities? This was the chant that greeted Jacques Parizeau on Referendum night (October 31, 1995) as he rose to acknowledge his defeat, covering himself with shame as he blamed the whole thing on "*money and the ethnic vote*." Predictably, hateful anti-English and antisemitic graffiti appeared throughout Montreal the following day.

To placate PQ extremists in the fall of 1996, the government of Québec decided to change the telephone answering practices of its various departments and agencies. Despite the fact that the language law did not require the government of Québec to provide bilingual telephone answering services, it had apparently become the practice of some departments to do so. This might have reflected the desire of the service-providers to be courteous toward their clients. But, no more! French-only service was commanded from then on.[6] It obviously made political sense to irritate a large number of fellow citizens--who always voted for the opposition anyway--in order to placate the mouth-breathers in the PQ who see an English menace behind every blade of grass.

And then there was the case of the parrot that could not speak French. This took place in 1996 when a woman entered a pet store in Montreal looking for a parrot that spoke French. When told that the store's single parrot only spoke English, she flounced from the premises proclaiming indignantly that she was going straight to *L'Office de la langue française* to lodge a complaint. Imagine, selling parrots that could not speak French! When this story, sworn to be true, gained the attention of journalists, it was treated as a huge joke. When *L'Office* was asked by giggling anglophone journalists if the complaint had in fact been lodged, its spokesperson rolled her eyes and treated the whole issue as a great hoax meant to make Québec's language laws look silly. Whether this preposterous complainant ever went to see *L'Office* will never be known. If she had indeed lodged the complaint, *L'Office* would have been too embarrassed to admit it. After all, *L'Office* does not engage in trivial matters! Oh no?

Item: A convenience store near Montreal was told that its perfectly legal sign was in contravention of the law because the sign contained more English than French words. That it was impossible to reduce the number of English words or increase the number of French words had no effect on the earnest language inspector.[7]

Item: A Montreal businessman was criticized by the language police because he had two business cards, one in English, the other in French.

He should apparently not have had an English card.

Item: Another businessman was told that his English language Internet web site was illegal despite the fact that the government of Québec has no jurisdiction in this area. To the extent that the Internet can be controlled at all, it lies within federal jurisdiction.

When these three items were brought to the attention of Louise Beaudoin, the Minister responsible for Québec's language laws, her first reaction was to cite them as examples of continued English disrespect for French, disrespect that went back to 1763! And I thought the Irish had long and selective memories! When she finally regained her senses, she apparently told the language police to cool it and not to be so picky.[8]

And, what about the language-bureaucrats' assault in 1998 on the small Chinese Hospital in Montréal? All of the hospital's 108 patients were Chinese-speakers, most over the age of 85, few of whom even understood English or French. Nevertheless, these bureaucrats insisted that, when hiring a new head nurse, preference be given to francophone candidates even if they could not speak or understand Chinese. Got that?

One of the consequences of this type of deplorable social behaviour is the rise of the infantile practice of saying "my *culture is better than yours.*" It is not unlike the claim of some of my boyhood friends who used to boast: "*My dad can beat your dad.*" Fortunately, our fathers generally ignored our efforts to foment war. Not so innocent are boasts from some anglophobes. How often have we heard that *Québécois* popular culture is superior to the anglophone variety? Why? Because it is home grown in Québec while English Canada simply imports its culture from the United States. Why one would even bother making such a claim is beyond me ... other than to be mischievous, of course. In any event, the claim is either untrue or irrelevant.

First, francophone imperatives in Québec impose demands that simply do not obtain among anglophones. Thus, French TV soaps, for instance, will either be translations of American programs or be developed in French by local artists. If they are translations, how can they be any better than the original American version? The dialogue is simply expressed in one language rather than another. Much the same can be said for French originals--except that their subject matter might better reflect local socio-political and historical imperatives. But then again, a soap is a soap is a soap, and it ain't Shakespeare or Molière! On the other hand, developing local playwrights is not to be denigrated. However, anglophone playwrights have been known to develop their skills in the United States, a not inconsiderable feat. And on and on.

Second, even if true, the claim is irrelevant. That is, am I culturally deprived watching Shakespeare on American TV as compared to my *Québécois* cousin who spends his time watching locally produced soaps? I think not. Moreover, the claim is simply incorrect. The nationalists who make this preposterous claim assume that culture in English Canada is not only monolithic but American. If true, so what? What is wrong with imitating the Americans? Even *Québécois* imitate the Americans--in French of course. In any event, some parts of Canada are culturally quite unique. Consider, for instance, the popular singing groups that come out of Newfoundland and Cape Breton. You will not find their equal in number and character anywhere else in Canada--even in Québec. Or what about Newfoundland comedians? You will have to go a long way to find their equal elsewhere in Canada--except in Québec. Or what about international musicals? Can anyone compete with Toronto? Some nationalists would of course sniff that "Showboat" is after all an American musical. Not at all like the Montreal Jazz Festival which celebrates the genius of that well known *Québécois* musician Duke Ellington; or like the annual rodeo at St. Thècle which celebrates Québec's non-existent cowboy heritage!

Clearly, those who put this juvenile spin on cultural differences eventually find themselves exposed to well deserved ridicule. For instance, although some of Canada's finest writers may be *Québécois* who write in French, the most internationally acclaimed Quebecers were/are Montreal anglophones: Hugh MacLennan in the 1940s and Mordecai Richler today. Richler must really irritate ardent *Québécois* nationalists because he misses few chances to expose to the world the idiocy of Québec's language laws. But, one does not criticize Québec's most sacred cows with impunity. To celebrate the 20th anniversary of the adoption of Bill 101, Québec's revered language law, the government of Québec named each of 101 islands in a large northern reservoir after 101 deserving works of fiction written in Québec in French since WW II. Three were French translations of work written originally in English. I have heard of one of the three anglophone authors, Neil Bissoondath: The translation of his Digging Up The Mountains was deservedly honoured. The two others were poets whose names and poems are unknown to me.[9] But the poems, however obscure, were obviously of sufficient importance to warrant selection over an internationally acclaimed writer like Mordecai Richler whose work has also been translated into French. Take that, Richler!

In the realm of more popular culture, consider Céline Dion. She is a *Québécoise* singing star admired by all, first, because she is apparently an excellent singer, and second, because she performs internationally. But what her admirers are loath to admit is that her international popularity derives in part from the fact that she generally sings in English! But, notwithstanding her international success in English, Dion showed the really mean minded side of political correctness in Québec when she refused an award as Québec's most outstanding singer in English ... because she was *Québécoise* not anglophone![10]

Finally, those who trumpet Québec's *cultural superiority* conveniently forget the most important cultural indicator of all, the educational level of the population. And here, *Québécois* unfortunately find themselves at or near the bottom of the cultural barrel.

It should be clear from these examples that:

1.   *Québécois* have been set against other ethnic groups in Québec by the anglophobic policies of their provincial government.

2.   This has given rise to an unfortunate backlash in the rest of Canada against all *Québécois* instead of against the culpable *Québécois* élite.

3.   These ethno-centric policies must inevitably lead to disgraceful consequences, the public discussion of which is generally avoided.

Flight of Anglophones: Ethnic Cleansing

Ethnic cleansing is a term that takes your breath away. So is the word racist. Neither should be used frivolously. Calling someone a racist is not in the same league as describing the same unfortunate as a son of a bitch. When I refer to someone as an SOB, I mean simply that he is not very nice. But when I use the word racist, I am describing someone so low in the food chain that public censure is warranted. In other words, where SOBs are merely pains in the butt and to be ignored, racists are contemptible and should be crushed.

So also with the term ethnic cleansing, a term one must use cautiously ... and only with evidence to back it up. By ethnic cleansing I mean the involuntary exodus of a minority for the benefit of the majority as a result of force or intimidation by the majority. Although there is no evidence to suggest that force has been used for this purpose in Québec, there is ample evidence to conclude that the precipitous decline of the anglophone population of Québec is explained by the intimidation and public censure that has been visited upon them by the ethnically-based policies of the governments of Québec since about the mid-1970s. Let's examine the record.

First, it is in the interests of secessionist *Québécois* nationalists to reduce the influence of non-secessionists. Anyone doubting this need only consult the results of the 1980 and 1995 referenda in Québec. Second, the debates during these two referenda were full of statements by many nationalists suggesting that non-*Québécois* refrain from casting their anti-secessionist votes. This sentiment was underlined every time we heard the hymn "*Le Québec aux Québécois*," a clear demand from the majority that minorities leave Québec.

Now comes the tough question: Does the intent of this disgusting hymn derive from the objectives of public policy, or is it merely a tasteless means of letting off steam? If it is the latter, it will annoy many non-*Québécois* and demean all *Québécois*, but no more. On the other hand, if its hateful message is found in, or is a reflection of public policy, I would argue that the involuntary emigration of non-*Québécois* was its intended result. And that, of course, is ethnic cleansing. For instance, the legislation that reserved Québec's English schools for the children of those who had received their education in English in Québec was clearly intended to at least reduce the growth of Québec's anglophone community. As a result, those moving to

Québec (Albertans, for instance), who would normally have sent their children to English schools, had to send them to French schools. Québec anglophones henceforth had to seek population growth in their own bedrooms rather than by having their schools assimilate immigrants and migrating Canadians. Although I think that this restriction of access to English schools was bad public policy, I was initially reluctant to associate it with ethnic cleansing. That is, if the anglophone community was not otherwise threatened, how can anyone call it ethnic cleansing if the community continued to grow and prosper? Read on.

When questioned, nationalist leaders claim solemnly that their language legislation is not anglophobic, that it is only intended to protect fragile French culture. For example, the law that infringes on free speech by prohibiting or limiting the use of English on public signs is intended to protect French, not to outlaw English. That is, a completely French sign protects French while a bilingual (French-English) sign endangers French culture!

Supporting the drive to protect French culture are two major assumptions. The first is that *Québécois* culture and the French language are synonymous; the second that the use of French is declining or in danger of declining in Québec. As argued earlier, it is absurd to claim that language and culture are necessarily correlated. Moreover, the historical record shows clearly that the use of French has not declined in Québec. On the one hand, the francophone share of the population of Québec did not decline during this century; on the other hand, the use of French cannot be declining when all allophones, as well as an increasing number of anglophones, are taking all or part of their schooling in French. When you add these multilingual allophones and bilingual anglophones to the majority francophones, you must conclude that more people speak French today than ever before. True enough, but there is a fatal flaw in my argument. *Québécois* nationalists are not interested in bilingual anglophones or allophones even if they are fluent in French. They are not French, you see, they are not *one of us*.

Since the justification for Québec's language legislation cannot logically have been cultural or linguistic, it must have been administrative or political. Since I am not prepared to waste time on the theoretically possible though highly improbable administrative option, I will conclude first that the justification was in fact political, and second that, since about 1960, these laws were used to further the interests of the secessionist movement in Québec.

Central to secessionist interests was the need to reduce the political influence of non-secessionists. That is, if the electorate is split between *Québécois* and non-*Québécois* in the proportion of about 82:18, and if non-*Québécois* vote massively against secession, it would require a pro-secessionist vote of about 61 percent of *Québécois* to obtain 50 percent of the overall vote (82 x .61 = 50 percent). However, if they could erase the effect of the non-*Québécois* vote, secessionists would need only 50 percent of the *Québécois* vote, and 50 percent is much easier to obtain than 61. Thus, ridding Québec of non-*Québécois*, though odious, makes a lot of political sense ... to secessionists.

Table 7-1: Ethnic Cleansing

Population by Mother Tongue - m

	French	English	Other
1996	5,783	595	658
1991	5,745	617	532
1986	5,521	602	409
1981	5,307	706	425
1976	4,989	801	444
1971	4,866	789	373
1961	4,270	697	292
1951	3,342	558	150
1941	2,717	469	146
1931	2,292	430	152
1921	1,889	357	115
1911	1,605	316	84
1901	1,322	290	37

Source: StatCan Censuses

However, *Québécois* leaders insist that their language laws are meant to protect French culture, not to oppress non-*Québécois* or drive them from Québec. That this is a bald-faced whopper is obvious. First, as shown previously, legislation cannot protect culture. Second, because of ethnically-based employment practices, non-*Québécois* have been finding it increasingly difficult to find work in Québec. For example, even bilingual anglophones have been effectively excluded from working in the Québec public service where 99 percent of the workers are *Québécois*. I should add that this is also becoming the norm in the *federal* public service in Québec! Even in the private sector, hiring practices have favoured *Québécois* since the 1960s. Third, the provisions of certain sections of the law, those dealing with the language of signs, for instance, are so vexatious and insulting that they can have no other intent than to harass non-*Québécois* in general and anglophones in particular. Their message is clear: "*You are not welcome in Québec*: *Le Québec aux Québécois.*"

And how have non-*Québécois* reacted to this abusive environment? The answer is to be found in the historical record in Table 7-1. What leaps from these data are two points: First, the francophone population of Québec has never stopped growing; second, after almost a century of steady growth, the populations of both anglophones and allophones (others) in Québec started to decline precipitously after 1976: In the period 1976-1986 anglophone numbers declined by 25 percent, allophones by 8 percent. From then on, steady and uninterrupted allophone growth again became the norm. Not so with anglophones: After a short period of modest growth (2.5 percent between 1986 and 1991), the decline continued. In summary, during the 20-year period ending in 1996, the anglophone population of Québec fell by 26 percent. What happened to cause this historical anomaly?

Well, the first restrictive language law was passed in 1974 and Québec's first explicitly secessionist political party came to power in 1976. Following these two events:

1.   Anglophobia moved from the background to the foreground of political discourse.

2.   Language laws became more vindictive.

3.   Private sector employers started to imitate the francophone-dominated public sector by discriminating in favour of *Québécois*.

4.   Job-creating business investment started to dry up.

5.   Many anglophones, some allophones (and some *Québécois*), seeing the writing on the wall, started to leave Québec. This was repeated following the re-election of the secessionist *Parti Québécois* in 1994.

Had there been no forced exodus, the anglophone population of Québec would have grown by about 14 percent between 1976 and 1996 instead of falling by 26 percent. That is, there would have been about 910,000 anglophones in Québec, not the 595,000 resident there in 1996. For those unfamiliar with higher mathematics, this translates into a 35 percent loss to the anglophone population of Québec! Thus, whether it was the language laws, the threat of secession or the inability to find work, or all three, that caused Québec's anglophones to flee, the flight was real and unprecedented ... in Canada. Moreover, if the anglophone population continues to decline at this rate (about 100,000 per decade), it will obviously not be long before Québec's anglophones are reduced to political insignificance.

To give this emigration an international and historical perspective, compare the 1976-81 exodus of anglophones from Québec with the 1933-38 flight of Jews from Germany--before the Nazis resorted to state-sanctioned, organized mass murder in the post-1939 Holocaust. Between 1976 and 1981, anglophobia and its related public policies and practices in Québec reversed more than a century of anglophone population growth in that province. That is, during that five-year period, Québec's anglophone population *declined* by 12 percent instead of continuing to grow. On the other hand, during the first five years of Hitler's reign (1933-38), German Jews were subject to harassment of unprecedented proportions, the purpose of which was to *encourage* them to leave Germany. And they did: 25 percent of Germany's Jewish population in 1933 had left that country by 1938.[11] I would argue that, even if the Nazis had not followed up this expulsion with the murderous Holocaust after 1939, they would still have been guilty of ethnic cleansing because of their egregious behaviour toward German Jews between 1933 and 1938. Based on these data, can we conclude that the cleansing of anglophones from Québec was about half as serious as this Jewish expulsion from Germany (12 versus 25)? Perhaps, but I am not prepared to be that mathematical. However, I do argue that the anglophone exodus from Québec was not the result of normal migration imperatives, that it was instead involuntary and the product of the ethnic cleansing policies and practices of the *Québécois* élite. And, in one of life's tragic ironies, some of the victims of the German expulsion found themselves among those fleeing Québec. Finally, remember that the non-secessionist side won the 1995 Referendum in Québec by only 50,000 votes. Thus, before 2000, the 1995 non-secessionist majority in Québec will have been neutralized. And, if this is not ethnic cleansing, what is it? And then there was the parallel exodus of head offices.

Flight of Head Offices

Since major decisions are made at corporate head offices, their location is important to those wishing to influence its decisions--politicians, for instance. Moreover, head offices mean relatively high paying jobs for both their occupants and those working at local companies supplying them with goods and services. To the computer salesman, for instance, the head office is where are located the people who decide whose computers the company's branch offices will buy. In addition, the head office location tells the world that that company considers that location to be a good place in which to invest and do business.

But, on the flip side of the coin, when a company moves its head office, it also conveys a message. In some cases the message is innocuous. For example, if an oil drilling company moved its head office from Halifax to Calgary to be near its operations in central Alberta, the move would likely have no ripple effect among other head offices in Halifax. However, if the move was being made because the company was dissatisfied with the policies of the government of Nova Scotia, you can bet that there would be a few ripples. Not only might other head offices decide to move, but foreign manufacturers of widget wings, for instance, might decide to build a plant in New Brunswick rather than in Nova Scotia. Clearly, the movement of a head office is economically and politically significant.

Until the 1970s, Montreal was the head office capital of Canada. Far behind in second place was Toronto. Coincidentally, Montreal's economy was then vibrant and growing. Then, along came the first restrictive language law in 1974 followed by the election of the secessionist *Parti Québécois* in 1976. After a suitable pause to assess the new environment, the first head office moved, then another and another, and then it became a flood. By the early 1990s, Montreal had not only lost its title to Toronto, it had fallen behind second place Calgary and was losing ground to fourth place Vancouver. In less than one generation Montreal had fallen from world class to regional class and Québec's economy along with it. Job-creating investments were being made in Ontario and New Brunswick instead of in Québec.

But no matter, say some nationalists, those jobs were filled by anglophones in any event, not by *Québécois*. Fools! Not only were most of those jobs in fact filled by *Québécois*, the spillover economic effect of this exodus was catastrophic for Québec. As a result, these same *Québécois* are either working in the same head offices, but no longer in Québec, or are under-employed in Montreal. Moreover, those who worked for smaller companies (supplying pencils and accounting services, for instance, to those head offices) are probably suffering tough times: They also are either under-employed or seeking work since their former employers closed down or reduced the size of their Montreal operations to follow their head office clients elsewhere. To get a feel for this malaise, just walk down any street in downtown Montreal and take note of the decay. There are indeed consequences to misguided or mischievous public policies, and they are all bad.

Flight of Business Investment

And how might one expect business investors to behave in an environment where the workforce was relatively uneducated, where ethnic tensions dominated the social climate and where public policy was driven by bureaucratic and secessionist imperatives? Obviously, one would expect them to be reluctant investors under such conditions. They would invest instead in politically more stable jurisdictions and/or where social peace prevailed and/or where workers were better educated. And, since business investment creates jobs, it follows that, when businessmen do not invest, increased unemployment is the result. Before dealing with the history of business investment in Québec, let us consider the structure of investment across Canada.

Even in provinces such as Nova Scotia that are relatively more reliant than others on government investment, business is still dominant (Table 7-2). In Québec and Ontario, for instance, business investment accounts for about 89 percent of all investment. That is good since, as shown earlier, business investment creates jobs where government investment does not--or at least not very many. Thus, those who believe that one can run an economy on government investment must not be aware of the facts or else be privy to information not available to ordinary mortals.

Then when we consider inter-provincial comparisons for business investment, we see that the leading provinces are dominated by the resource sector (Alberta and BC) or by large scale agriculture (Saskatchewan). Thus, comparing industrial Québec or Ontario to these three would be like comparing apples with oranges. On the other hand, since Québec and Ontario have structurally similar economies, it makes sense to compare their respective investment patterns. Thus, the fact that per capita business investment in Québec lagged 13 percent behind Ontario (3,867 vs 4,445) in the 1986-91 period is significant. I would argue that this investment shortfall is the logical consequence of Québec's poisoned social and political atmosphere. That is, given a choice between investing in turbulent Québec and pacific Ontario, why wouldn't a prudent investor put his money in Ontario! Moreover, when we take a

Table 7-2: Investment, 1986/91

$ Per Capita Per Year

	Gov't.	Bus.
Alberta	820	6,303
BC	664	5,161
Sask.	644	4,567
Ontario	564	4,445
Québec	538	3,867
Manitoba	553	3,225
NScotia	688	3,188
NB	659	3,066
NFLD	657	2,845
PEI	753	2,610
Canada	614	4,396

Source: StatCan 93-328, T 2

Table 7-3: Business Investment (BI)			
A: BI % of Total Investment			
B: BI Per Capita, Qué vs Ont			
	A		B
	Qué	Ont	
1994	87	88	- 8.4 %
1991	88	88	- 14.9 %
1981	88	90	- 20.6 %
1971	76	84	- 34.8 %
1961	84	81	- 16.5 %

Source: StatCan 13-213,61-202, 93-320

longer term perspective, it would appear that this business investment deficiency with Ontario seems to have been a relatively constant 15 percent or so since the onset of the Quiet Revolution in 1961 (Table 7-3). However, since the trend in column B, suggests a closing of the gap rather than its maintenance, let me explain.

First, the 8.4 percent gap in 1994 is misleading. Since both provinces were caught in a recession in the early 1990s, per capita business investment fell in both provinces, but more in Ontario (10 percent) than in Québec (3 percent). Without a recession, Québec would have maintained its 15 percent business investment gap with Ontario. Why business investment during this recession fell more in Ontario than in Québec is an open question. I would argue that, because of the conditions described previously, normal investment in Québec was as low as it could get with the truly discretionary investment going to Ontario. Thus, since recessions cut first into discretionary spending, the recession of the early 1990s would have hit business investment more severely in Ontario than in Québec. For this hypothesis to be proven valid, investment will have to recover more quickly in Ontario than in Québec at the end of the recession. It did.

The second anomaly is in the year 1971 when business investment in Québec fell 34.8 percent below Ontario. It would appear that this was the result of unique conditions in Québec at that time. Thus, I would conclude that business investment in Québec has lagged behind Ontario by about 15 percent per year since the beginning of the Quiet Revolution.

Moreover, when we split this business investment into its two strategic components, an even more telling story emerges. That is, investments are made either to maintain existing facilities or to build new productive capacity. The first maintains existing plants in good repair but creates no new jobs; the second provides for growth and hence creates new jobs. In the period 1986-91, business investment in new or expanded facilities was 24 percent lower in Québec. Hence, in order for Québec to be 15 percent lower in total business investment and 24 percent lower in new investment, its investment in existing facilities must have greater than Ontario's. Although investment in existing facilities is not a bad thing, inadequate investment in new facilities is definitely not good--unless you are planning to dispose of your business and retire. But, economies do not retire, they either grow or they stagnate. Québec's investment pattern is thus characteristic of a stagnating economy.

It is axiomatic that this type of investment deficit must inevitably have translated into a job deficit. And, it did (Table 7-4). Note that

Table 7-4: Jobs Per 1000 People

	Qué	Ont	Québec vs Ont
1991	506	533	- 5.1 %
1981	472	515	- 8.3 %
1976	420	457	- 8.1 %
1971	397	422	- 5.9 %
1961	346	385	-10.1 %
1951	360	407	-11.5 %
1946	368	416	-11.5 %

Source: StatCan 1991 Census, 93-324,T3

the 1960s appears to have been a pivotal decade: The job deficit with Ontario was reduced significantly in the 1960s but has not improved since then despite the apparent improvement in 1991. That is, as noted earlier, if the recession of the early 1990s had been as hard on Québec as it had been on Ontario, Québec's job deficit in 1991 would have been closer to 8 percent than to the 5.1 percent shown here. That it was not hit as hard as Ontario has already been explained. It would appear, therefore, that Québec's normal job deficit with Ontario is in the order of 8 percent. And the reasons are obvious. In the 1960s, buoyed by the liberating expectations of the Quiet Revolution, business and government invested heavily in Québec. As a result, in that one decade, Québec's job deficit with Ontario was cut almost in half (from 10.1 percent to 5.9). To have predicted at that time that this job deficit would disappear within the next decade or so would have been considered a normal, even unremarkable forecast. But, it did not disappear; it did not even improve very much. The businessmen who invested with such gusto in the 1960s became turned off in the 1970s, 1980s and 1990s because of the adverse social and political climate described earlier.

This puts into perspective the failure of Québec Inc., that fabled partnership of Québec's public sector and *Québécois* businessmen: They were going to make Québec prosperous no matter what investment decisions were made by others. Those familiar with the debates preceding the Free Trade Agreement with the United States may recall that Québec was contemptuous of the rest of Canada: Where Québec lusted after free trade so that it could show how competitive it was in international markets, the other provinces tended to be relatively timid and protectionist. In a word, they were wimps.

But, talk is cheap. If Québec Inc. had been effective, the Québec economy would have seen higher levels of investment and more jobs. The record shows that neither was the case. Moreover, had Québec Inc.'s aggressive support of the Free Trade Agreement been more than a boastful taunt, Québec would have had a healthy export sector. But it didn't. Consider the import-export balance in Québec and Ontario since 1960, the period during which Québec Inc. was supposed to have been producing its miracles (Table 7-5). These data depict the net of exports over imports, expressed as a percentage of the provincial Gross Domestic Product. A

Table 7-5: Net Exports As % GDP

	Qué	Ont
1990s	-2.5	3.2
1980s	-0.2	6.5
1970s	-0.6	6.4
1960s	3.9	6.0

Source: StatCan 13-213, T2

positive number means that exports exceed imports and that new jobs had been created, and that is good; a negative number that imports exceeded exports and that jobs had been exported, and that is generally not good.

Throughout this period, where Ontario's was obviously an exporting economy, Québec's, with the exception of the 1960s, was just as obviously an importing economy. Where businessmen had clearly continued to invest in export-oriented facilities in Ontario, they had just as clearly turned their backs on Québec. Obviously, Québec Inc. failed to produce jobs. Although it is always pleasing to make braggarts eat crow, this failure was devastating for the Québec economy. Because Québec government policies since 1960 have arguably tended to discourage job-creating business investment, it became imperative that Québec Inc. succeed. Since it did not, the great Québec gamble came up snake-eyes and Québec workers were up the creek ... again.

The consequence of this investment deficiency is also evident in the unemployment statistics: From 1941 to 1991, whatever the unemployment rate was in Ontario, it was about half-again as high in Québec (Table 7-6). For example, in 1941, Québec's unemployment rate of 7.5 percent was exactly half-again as high as the 5.0 rate in Ontario. One need not be a rocket scientist to conclude that employment prospects in Québec relative to Ontario have not changed since 1941. Thus, the Quiet Revolution had no more impact on closing the economic gap with Ontario than had the Church-dominated economy that preceded it. A discriminating observer might well ask: "*Since the people obviously did not benefit from this revolution, who did?*" Read on.

Table 7-6:	% Unemployed	
	Qué	Ont
1991	14.3	10.9
1981	13.6	8.2
1971	10.1	6.9
1961	9.2	5.5
1951	2.9	1.7
1941	7.5	5.0

Source: StatCan, 1991
Census, 93-324, T3

Since this job gap was caused by more than a century of investment neglect, it will take decades of extra investment to redress this deficiency. Whether this will ever happen is an open question. I would argue that business investment will not improve markedly in Québec unless the social and political climates improve substantially. That was also the view of the *Québécois* businessmen who attended Québec Premier Bouchard's economic summit on Oct. 30, 1996: They told him that the never-ending threat of Québec secession, as well as the abrasive features of the province's language laws, had had and would continue to have a negative effect on job-creating business investment in Montréal.[12]

An Economy in Decay

The evidence so far suggests that a relatively uneducated workforce as well as a society buffeted by social and political strife have tended to turn potential investors away from Québec. As a result, Québec's per capita Gross Domestic

Table 7-7:	GDP	
	$ Per Capita	
	Qué vs Ont	
1993	- 17.1	%
1990	- 18.3	%
1980	- 15.6	%
1970	- 24.0	%
1961	- 24.6	%
	Source: StatCan	
	3-213, 15-203	

Product (GDP) stood fourth in Canada in 1990, 18.3 percent behind second place Ontario. Resource-rich BC and Alberta were first and third respectively. In Québec, about 71 percent of the GDP was paid out in the form of wages (or their equivalent for farmers and small businessmen) versus 74 percent in Ontario. Advantage Ontario workers.

Moreover, these GDP deficits with Ontario are not of recent vintage: They have existed for some time (Table 7-7). Also, it appears that, after improving during the 1980s, Québec's relative position with Ontario started to deteriorate once again. Anyone at all attentive to the news of the day will recognize that this downturn in the 1980s coincided roughly with two items. The first was the first practical implementation of the most abrasive aspects of Québec's language laws, the second, the realization by potential investors that, with the election of the *Parti Québécois*, the secessionist threat in Québec had to be taken seriously. At this point it is tempting to bring the discussion to a close with the observation that, after a very brief improvement, the economic lot of *Québécois* is dropping to historic lows. What else is there to explain? Well, it is worth explaining where Québec's economy got off the rails ... because worse is yet to come.

Although the Québec and Ontario economies are structurally similar to one another, they are not identical. Moreover, their structural differences tend to favour Ontario. For example, when we earlier split the Canadian economy into its private and public sector components, we found that there was a strong correlation (R^2 of 0.75) between overall employment income and GDP in the private sector. That is, 75 percent of the interprovincial variation in per capita employment income was explained by interprovincial variation in private sector GDP. On the other hand, there was an almost non-existent correlation (R^2 of 0.06) between overall employment income and GDP in the public sector. Thus, workers tend to be better off in economies that favour the private sector. Furthermore, Québec's 18.3 percent GDP deficit with Ontario was made up of a 21 percent deficit in the private sector coupled with a more modest 5 percent public sector deficit. That is, Québec was relatively more reliant on the job-poor public sector than on the job-rich private sector. Advantage Ontario workers.

In addition, when we split the Canadian economy into two other major components, services (accounting, for instance) and goods (manufacturing), we found a very high correlation (R^2 of 0.84) between overall employment income and the services sector GDP. In other words, 84 percent of the interprovincial variation in employment income was explained by the interprovincial variation in GDP in the services sector. The correlation between overall employment income and the goods sector was not as good (R^2 of 0.54).

Thus, workers tend to be better off in economies where services dominate the goods producing sector. In 1990, Québec's 18 percent GDP deficit with Ontario was made up of deficits of 20 percent in the services sector and 16 percent in the goods sector. Again, Québec's greatest deficit was in the sector that produced the most or best paying jobs. Advantage Ontario workers.

Moreover, when we split the Services Sector GDP into its private and public sector sub-groups, we find quite different correlations between overall employment income and GDP. That is, there was a high correlation (R2 of 0.82) between overall employment income and private sector services, and a poor correlation (R2 of 0.27) between overall employment income and public sector services. In this particular case, Québec's GDP was running 28 percent behind Ontario in private sector services, 7 percent behind in public sector services. Here again, Québec was overly reliant on the job-poor public sector. Advantage Ontario workers. Finally, the best correlation (R2 of 0.98) between employment income and GDP was obtained when two sub-groups were combined: Private sector services (R2 of 0.82) and manufacturing (R2 of 0.72). That is, workers are best off in an economy where private sector services and manufacturing lead the way. Québec lagged behind Ontario by 28 percent in per capita private sector services GDP in 1990, by 24 percent in manufacturing. Advantage Ontario!

Before we dig deeper into private sector services and manufacturing, let's have a look at two special sub-groups: Provincial Services and Utilities. Consider first the sorry history of that portion of the provincial economy called Provincial Services, the cost of administering the province (Table 7-8). Note that, not only does provincial administration cost more in Québec on a per capita basis, it even cost more in *absolute* terms during much of the 1970s and 1980s--and Québec's population is about one-third smaller than Ontario's! That the Québec public service was bloated has long been a matter of public knowledge and the object of popular ridicule; that it could have been this bloated even the most cynical might not have imagined. In fact, I would argue that it is more than bloated, it is obscene. If the reader considers the word obscene too strong, consider this.

Québec's provincial politicians are the highest paid in Canada because of salaries they grant themselves, the cost of which is obviously borne by Québec's taxpayers. The same politicians decide who and how much to tax and how to allocate tax revenues. They evidently decided that it was more important to surround themselves with an expensive

Table 7-8: Provincial Services GDP				
	Absolute: $ M		$ / Capita	
	Qué	Ont	Qué	vs
			Ont	
1991	3,521	4,001	+ 30.1	%
1986	2,768	2,697	+ 44.4	%
1981	2,244	1,941	+ 55.5	%
1976	1,150	1,090	+ 38.5	%
1971	428	529	+ 14.3	%

Source: StatCan 61-202, 1983
15-203, 84/93

and bloated public service than to invest in other areas such as public education. Had these politicians provided themselves with a public service that was only proportionately equal to Ontario's, they could have saved over $800 million in 1991! When I say equal to Ontario, I am not referring to an inefficient standard: As I write (April 1996), the government of Ontario is planning to reduce its fat public service by about 15 percent! Therefore, Québec's reduced public service would still have been fat.

Then, had this annual $800 million saving been invested in public education, increasing spending there by about 20 percent per year (by hiring more teachers, for instance) the government of Québec might have been able to do something about correcting the educational deficiencies described earlier. For instance, they surely could have helped reduce Québec's horrendous school drop-out rate. Wouldn't it have been more desirable to keep hundreds of thousands of vulnerable kids in school rather than pad an already bloated public service? The question is obviously rhetorical and the answer must be a resounding yes! But logic played no part in this area. Québec's politicians obviously preferred to provide for themselves and their fellow travellers rather than minister to the greater needs of the people. Worse still, the people were taxed to pay for this extravagance. Still troubled by the word obscene?

The utilities sector in Québec means Hydro-Québec, the very symbol of Québec's economic rejuvenation since the earliest days of the Quiet Revolution. In fact, a provincial election was fought in the early 1960s with the slogan "*Maitres chez nous!*" The slogan called upon *Québécois* to become economic masters in their own *patrie* by nationalizing private sector hydro-electric companies to form the modern Hydro-Québec, the expected engine of economic growth. Let it be noted in passing that this revolutionary act followed by only 50 years similar action by the very conservative government of Ontario.

At first blush, the Québec expectation seems to have been realized: The per capita utilities GDP in Québec that was about one percent *behind* Ontario in 1971 was 20-percent *greater* in 1990. Impressive performance in Québec! However, if the generation of hydro-electric power was really the engine of economic growth, the spark required to industrialize Québec, how does one explain the following anomaly: Although Québec's Utilities' GDP was 20 percent greater than Ontario's in 1990, its manufacturing GDP was almost 25 percent lower? Stated another way, for every dollar of utilities GDP, $5.45 of manufacturing GDP was produced in Québec in 1990 versus $8.58 in Ontario. These data suggest that Hydro-Québec was about 36 percent less effective than Ontario-Hydro as an engine of economic growth.

Was Hydro-Québec in fact less efficient? It depends on how one defines efficient, I suppose. If it is defined in terms of costs of power generation, Québec must have been more efficient. Where Québec uses the cheapest form of generation (hydro-electric dams), Ontario has to resort to the most expensive (coal-burning and nuclear power plants). Thus, all other things being equal, Québec's costs of power generation must be lower than Ontario's.

Is part of the deficit explained by the fact that Hydro-Québec exported more of its production than did Ontario-Hydro? Probably. Hydro-Québec justified the building of huge, expensive hydro-electric dams in the remote and environmentally sensitive north by pointing to impending export contracts with the energy-hungry United States. Robert Bourassa, the Liberal Premier of Québec, apparently dreamed of Québec becoming the North American equivalent of OPEC, the crude oil producing cartel of some international repute. If OPEC was getting rich selling oil to the West, why couldn't Québec enrich itself selling electricity to the United States! Seemed logical. But the OPEC monopoly collapsed and the Americans later backed out of the energy deal with Québec, sticking Québec with costly and unnecessary power generating capacity. This suggests that Bourassa's assumptions and Hydro-Québec's analyses were not very well founded. Thus, if efficiency is defined in terms of accurate long-term planning and productive marketing, Hydro-Québec was obviously not very efficient. Clearly, the Québec economy, and the workers within it, would have been much better off had some funds been invested in public education rather than in hydro-electric facilities.

But back to the economic sub-sectors that really pay off: Business Services and Manufacturing. If we postulate an economy combining both, we end up with one having a near perfect correlation ($R2 = 0.98$) between employment income and the economy. Thus, workers are best off in an economy dominated by the private sector where services predominate. In Ontario, Private Sector Services are about 33 percent greater than manufacturing; in Québec about 26 percent greater. Consequently, we would expect the average worker to have been better off in Ontario than in Québec in 1990. He was ..... 27 percent better off!

Let us now peel another layer from the onion to see why Québec lags so far behind Ontario in these two private sector areas, starting with Services (Table 7-9). The data again demonstrate the relative weakness of the Québec economy. Not only is Québec at a substantial deficit in this, the most important sub-sector, it's relative position deteriorated in six of its eight sub-groups between 1971 and

Table 7-9:   Private Sector Services GDP, $ Per Capita

	Que	Ont	Que versus Ont	
	1990	1990	1990	1971
Finance/Real Estate	1,359	1,932	- 29.7 %	- 24.7 %
Dwellings	1,171	1,669	- 29.8 %	- 34.5 %
Business Services	877	1,292	- 32.1 %	- 25.4 %
Tourism	491	591	- 16.9 %	- 9.8 %
Health Services	377	558	- 32.4 %	- 22.3 %
Recreation	208	210	- 0.8 %	+ 2.5 %
Household Services	200	252	- 20.6 %	- 19.9 %
Private Schools	82	34	+141.2 %	+ 44.0 %
All P Sector Services	5,109	7,043	- 27.5 %	NA

Source: StatCan 15-203.

1990. Note also that the two sub-groups where Québec led, Recreation and Private Schools, are either insignificant or irrelevant.

The data for recreation suggest that leisure was an equally popular activity in both provinces. But, since one does not run an economy on leisure services--Nevada's legal brothels notwithstanding--I shall allow this segment of the economy to pass without comment. Private schools, on the other hand, require special comment. Québec's private school system is the largest in Canada, well ahead of second place British Columbia and miles ahead of fourth-place Ontario. Furthermore, Québec's private school system is large because Québec's parents have lost faith in the province's public school system. Moreover, it would appear from the historical record that this loss of faith increased in intensity between 1971 and 1991, the period during which Québec was in the throes of all sorts of reforms to its school system. Clearly, Québec's parents must not have been very impressed by these reforms. Hence, it can hardly be considered an honour for Québec to be so dominant here.

And this brings us to the service sub-sectors that do have a significant economic impact on the people: Financial/Real Estate, Business and Tourism. The first two can be grouped together under a general business umbrella that we can call Commercial Services. This umbrella group would include all those services that businesses need to function efficiently. From these data we can conclude that, in the Commercial Services sector, Québec lost ground: It went from a combined deficit with Ontario of approximately 25 percent in 1971 to a deficit of about 30 percent in 1991. Much of this deterioration can be attributed to the flight of head offices from Québec, a flight that started in the mid-1970s. Since the causes of this exodus were described earlier, I will not repeat them here.

Tourism, however, needs some discussion. Here again, the deficit with Ontario worsened considerably between 1971 and 1991. How does one explain a tourism deficit in Québec that was about 10 percent below Ontario in 1971 and 17 percent below in 1990? To argue that it is because Ontario is objectively more attractive than Québec or that it was less attractive in 1990 than it was 1971 is absurd. Though I may concede that Niagara Falls is better known internationally than Montmorency Falls, I refuse to accept the notion that Toronto is more appealing than Montréal; or that there is any city in Ontario that can match the charm of Québec City; or that Ontario has anything comparable to *La Gaspésie*; or to the Eastern Townships; or to the ski hills of *Les Laurentides* or *Mont Sainte-Anne*. I would argue that it is because neither the Québec tourism industry nor the various governments of Québec have been very effective in promoting Québec's obvious tourist potential. Of course you can point to prestigious projects such as the 1967 World's Fair and the 1976 Olympics, both of which were held in Montréal. Did they not enhance Québec's international image? Apparently not enough. And what about the Québec Winter Carnival, the most famous winter carnival in the world; or the festivals that sprung up in Québec in the last few decades celebrating everything from cowboys and fireworks to hot air balloons, jazz and humour? According to the evidence, they apparently were not effective enough to offset Ontario's appeal.

It appears as if Québec is fairly adept at hosting prestigious events such as the very costly and heavily subsidized Olympics,[13] but is quite inept at convincing New Yorkers or Ontarians to vacation in Québec during ordinary times. And to rub salt in the wound, consider the provincial ranking for per capita tourism GDP in 1990: First was BC with $718, second was Alberta with $667, third was Ontario with $591, fourth was Manitoba with $521 and *fifth* was Québec with $491, just ahead of Saskatchewan with $490 and PEI with $481.[14] Without being unkind to Saskatchewan or Manitoba, who would ever have believed that tourists would have preferred the flat Prairies to Québec?

Clearly, these data show that Québec has not been very effective developing its tourist industry. And it is not because promoting tourism is akin to rocket science. All it takes is modest long term funding, reasonably competent marketing and a reordering of priorities to recognize the economic importance of tourism. Clearly, all the wonderful things done as a result of the Quiet Revolution did not include any attempts to reduce the tourism gap with Ontario. In fact, whatever was done made the gap worse.

And what does all this tell us? Bear in mind that the Private Sector Services Sector is the most important economic sector in any modern economy. During this period, Québec's deficit with Ontario not only did not improve, it worsened, and shows little prospect of improving in the near future. Moreover, the largest sub-sectors were those that fared the worst; they were also the ones most adversely affected by the language and secessionist policies of the government of Québec. And the available evidence suggests that the situation is not likely to improve any time soon: The secessionist movement is not in retreat; there are increasing outcries from nationalists to restrict further the use of English and services to anglophones. Thus, the most important economic sector, the Private Sector Services Sector, is being savaged to satisfy the whims of the idiotic wing of the *Québécois* élite. And they are getting away with this by calling it sacrifice by all in the name of common cultural survival. The only problem is that the sacrifice is being borne by the masses, not by the élite.

Now on to manufacturing, the second most important economic sector. At a general level, the number of manufacturing jobs per capita was 16 percent lower in Québec than in Ontario in 1961; 20 percent lower in 1990. If Québec had gained ground on Ontario in the Services Sector during this period, one might properly conclude that losing ground in manufacturing was explained by a corresponding improvement in services. But that did not happen: Québec lost ground there as well. Hence, losing ground in both sectors meant that workers in Québec were hit with a double whammy. Advantage Ontario.

Furthermore, the average manufacturer employed 40.3 workers in Québec in 1961, 38.3 in 1990; the comparable figures for Ontario were 51.4 and 60.8. Clearly, not only were Québec's manufacturers much smaller than

Ontario's to begin with, they became smaller while Ontario's grew. That is, the average manufacturer in Québec employed about 5 percent fewer workers in 1990 than in 1961; the average manufacturer in Ontario employed 18 percent more workers in 1990. One might argue that this was a sign of greater operating efficiency in Québec or that it was the necessary consequence of an expanding economy where small new companies were starting up. However, both would have required a large dose of new capital investment for which there is no evidence. Therefore, this 5 percent decline in Québec is probably best explained by a simple deterioration in production.[15] Moreover, since better wages tend to be paid by larger companies, these data suggest that workers in the Ontario manufacturing sector were and are better paid than their opposite numbers in Québec. In fact, they were and are. Advantage Ontario.

And why were/are manufacturers so much smaller in Québec than in Ontario? Although some analysts might wax long in response, let me suggest two possibilities. The first is that the Québec economy is only capable of supporting small businesses, the second that social and political conditions generally did not encourage large business investments in Québec. Although there is no evidence to support the first option, there is abundant evidence to support the second. For example, I argue, first, that Québec's poorly educated workforce discouraged business investment in modern enterprises, and second, that Québec's irritating language laws as well as the province's omnipresent threat to secede make large business investments there too risky for prudent investors. Thus, advantage relatively well educated and tranquil Ontario.

Much the same conclusions can be derived from a more detailed analysis of the manufacturing sector where Québec reduced its manufacturing GDP deficit with Ontario substantially, going from a 34 percent deficit in 1971 to a 23 percent deficit in 1990. And that was good ... or was it? Let us dig a little to see what the data tell us.

In Table 7-10 are listed in order of their relative size the major sub-sectors of the manufacturing sectors in Québec and Ontario. Note that the unfavourable GDP gap with Ontario improved (*) in eight sub-sectors and worsened in six between 1971 and 1990. Apart from Food, the six losers tended to be among the smallest, the eight winners among the largest. And that should auger well for Québec. But does it? At present trends, it will still take about 40 years

Table 7-10: Manufacturing GDP/Capita

	% Difference Qué versus Ont		
	1990	1971	
Food	- 18	- 14	
Autos	- 60	- 74	*
Paper	+ 33	+ 28	*
Chem. Prods.	- 27	- 38	*
Elec. Prods.	- 40	- 47	*
Primary Metals	- 6	- 56	*
Printing	- 27	- 34	*
Fab'd Metals	- 37	- 50	*
Clothing	+ 193	+ 229	
Wood	+ 80	+ 32	*
Primary Text.	+ 59	+ 76	
Machinery	- 50	- 70	
Mineral Prods.	- 38	- 33	
Furniture	- 8	0	
All Mfging	- 23	- 34	

Source: StatCan 15-203

to close the overall manufacturing gap with Ontario--a not very exciting prospect for those looking for a little help with tomorrow's bills or for those hoping for better job prospects for their grandchildren. Moreover, when we look at the eight winners and ask when they will eliminate their GDP deficits, we realize that the term winner may need a little explaining. That is, two of the eight are currently at a surplus with Ontario (Paper and Wood); one (Primary Metals) needs only about a year to close the gap; the other five will require from 50 to over 100 years to close the gap! This is clearly an unsatisfactory state of affairs. And when we delve below the surface still more to examine the two largest winners, Autos and Paper, we see disaster looming on the Québec horizon.

In the Autos sub-sector, for example, the favourable trend suggested in Table 7-10 has already been arrested since publication of these data. Hyundai and Kenworth closed their assembly plants in Québec in the 1990s. Only GM remains, and it is talking of a possible transfer of some of its Québec operations to plants elsewhere in North America. The Autos sub-sector, therefore, is likely to deteriorate in Québec rather than recover.

In the Paper sub-sector there looms an even greater potential threat: Recycling. At one time, paper mills were located close to their raw material supply, nice big trees in northern Canada, mostly in Québec. But when they discovered how to make decent paper from trees of lesser quality in the southern USA, they effectively stopped building new paper mills in Canada. Eventually, paper mills will start moving closer to their new source of raw material, recycled newspaper in large cities ... in the USA! The changing dynamics in the paper industry suggest that, in the long run, paper mills will move from the Canadian north toward large metropolitan areas, especially in the USA. And since Québec is the heart of the Canadian newsprint industry, it will be the hardest hit. Hence, Québec's currently favourable position in this industry relative to Ontario may be chimeric. As the industry declines in both provinces, Québec's relative advantage will become irrelevant. Proof of the unhealthy state of this industry in Canada is the spate of paper mill closings that were averted in the past few years only by virtue of government intervention in the form of loans and cash grants or by major wage concessions from paper mill workers. Sounds like an industry gasping for air as it goes down for the count.

And, lest anyone point with pride to Québec's strong position in the Clothing and Textiles sub-sectors, let me point out a few caveats. First, these two sectors are among the smallest on the list; second, as will be shown later, the wages paid in these two areas are among the lowest in the economy; and third, with the tendency of these sub-sectors to seek even lower cost sources offshore, wages are likely to always be marginal. So, who needs them?

It would appear then that Québec's manufacturing gap with Ontario will probably worsen. When you couple this prognosis with the previously described disaster in the services sector, we must conclude that the Québec economy will continue to lose ground to Ontario for a long time to come--with the attendant adverse consequences on workers' incomes.

Crumbs for the People

Time to summarize. Because potential investors tended to shun Québec, its economy (per capita GDP) stood fourth among Canada's ten provinces in 1993, 17.1 percent behind second place Ontario. In the same year, Québec's per capita income from employment lagged 17.4 percent behind that of its sister province. Moreover, this employment income deficit has been the norm since at least the end of WW II (Table 7-11). And, efforts to close this gap were stymied by the evil twins of the Quiet Revolution: Language laws and threats of secession.

But, the situation could have been much worse had the people not adjusted their breeding habits. Because of changing attitudes toward procreation, the size of the average Québec family declined considerably between 1961 and 1993. Since the average Québec wage earner thus had fewer mouths to feed, per capita employment income increased proportionately. In fact, had the size of the average Québec family not changed in this period, per capita income from employment in Québec would have deteriorated from a 24 percent deficit with Ontario in 1961 to a 41 percent deficit in 1993. Even if the size of the average Québec family had declined in line with the Ontario decline, per capita income from employment in Québec would still have deteriorated to a 29 percent deficit with Ontario. Only by under-producing Ontario in the bedroom was Québec able to reduce its per capita employment income deficit with its neighbour! In other words, it took a change in the private bedroom practices of the people to overcome the adverse economic effects of the public policies of the *Québécois* ruling classes!

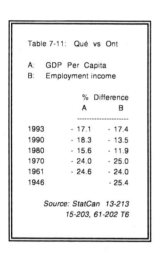

Table 7-11: Qué vs Ont

A: GDP Per Capita
B: Employment income

| | % Difference | |
	A	B
1993	- 17.1	- 17.4
1990	- 18.3	- 13.5
1980	- 15.6	- 11.9
1970	- 24.0	- 25.0
1961	- 24.6	- 24.0
1946		- 25.4

Source: StatCan 13-213
15-203, 61-202 T6

As described earlier, the income from employment of workers in Québec is adversely affected by the very structure of the economy. For instance, that the Québec economy is more dependent on the public sector than on the private sector is bad news for workers; so also is the fact that Québec depends more on *old fashioned* manufacturing, particularly on relatively small and vulnerable manufacturers. Ontario workers do well because their economy depends more on the private sector, on *modern* services and on larger, more mature manufacturers. But, apart from structure, we can be more precise about the elements that influence the level of employment income in Québec.

Since the economy must provide for all the people in it, not just for employed workers, employment income *per capita* (or *per family*) is still the relevant statistic to use in measuring the worth of any economy. Moreover, I have postulated a correlation between per capita employment

Table 7-12: Québec versus Ontario

A: Employment Income Per Capita
B: Average Weekly Wages
C: Workforce Per 1000 People

	Percent Difference Québec versus Ontario			Unemploy'nt Rates - %	
	A	B	C	Qué	Ont
1991	- 19.7	- 6.7	- 5.1	14.3	10.9
1986	- 18.7	- 4.8	- 8.2	14.6	8.3
1981	- 13.1		- 8.3	13.6	8.2
1976	- 18.9		- 8.1	8.3	6.6
1975	- 19.3	- 2.7	- 6.8	8.8	6.0
1971	- 23.9	- 7.7	- 5.9	10.1	6.9
1961	- 24.0	- 7.2	- 10.1	9.2	5.5
1951	- 28.4	- 8.4	- 11.5	2.9	1.7
1946	- 25.4	- 3.7	- 11.5	4.0	2.8
1941	- 30.2	- 11.0		7.5	5.0

Sources: Statcan 1991 Census, 93-324, T3

income and three conditions in the economy (Table 7-12). The first condition is the relative size of each potential workforce: The total number of people of working age per 1,000 of population. In 1991, for instance, there were 506 people of working age per thousand people in Québec, 533 in Ontario. Why would Québec have about 5 percent fewer people in this category? Did it have a relatively younger population? Yes. Had relatively more of its older people emigrated in search of work? Yes again. In any event, because there were about 5 percent fewer potential workers, we would expect per capita employment income in 1991 to have been in the order of 5 percent lower in Québec.

The second condition is the rate of unemployment which has always been higher in Québec than in Ontario. In fact, the relationship between the unemployment rates in the two provinces is almost constant: Québec's rate is about half-again as high as Ontario's. If we consider the opposite side of the unemployment coin, there were recent *employment* rates of about 85 percent in Québec and 90 in Ontario. Thus, again all other things being equal, we would expect per capita employment income to be about 5 percent lower in Québec.

The third condition is the average weekly rate of pay, the average weekly wage that was actually paid to people with jobs. In 1991, it was about 7 percent lower in Québec.

Taken together, these three conditions suggest that per capita employment income could have been in the order of 17 percent lower in Québec in 1991: It was in fact about 20 percent lower. It appears therefore that changes in per capita employment income can be largely explained by changes in these three conditions, each one responsible for about one-third of the total change. In fact, when we crunch these data in a regression model, we obtain an almost perfect correlation: $R2 = 0.98$. Hence, if we study the behaviour of these three variables, potential workforce, wage rates and unemployment rates, we should get a reasonable explanation of Québec-Ontario employment income disparities.

In the 15 years following WW II, Québec's workforce deficit with Ontario improved only a little, going from an 11.5 percent deficit in 1946 to 10.5 in 1961. By 1971, however, the deficit had narrowed substantially to 5.9 percent.

Table 7-13: Wage Rates		
Qué vs Ont		
1976-90	- 4	%
1961-75	- 6	%
1946-60	- 7	%
1941-45	- 9	%
1926-40	-12	%
1901-25	-10	%
Source: StatCan Historical Statistics		

This suggests that the population was getting older, and/or that more working-age *Québécois* remained at home during this period instead of migrating in search of work. Whether one or the other, or both, the improvement can be explained in part by the considerable investment made in the Québec economy during the 1960s as well as by the yet-to-be-really-felt impact of the birth control pill. Then, following the decline in business investment, this deficit worsened and has remained at about 8 percent ever since. However, as birth control really takes effect in Québec, this workforce deficit with Ontario should disappear before very long ... if jobs become available in Québec in sufficient numbers to discourage job-related migrations. During the same post-war period, Québec's unemployment rate remained at a level about half-again as high as Ontario's. Thus, one might argue that employment in Québec was influenced more by spillovers from Ontario than by initiatives within Québec.

The other major cause of the deficit in employment income was the deficit in wage rates which may be related to the unemployment problem. With unemployment in Québec consistently above that in Ontario, wage rates could indeed be lower in Québec: All other things being equal, low wage rates and high unemployment tend to go hand-in-hand. Supply and demand! Another possible factor is the generally lower level of skills in Québec that go hand-in-glove with the province's lower level of education.

At any rate, unemployment and other factors notwithstanding, the wage-rate gap with Ontario has narrowed over time. Note that weekly rates of pay are related to but not identical to weekly wages. That is, an average weekly wage can change for several reasons, one of which is a change in the rate of pay; another is overtime; another is job mix. But, no matter which definition is used, the general conclusion is the same: Except for the period of the Great Depression (1926-40 in Table 7-13), the wage rate gap with Ontario has been narrowing throughout the 20th-century. Thus, those who associate this narrowing with the advent of the Quiet Revolution in the 1960s have obviously never properly informed themselves. Also, it appears that Québec's wage rate deficit with Ontario has stabilized at about 4 percent.

Table 7-14: National Rankings		
1 : Highest		
10 : Lowest		
	Qué	Ont
Spending	1	5
Deficit	1	2
Debt	1	4
Taxes	1	2
Ottawa Citizen March 27, 1997 Can. Tax Foundation StatCan 68-212-XPB 1995-1996		

Thus, based on the evidence advanced here, it is difficult to envision any significant lowering of the per capita employment income gap with Ontario. That is, there is no evidence to suggest how or why average wage rates in Québec should improve further relative to Ontario. However, Québec's workforce deficit is likely to improve as the birth rate declines ... if adult *Québécois* do not migrate in search of work. But, the combination of secessionist threats, abusive language laws and a relatively uneducated workforce, will tend to discourage investors. Hence, Québec's unemployment rate will likely remain relatively high. And, to top it all off, the policies and profligate spending practices of Québec's politicians have made *Québécois* the most highly taxed and indebted people in Canada (Table 7-14). Small wonder then that Québec has the highest poverty rate and Ontario the second lowest of Canada's ten provinces.[16]

Three Classes of Workers

Although there is no evidence to suggest that average wage rates in Québec will improve very much relative to Ontario in the near future, there is more than a suggestion that public policy in Québec will continue to favour some workers over others. In 1992, for instance, salaried workers in Québec were paid 11 percent less than their Ontario counterparts. On the other hand, those who were paid by the hour were paid only 5 percent less. What explains this anomaly?

Consider Figure 7-15 where the major economic sectors are listed in order of hourly wage rates: Mining is at the top (about $20 an hour) and Trade at the bottom (about $10 an hour). Now, let us divide this list in two to see what the data can reveal. The first group (*) encompasses the economic sectors that obviously belong in the private sector: Mining, Forestry and Manufacturing. The second includes the remaining five, all of which are generally more influenced by government intervention. When we do some rough averaging, we find that, relative to Ontario, salaried people fared equally poorly in both the private and government sectors: As cited above, the average weekly wage of salaried workers was running about 11 percent behind Ontario in 1992. Although the explanation for this differential is of course arguable, all I wish to conclude here is that, whatever the explanation, it did not appear to discriminate in behalf of or against any particular economic sector. In other words, the wage rates of salaried workers appear to have been set by the market.

Not necessarily so with those paid by the hour. Those working in the private sector (Mining, Forestry and Manufacturing), fell behind Ontario by an amount roughly equal to their salaried colleagues (about 11 percent). Here again, the market seems to have prevailed. On the other hand, hourly rated workers in the

Table 7-15:	Wage Rates, 1992	
	% Difference Québec vs Ontario	
	Salaried Staff	Hourly Rated
Mining	- 11.1	- 9.3 *
Construction	- 19.3	+ 10.2
Transp/Utilities	- 3.1	+ 1.3
Forestry	- 18.9	- 21.2 *
Manufacturing	- 8.0	- 12.6 *
Services	- 3.5	+ 3.1
Finance	- 13.3	+ 8.8
Trade	- 19.3	- 6.2

Source: StatCan 72-002
July 1992, T 8

other group (Construction, Trade, etc.) were paid an average of about 4 percent *more* in Québec. Because construction unions in Québec have been sheltered by provincial legislation since about 1960, the salaries of their hourly paid members have consequently tended to be quite high, about 10 percent higher than Ontario by the looks of it. If anyone needs a memory check on this, simply consult any newspaper report on the wage concessions made by the Québec government to satisfy the demands of construction unions working on Québec's various hydro-electric projects. The notion of craven capitulation to thuggery and blackmail may come to mind. Similarly, hourly rated workers in sectors such as Transportation and Utilities (Hydro-Québec!) benefitted from negotiating with a compliant Québec government. Others, such as those working in the Finance, Services and Trade sectors, benefitted from the upward pressure from relatively generous, government-imposed minimum wage rates.

Whether these wage premiums in the hourly rated sector were gained at the expense of jobs is of course arguable. Let us examine the data and see for ourselves. In the goods producing industries (manufacturing, for instance), Québec had 25.5 percent fewer salaried workers per thousand of population than Ontario; it also had 28.7 percent fewer hourly rated workers (Table 7-16). This is an almost one-to-one relationship, about what one might have expected. On the other hand, in the service producing industries (Trade and Finance, for instance), where Québec had 16.5 percent fewer salaried workers than Ontario, it had 25.3 percent fewer hourly rated workers. Something appears to be out of whack here: If the trend for salaried workers was the norm, there should have been 18.6 percent fewer hourly rated workers in Québec, not 25.3 percent fewer. What explains this variation which amounts to about 4.75 jobs per 1,000 people, or 33,000 jobs in total? Some of these 33,000 missing jobs were never created because of a lack of business investment, others because employers simply found a way to do without relatively expensive hourly rated employees. Furthermore, whether the loss of 33,000 jobs was a reasonable social price to pay so that 350,000 workers might enjoy a pay premium of less than $1 an hour, is not clear. Consider the evidence.

It seems to me that minimum wage laws applied originally to part-time workers such as my teenage children working for pin money. In that case, I favour keeping minimum wages low to maximize the number of pin money jobs. On the other hand, when people started flipping hamburgers to support families, the social dynamics changed: Pressure was on to increase the

Table 7-16:	Jobs per 1,000 People	
	Goods	Services
	Salaried	Workers
Québec	16.4	94.4
Ontario	22.1	113.0
Qué vs Ont	- 25.5 %	- 16.5 %
	Hourly Rated	Workers
Québec	28.6	52.9
Ontario	40.1	70.8
Qué vs Ont	- 28.7 %	- 25.3 %
Source: StatCan 72-002, T 4.2, Dec. 1990		

level of minimum wages to accommodate this new imperative. These higher wages obviously caused hamburger flipping companies to look closely at their labour costs, seeking savings wherever possible. As a result, labour saving devices and procedures entered the hamburger flipping market at the expense of jobs. Furthermore, as minimum wages rose in the hamburger flipping sector, say from $5 to $6 an hour, service jobs in the industrial sector rose accordingly: For instance, $9 jobs became $10 jobs. Here again, in reaction to this increase in labour costs, employers turned to appropriate labour saving practices.

So, in both cases, relatively high minimum wage levels could be held responsible for job losses. Nevertheless, better, I would argue, that some make $10 an hour than that everyone struggle at $9; better that the displaced seek employment elsewhere. Therefore, the policies of the government of Québec that drove up minimum wage levels were commendable, the loss of 33,000 jobs notwithstanding ... if there were 33,000 other jobs to go to.

But, there weren't. As argued earlier, since 1960, the policies of the various governments of Québec have had the effect of discouraging job creating business investment, investment that could have created manufacturing jobs that paid average wages three-times the minimum rate! Therefore, creating unemployment while simultaneously throwing a few crumbs to the lowly paid must be called by its proper name: A cynical gesture by a political class more interested in its own political agenda than in the people's economic interests.

So, in Québec we have three classes of worker:

1. Those on fixed salaries whose pay rates are set by competitive forces.

2. Those relatively highly paid hourly rated workers whose rates of pay are set in negotiations with the government of Québec.

3. Those relatively lowly paid hourly rated workers whose rates of pay, although low, are higher than they would otherwise be because of upward pressure from Québec's minimum wage laws.

Clearly, not all workers in Québec fared badly from its public policy initiatives. In the three classes described, two owe their relative affluence to preferential treatment from the government of Québec. That is, while workers in the first class have to compete within a normal market economy, those in the other two benefit from the shelter provided by the protective policies of the government of Québec. In the Distinct Society, some workers are more equal than others.

Economic Apartheid

This inequality among working people also had related class and linguistic dimensions. In Table 7-17 are listed some important socio-economic indicators for three geographic areas in Québec and Ontario. Although setting the

Table 7-17: Economic Apartheid, 1991

	Pop'n % Prov	French % Pop'n	<Grade9 % Pop'n	UnivDeg % Pop'n	EmployInc $/Family	LowInc %	Unemploy %
Montreal Island	25.8	58.5	19.5	15.6	36,348	23.1	13.2
Other Major Areas	14.6	89.9	15.2	12.8	40,846	15.5	9.4
Hinterland	59.6	92.9	21.7	7.2	34,782	13.6	12.3
All Québec	100.0	83.8	20.1	10.3	36,062	16.2	12.1
Metro Toronto	22.6		13.2	17.9	47,531	16.3	9.6
Other Major Areas	38.1		9.0	14.9	51,840	9.3	7.6
Hinterland	39.3		12.9	8.1	37,742	9.4	7.4
All Ontario	100.0		11.5	13.0	45,209	10.9	8.5

Source: StatCan 95-338, 1991 Census

boundaries of these areas is arguable, my intention was to divide each province into relatively comparable economic areas. The first area includes the main urban agglomerations: Montreal Island in Québec, Metro Toronto in Ontario. The second area takes in other major urban centres that have significant impacts on the economies of each province. The third area is simply everything that is left over, the economic hinterland that stands apart from and is supposed to nourish the first two areas with people and resources.

The second area includes three urban centres in Québec and eight in Ontario. In Québec these are Laval, Metro Québec City and the Outaouais metropolitan area. The first centre, Laval, is Québec's second largest city and is adjacent to Montreal Island; the second is the capital of the province; the third is a group of bedroom communities for federal public servants working in the nearby national capital in Ottawa, Ontario. Laval's economic life depends on its proximity to Montreal; Québec City and the Outaouais are obviously buoyed economically by the presence of major provincial and federal government bureaucracies. These three urban centres had an average population of 335,000 people in 1991. Since Québec City and the Outaouais had a combined population equal to 69 percent of the total population in this second economic area, I would conclude that its overall level of prosperity was far more dependent on government largesse than on private sector paychecks.

In Ontario, the eight urban centres in this second economic area averaged 480,000 people, 43 percent higher than the related Québec average. The Ontario municipalities were London, Waterloo, Hamilton, Oakville, Mississauga, York, Oshawa and Ottawa. Apart from Ottawa, this second area is in effect an extension of the Metro Toronto economic area and forms part of the so-called Golden Horseshoe. Moreover, Ottawa, with 18 percent of the population of this second area, was the only one whose well being depended on government. Clearly, this second economic area was far less reliant on government than was its counterpart in Québec.

The third area, the hinterland, is not entirely rural since some important urban centres are included in it. However, they were not significant enough to warrant inclusion in the second area. I should point out again that hinterlands traditionally supply the major economic areas of any modern economy with goods, services and people. Thus, as a modern economy expands, we would expect to see people migrating from the hinterland to areas of greater economic potential. And, this did indeed happen in Ontario, but not in Québec.

In 1991, the hinterland accounted for 59.6 percent of Québec's population and 39.3 percent of Ontario's. To put these relative percentages into absolute perspective, note that, although Québec's total population was about 32 percent less than Ontario's, its absolute hinterland population was about 4 percent *greater* than Ontario's in 1991. Further, if much of the economic development took place in the first two economic areas, as it did, it follows that the hinterland would be relatively less developed, and it was. This may surprise some since Québec's two most important manufacturing industries, pulp and paper and automotive, are located in this hinterland. Let it also be noted that they are both in danger of imminent and serious decline.

The most significant statistic in Table 7-17 is the relative size of the hinterland in each province: 59.6 percent of Québec's population, 39.3 percent of Ontario's. That is, because Québec's economy outside Montreal Island did not develop to the same extent as its Ontario counterpart, one-third of the population in this hinterland area, over 1.4 million people, about 20 percent of the population of Québec, had to put up with a standard of living that was lower than necessary. That is, had the *Québécois* élite done their job, there would have been greater economic development in this area and incomes from employment would have risen (a) by 17 percent to equal their more fortunate cousins in the second sector who were sucking on the public teat in Québec City and the Outaouais, and their other cousins in Laval living off the avails of their proximity to Montreal, or (b) by 50 percent to equal the average in the second economic area in Ontario. To conclude that these hinterland *Québécois* have been had is, of course, a considerable understatement.

And when we consider the evolution of these three areas from 1961 to 1991, we see how bankrupt were Québec's economic policies. The poverty rate went from 27.9 percent of Québec families in 1961 to 16.2 percent in 1991. This gives the illusion of great progress until we note that Québec's poverty rate went from Canada's *second* highest in 1961 to its *highest* in 1991.[17] The comparable figures for Ontario were 18.6 percent in 1961 and 10.9 percent in 1991.[18] Moreover, the relative economic condition of the average Québec family deteriorated significantly in this 30-year period: Average family income from employment was 11 percent behind Ontario in 1961, 20.2 percent behind in 1991, 30 years after the start of the Quiet Revolution. Some revolution!

The major reason for this inability to improve the economic lot

Table 7-18: Economic Apartheid, 1961

	Pop'n % Prov	French % Pop'n	ElemSchl % Pop'n	UnivDeg % Pop'n	EmployInc $/Family	LowInc %	Unemploy %
Montreal Island	33.2	67.7	34.7	4.2	5,310		
Other Major Areas	11.2	89.1	37.3	3.2	4,872		
Hinterland	55.6	90.7	44.2	1.6	4,112		
All Québec	100.0	81.2	40.0	2.7	4,694	27.9	9.5
Metro Toronto	24.3		32.7	4.5	5,796		
Other Major Areas	27.0		33.6	4.3	5,659		
Hinterland Ontario	48.7		40.5	2.1	4,780		
All Ontario	100.0		36.7	3.3	5,274	18.6	5.5

Source:StatCan 93-519, 1961 Census; 93-328 T1, T74; 99-544, t*.1, 1991 Census

of *Québécois* is clear: Where Ontario decreased its hinterland population by moving people into major economic areas, Québec instead increased its hinterland population (by starving Montréal). That is, where Ontario decreased its hinterland from 48.7 to 39.3 percent of the provincial population, Québec increased its hinterland from 55.6 to 59.6 percent. This meant that a significant number of hinterland Ontarians were able to compete for jobs that paid about 37 percent more than jobs in the hinterland. Advantage Ontario.

Moreover, in both provinces the data suggest that the highest paying jobs moved from the major metropolitan areas (Montreal and Toronto) to other major economic areas. That is, where the highest family incomes were found in these major metropolitan areas in 1961, by 1991 they had migrated to the sector called "Other Major Areas" in Tables 7-17 and 7-18. Since this sector is dominated by government spending in Québec and by private sector activity in Ontario, this is further evidence of the division of Québec into two economic solitudes: Those who have access to the public trough and those who do not.

And, things get worse ... in Montreal.

Although one may argue that *Québécois* have not been very successful in any of these three areas, they were especially unsuccessful in Montreal. Why? To help answer this question, I divided Montreal Island into Franco-Montreal and Anglo-Montreal (Anglophone/Allophone Montreal for purists--the abbreviation anglo is used here only for convenience). Franco-Montreal included all census areas whose 1991 populations were more than 50 percent francophone; the balance were considered to be part of Anglo-Montreal. The population distributions in 1991 are shown in Table 7-19. Since average family income from employment was 50-percent higher in Anglo-Montreal in both 1961 and

Table 7-19: Montréal Island, 1991		
Demographic Distribution - %		
	Franco Montréal	Anglo Montréal
Francophones	67.6	34.6
Anglophones	16.5	49.5
Allophones	15.9	15.9

1991, let's for the moment consider these linguistic labels as metaphors for successful (Anglo-Montreal) and unsuccessful (Franco-Montreal). Then, let's restate the data in another way: 54 percent of anglophones on Montreal Island lived in Anglo-Montreal in 1991 and hence could be considered successful; so did 16 percent of francophones and 28 percent of allophones. The obvious question then is: "*Why weren't more francophones successful?*" When you look at the data, an obvious answer leaps from the page: The residents of Franco-Montreal were relatively poorly educated.

If the school system in Franco-Montreal had improved its performance, permitting *Québécois* to be as successful as allophones, another 115,000 *Québécois* would have joined the successful category; if it had done a good enough job to permit *Québécois* to be as successful as anglophones, 370,000 Québécois would have joined the successful category. Since there is no reason to suppose that *Québécois* could not have been as successful as anglophones, I would conclude that about 370,000 people in Franco-Montreal (38 percent of the population of Franco-Montreal) were living in strained economic conditions, conditions that could have been avoided had the Québec Minister of Education done his/her job! Had the schools done their job, these losers might have had a chance to increase their incomes by 50 percent in the same types of jobs as those enjoyed by residents of Anglo-Montreal. But, because they were trapped in Franco-Montreal, their family incomes remained 33 percent behind. No relative improvement in 30 years! This explains why Franco-Montreal's poverty rate was almost twice as high as the rate in Anglo-Montreal, or in the area called "Other Major Areas," or even in the hinterland.

Moreover, although the population of Anglo-Montreal increased by 273,000, Franco-Montreal's *decreased* by 192,000 in this period. Some of the more successful among these *emigrants* from Franco-Montreal moved into Anglo-Montreal, some into Laval; some also left Québec for greener pastures elsewhere. If history is any guide, one would have expected people to move steadily from the hinterland into Franco-Montreal in sufficient numbers to increase its population. But, that did not happen: The exodus from Franco-Montréal was greater than the intake from the hinterland. And the reason is obvious: Where, in 1961, family incomes were 22 percent higher in Franco-Montreal than in Québec's hinterland, the reverse obtained in 1991 when Franco-Montreal incomes were 9 percent *lower*. So why would you move to the city when you could do better on the farm? Clearly, the Quiet Revolution did a better job than the Church in keeping the faithful away from Montreal!

In 1991, it would appear that about one-third of *Québécois* were economically deprived either because of poor education or inadequate

Table 7-20:	Québec, 1991			
	Pop'n % Prov	French % Pop'n	EmployInc $/Family	Poverty Rate-%
Hinterland	60	93	35,000	14
Franco Mtl	19	68	32,000	27
Gov't Areas	14	90	41,000	15
Anglo Mtl	7	35	47,000	14

economic development, or both. Moreover, the data suggest that Québec's economy is divided into four fairly distinct economic ghettos. In order of population size, they are shown in Table 7-20. Clearly, although the winners and losers in this list are both *Québécois*, the biggest losers are those in Franco-Montreal, the poorest among them having become Québec's underclass. And, given their current school drop-out rate of over 50 percent, they are not likely to close the education gap with Anglo-Montreal any time soon. Moreover, since they are not being nourished by significant migrations from the hinterland, they will continue to stagnate culturally and economically. As a result, they may even become Québec's permanent underclass.

Moreover, with a growing hinterland isolated from a stagnating inner city, with a "Successful Montreal" dominated by anglophones who are being driven from Québec, and with economic development outside of Montreal dominated, not by the job-creating private sector but by public administrations that are being downsized, it is easy to describe the Québec economy as an assortment of deteriorating ghettos. Moreover, since the economies in these ghettos are influenced largely by misguided or mischievous government policies, it is difficult to hold out much hope for improvement in the near future. Consequently, to improve their economic lot, *Québécois* have not much choice but to leave Québec ... or do something about their leaders.

Plight of Québécois

Fortunately, being resourceful and persistent has always been a characteristic of the people of Québec. For instance, during the French régime, the male colonists had to be particularly persistent in their search for mates since the colony counted about six men for every four French women. Hence, the surplus males had either to be celibate or select mates from nearby Indian settlements. Although celibacy might have suited some, the historical record shows that inter-ethnic coupling and more than the occasional marriage was the norm. My family tree, for example, contains more than one reference to a female aboriginal ancestor. Hence, it is likely that about a third of *Québécois* have aboriginal blood in their veins. Thus, when Lionel Groulx and his modern apologists insist that today's *Québécois* are unadulterated descendants of the original French settlers, they are obviously being inventive.

The colonists also had to be resourceful in the pursuit of their economic interests which sometimes required them to seek greener pastures beyond the confines of New France. In fact, the colonial administration and the

Church fought a losing battle trying to keep the young men at home. The historical record is rife with accounts of young bucks fleeing the colony to seek their fortunes in the western fur trade. As proof of this, simply cast your eyes across a map of North America to see the consequences of their migrations: Cities like Detroit, Michigan and Butte, Montana; and progeny that cover the continent. It is estimated that the original 10,000 French colonists produced about 12 million progeny, only half of whom live in Québec. Particularly significant was the great exodus of about 500,000 *Québécois* to the United States between 1850 and 1930. To put this into perspective, this represented an average annual emigration about nine-times as great as the 1991 emigration rate.[19] And this took place for only one reason: There were jobs in the United States, but few at home. As a result, French Canadian names are common in the United States, especially in New England.

But, times have changed. Where brawn and good intentions were all that migrants needed to find work in those days, brain power is now much more important. Moreover, where there were few restrictions on those migrating labourers, the Americans have since restricted access to the very skilled: Ask anyone applying for an American work permit. The *de facto* dominance of the more educated among migrants is also evident in Canadian interprovincial migration statistics.[20] Between 1986 and 1991, of all those who moved from one province to another in Canada:

*   5   percent had less than grade 9 education.

*   12   percent were high school graduates.

*   26   percent had some college/non-university education.

*   34   percent had attended university.

Clearly, the less educated are less likely to migrate today. In the first three categories, Québec does not differ much from other provinces. But, the fourth is another matter. For instance, where 34-percent of Ontario's interprovincial emigrants were university educated, Québec led the nation with 41-percent. Québec is obviously losing its best. Moreover, since *Québécois* tend to be less educated than anglophone Québecers, we would expect to find an echo of this in other migration statistics, and we do. Between 1986 and 1991, 9.2 percent of Québec's anglophone population moved to other provinces versus 2.6 percent of allophones and 0.7 percent of *Québécois*. Since the anglophone exodus was in part the consequence of ethnic cleansing, it is not surprising that the anglophone exodus rate was the highest in Canada outside of agriculturally distressed Saskatchewan.[21] But, what is surprising is that *Québécois* were only about one-quarter as mobile as Québec allophones (0.7 vs 2.6).

I would argue that three factors explain this weak *Québécois* migration pattern. First, *Québécois* were obviously not affected by the ethnic cleansing that targeted anglophones;[22] second, the relatively poorly educated *Québécois* had no choice but to stay home; and third, they swallowed the line fed to them during the Quiet Revolution: By becoming masters in their own house, they would reap great economic benefits. Barnum was right.

To get an even more revealing perspective, let's compare the *Québécois* migration rate with those for other francophones in Canada. First, the *Québécois* migration rate of 0.7 percent of the francophone population (1986-1991) was the lowest of all francophones in Canada; second was New Brunswick with a francophone migration rate of 4.2 percent; Ontario followed with a rate of 8.1 percent. The average for all provinces outside Québec was about 11 percent. Clearly, while *Québécois* were the least mobile people in Canada during this period, other francophones were the most mobile! Thus, although *Québécois* had migrated extensively in the past to find the work that was not available at home, they now find themselves restrained, first by a lack of education, and second by misguided public policies that have not and cannot deliver jobs at home. As a result, *Québécois* have become trapped in their own ghettos with few encouraging prospects because:

* Montreal, the economic engine of Québec, is dying.

* In Montreal, there are two classes: the anglophone-dominated well educated *rich* and the *Québécois*-dominated uneducated *poor*.

* With the anglophones leaving Québec, Montreal will become a haven for the province's losers.

* Because of declining economic prospects in Montreal, people in the hinterland are finding better jobs *on the farm*. This represents a reversal of over two centuries of economic evolution and is probably unique among industrialized nations.

And to top it all off, the people of Québec will suffer the classical fate of suckers: If they vote in the next Referendum as they did in 1995, and Québec is partitioned to reflect their political choice, they will find themselves on the outside looking in as their leaders abandon them. The new, independent state of Laurentia will be formed from areas with secessionist majorities. And the record is clear: Laurentia will include the poorest and least educated areas of the Québec Hinterland, Laval and Franco-Montréal; the residual Canadian province of Québec will include the three northern territories that were transferred to Québec's jurisdiction by the federal government after the 1867 Confederation agreement, all of affluent Anglo-Montreal as well as the most affluent and best educated areas of the Hinterland, Laval, and Franco-Montréal. Obviously, the *Laurentiens* will be relatively poor and uneducated. However, most of the leading members of the *Québécois* élite currently live in those sectors of Montreal that will remain in Canada! Although the honourable among them will emigrate to Laurentia to make the best of a poor result, the less honourable will choose to remain in Montreal. And, you can bet your boots that the latter will outnumber the former. Thus, after following the advice of their leaders by voting to secede, the people will have the pleasure of being abandoned by them and of picking up the pieces by themselves: The sucker's fate. About all that other Canadians can do is to see to it that these scoundrels are punished severely if they ever again raise the spectre of secession in Canada.

Summary

Québec is reaping the disastrous consequences of over two centuries of misguided public leadership, including the deplorable rise of ethnic cleansing as an instrument of public policy. And, the reason is clear: It is in the interest of secessionist *Québécois* to reduce the electoral influence of the generally non-secessionist minority anglophones. Among the instruments of this policy are the province's secessionist movement and its anglophobic language laws. At any rate, the record is clear: The steady growth of the anglophone population of Québec came to an abrupt halt in the 1970s and has been declining steadily ever since. Since the anglophone exodus resembled the pre-Holocaust (1933-38) forced emigration of Jews from Germany, it can be called ethnic cleansing.

There was a parallel head office exodus and it also had serious economic consequences for Québec. The spillover economic effect of the forces that caused these two exoduses was catastrophic: Job-creating business investment in Québec declined and is now running about 15 percent behind Ontario in per capita terms ... every year. As a result, Québec's unemployment rate is consistently half again as high as Ontario's. Strange as it may seem, the Quiet Revolution has had less effect on closing the economic gap with Ontario than had the Church-dominated economy that preceded it.

Since this job gap was caused by generations of investment neglect, it will require decades of extra spending to redress the deficit. But, since language laws and secessionist imperatives are likely to continue dominating public policy, economic decline will continue in Québec.

And, the nature of this decline is evident in the very structure of Québec's economy. That is, economies dominated by the private sector pay better wages than those dominated by the public sector. Since Ontario is less reliant on the public sector than Québec, Ontario workers tend to be better paid.

Moreover, the administration of public spending in Québec is especially profligate and inefficient. For example, had the size of Québec's provincial public service been reduced from bloated to simply fat, the province could have saved enough to increase annual spending in public schools by about 20 percent. Imagine what this extra spending could have done to address Québec's horrendous school drop-out problem! But, keeping thousands of vulnerable kids in school was not considered as important as providing for a bloated public service. The same can be said for investment in Hydro-Québec, than which no Québec institution is more revered ... or more over-rated.

And, to top it all off, the profligate spending practices of Québec's politicians have made *Québécois* the most highly taxed and most indebted people in Canada. Small wonder then that Québec has the highest poverty rate in Canada, Ontario the second lowest.

So much for the public sector, but what about the private sector?

In economies dominated by the private sector, wage earners fare best when services and manufacturing lead the way. Since Québec lags substantially behind Ontario in both areas, the advantage is again with Ontario. Moreover, it appears that the Québec economy will continue to lose ground to Ontario for some time to come which augurs not at all well for Québec's workers. At the present time, income from employment in Québec is running substantially behind Ontario. And when we consider the elements that affect employment income, the prognosis for Québec workers is not promising. But that does not mean that all Québec's workers are equally disadvantaged. The record shows, in fact, that there are three classes of worker in Québec:

1.   Those on a fixed salary whose rates of pay appear to be set by normal competitive forces.

2.   Highly paid hourly rated workers whose rates of pay are set in negotiations with the government of Québec.

3.   Lowly paid hourly rated workers whose rates of pay, although low, are higher than they would otherwise be because of upward pressure from Québec's minimum wage laws.

Clearly, not all workers in Québec fared badly from its public policy initiatives.

Moreover, this inequality among workers also had related class and linguistic consequences. To get at this dimension, I divided Québec and Ontario into three orthodox economic areas:

1.   The dominant metropolitan areas: Montreal Island in Québec, Metro Toronto in Ontario.

2.   Major growth areas: Laval, Metro Québec City and the Outaouais in Québec, and most of the so-called Golden Triangle in Ontario.

3.   The balance of each province, the economic hinterland, which, in

growing economies, normally feeds people and resources either to the dominant metropolis or to the growth areas.

Between 1961 and 1991, the relative economic condition of the average Québec family deteriorated significantly: Where average family income from employment was running 11 percent behind Ontario in 1961, the deficit had increased to 20 percent in 1991; where Québec had the *second* highest poverty rate in Canada in 1961, it had the *highest* rate in 1991. And the reason for this deterioration is clear. Where Ontario decreased its hinterland population in this period, Québec increased the size of its hinterland (Table 7-21). That is, as rural Ontarians were flocking to high paying jobs in "Growing Ontario" or Metro Toronto, rural *Québécois* stayed at home to compete for more modest wages. Clearly, the Quiet Revolution did a better job than the Church in keeping the faithful on the farm.

Moreover, in both provinces, the highest paying jobs moved from the major metropolitan areas (Montreal and Toronto) to the areas of greater economic growth. Since this area is dominated by government spending in Québec and by private sector activity in Ontario, this is further evidence of the division of Québec into two economic solitudes: Those who have access to the public trough and those who do not.

Table 7-21: Québec vs Ontario		
Population Distribution - %		
	1961	1991
Metro Montréal	33	25
Growing Québec	11	15
Hinterland Québec	56	60
Metro Toronto	24	23
Growing Ontario	27	38
Hinterland Ontario	49	39

But, things get worse ... in Montreal.

If Franco-Montreal is defined as those census areas on the Island of Montreal where *Québécois* account for more than half the population, with the balance called Anglo-Montreal, each would have the demographic distribution shown in Figure 7-22. Because the residents of Franco-Montreal were relatively poorly educated in 1991, they earned one-third less than those living in Anglo-Montreal ... the same condition that obtained 30 years earlier! For those who dislike linguistic identifiers, these two Montreals can be re-labelled "Uneducated Montreal" and "Educated Montreal" respectively. In any event, about 38 percent of Franco-Montrealers are living in strained economic conditions that could have been avoided had Québec's schools done a better job, and had

Table 7-22: Montréal Island, 1991		
Demographic Distribution - %		
	Franco Montréal	Anglo Montréal
Francophones	68	34
Anglophones	16	50
Allophones	16	16

Table 7-23:   Québec, 1991

	Pop'n % Prov	French % Pop'n	Emploync $/Family	Poverty Rate-%
Hinterland	60	93	35,000	14
Franco Mtl	19	68	32,000	27
Growth Areas	14	90	41,000	15
Anglo Mtl	7	35	47,000	14

the secessionist movement not discouraged job-creating business investment.

In 1991, about one-third of *Québécois* were economically deprived either because of poor education or inadequate economic development, or both. Moreover, in 1991, Québec was divided into four distinct economic ghettos (Table 7-23). With a growing hinterland isolated from an economically depressed inner city (Franco-Montreal), with the economy in "Growth Areas" dominated by public administrations that are being downsized, and with "Successful Montreal" dominated by anglophones who are being driven from the province, it is not difficult to conclude that Québec is an assortment of economic ghettos. Moreover, since these ghettos owe their existence largely to misguided or mischievous government policies that are not likely to change, it does not auger well for Québec's economic future ... as either a Canadian province or an independent country. To improve their lot, *Québécois* haven't much choice but to imitate many of their ancestors and leave Québec or do something about neutering their leaders.

Migration, especially emigration has always been a constant in the life of the people of Québec. In colonial times, the civil administration and the Church fought losing battles trying to keep the young men at home. In the early years of the 19th-century, seasonal migrations to New England were common. But these seasonal migrations became permanent between 1850 and 1930 when about 500,000 *Québécois* emigrated to the United States to find work. Consequently, the descendants of the original French colonists are about as numerous outside of Québec as within its borders. But, times have changed. Where a strong back was all that migrants needed to find work in those days, proof of adequate brain power is now required with the passport. This is evident even in Canadian inter-provincial statistics: Migrants tend to be relatively well educated. In fact, migrants from Québec tend to be more educated than migrants from other provinces. And since *Québécois* are less educated than anglophone and allophone Québecers, their lower level of skills tends to keep them at home; the migrants are Quebec's well educated anglophones and allophones. Also constraining was the promise of the Quiet Revolution: As masters in their own house, *Québécois* were promised that economic benefits would follow. They believed and waited. The benefits were not forthcoming. They were duped.

Although *Québécois* migrated extensively in the past to find the jobs that were not available in Québec, they now find themselves trapped, first, by misguided public policies that have not produced and cannot produce jobs at home, and second, by a lack of education that makes migrating difficult.

Finally, there appears to be a good correlation between prosperity and education on the one hand, and the 1995 Referendum vote on the other: Those who voted for secession tended to be the poorest and least educated. If the secessionists win the next Referendum, as is probable, and Québec is partitioned, as is likely, the new state of Laurentia will be formed from the poorest and least educated areas of Québec while the residual Canadian province of Québec will include the most affluent and best educated. However, secessionist leaders tend to live in those parts of Québec that are likely to remain in Canada. While the more honourable among them will emigrate to Laurentia, the less honourable will not: The latter will probably outnumber the former. The people of Laurentia will have been abandoned by their leaders. Smells like Barnum, doesn't it?

Notes

1.   Montreal Gazette, January 5, 1996, p. B3.

2.   Ottawa Citizen, July 19, 1997, P. A4.

3.   Nadia Khouri, Qui a peur de Mordecai Richler, (Montréal: Balzac, 1995), p. 72.

4.   Ottawa Citizen, Dec. 18, 1997, p. A4.

5.   La Presse, March 2, 1995, p. B6.

6.   Ottawa Citizen, Nov. 14/15/23 ff, 1996.

7.   Expressions usually require more words in French than in English. One of the rare expressions is the term "convenience store." Its French equivalent is "dépanneur." So convenient is the French term that most anglophone Québecers have adopted it to replace the less elegant English term.

8.   CBC National News, June 19, 1997. Ottawa Citizen, June 20, 1997, p. A5.

9.   Le Jardin Au Bout Du Monde, Note Toponymique, Aout 1997; Commission de Toponymie, Government du Québec.

10.   Josée Legault, L'Invention d'une minorité: Les anglo québécois, (Montréal: Boréal, 1992), p. 97.

11.   D. J. Goldhagen, Hitler's Willing Executioners, (New York: Vintage Books, 1997), p. 139.

12.   From Oct 30, 1996 economic summit in Montreal as reported in the Ottawa Citizen and Montréal Gazette.

13.   This was the hugely expensive Olympics that generated so much fuss. However, its main promoter, Jean Drapeau, the mayor of Montreal, insisted that his Olympics could no more run a deficit than a man could have a baby. The cartoonists had a field day when it in fact did run a large budget deficit. For more on this, read Nick Auf der Maur's The Billion-Dollar Game: Jean Drapeau and the 1976 Olympics.

14.   StatCan Catalogue 15-203, 1990, S13M44.

15.   Derived from StatCan 31-203, 1990, Tables 25, 29.

16.   StatCan 93-331, 1991 Census, T 9. The rate cited by StatCan is actually called the Incidence of Low Income among families. Although the poverty rate may be lower than this Low Income Rate, its relative inter-provincial position would be the same as the relative Low Income position.

17.   Poverty is here defined by the Statcan definition: Incidence of Low Income and can be found in StatCan, 1991 Census, 95-326, 95-338, Part B, Vol 1.

18.   StatCan, 1961 Census, 99-544 T 8.1.

19.   500,000 over 80 years works out to about 0.60 percent of the average population of Québec during that period; in 1991, emigration from Québec accounted for about 0.07 percent of the population (StatCan 91-002, Oct-Dec 1991, T 4).

20.   StatCan 1991 Census, 93-322, T3.

21.   StatCan 1991 Census 93-322, T4; 1986 Census 93-102.

22.   Given the 2.6 percent exodus among Québec allophones, one would have expected, based on experience in other provinces, that the Québec anglophone migration rate would have been about 4.2 percent. Thus, it would appear that ethnic cleansing probably accounted for the balance, about 5 percent.

8

CONSEQUENCES: THE ÉLITE ARE AT THE TROUGH

Overview

Now comes the sordid part of this sorry tale.

So far, we have seen how the *Québécois* élite impoverished their own kin by promoting and implementing misguided social policies. First came the Church which laid the base for this unfortunate social evolution by promoting the preservation of faith and language at the expense of bread and butter. The Church was displaced in the 1960s by secular nationalists who gave us the Quiet Revolution where faith was dropped from the lexicon, concern for language accentuated, and the secession of Québec from Canada became imperative. The Quiet Revolution was also supposed to visit prosperity upon all *Québécois*.

During the Church's hegemony, the average *Québécois* family still succeeded in improving its economic lot, gradually closing the gap with Ontario. The admonitions of bishops could not compete with the desire of the faithful for jobs. But this gradual economic improvement came to an end during the Quiet Revolution. Between 1961 and 1991, the average Québec family lost ground with Ontario, going from an 11 percent income deficit in 1961 to a 20 percent deficit in 1991. Moreover, since Québec's poverty rate deteriorated from Canada's second worst in 1961 to its worst in 1991, it is obvious that the Quiet Revolution did not improve the relative economic position of *Québécois*.

But, in the same period, how did the *élite* fare financially? Note that the remuneration of all members of this élite was influenced, directly or indirectly, by the same public policies that impoverished the people.

The Church

Although the contribution of the Church to the impoverishment of the people is obvious and beyond dispute, its concurrent enrichment is not evident. Consistent with the history of the Church elsewhere, the Québec Church became rich in assets that are of little use for much else. The Cistine Chapel in Rome, for example, is probably worth several fortunes, but would the Church dare offer it for sale? Who would buy it? And for what purpose?

Consequently, as the faithful abandoned the Québec Catholic Church, it has been stuck with expensive real estate, a diminishing income base, and a growing inability to pay its bills: It costs a great deal to heat a house of worship built to medieval scale. As a result, some churches have been demolished. And the end is not yet in sight. Thus, I must conclude that, although the Church may have been largely responsible for the impoverishment of Quebec in the past, it did not appear to enrich itself very much in the process. But that should not prevent us from condemning it for its lack of simple wisdom, or for its abuse of the power that God allegedly gave it.

POLITICIANS

In 1993 the *Indemnities and Allowances Commission of the Manitoba Legislature* conducted an interprovincial study of salaries paid to members of Canada's ten provincial legislatures. The Commission had been asked to handle the hot potato that surfaces every now and again in legislatures everywhere: How to increase the compensation of politicians without suffering at the polls. The Commission tabled its report in March 1994, predictably tossing the hot potato back to the members of the Legislature. Apart from their use to justify pay increases, the report's statistics were quite revealing of Québec largesse. What was particularly striking in the news item that brought this obscure report to my attention, was the astonishing fact that, where members of the Québec Legislature were the highest paid in Canada, welfare benefits in Québec were among the lowest. And the Québec Legislature set both the salaries of its members and the welfare benefits of their disadvantaged kin! Whatever happened, thought I, to the vaunted solidarity between the *Québécois* élite and ordinary *Québécois*? Something was starting to smell. After consulting the actual report, the smell became a stench!

The data in the report comparing Québec with Ontario were especially revealing (Table 8-1). Remember that these two provincial economies are structurally similar to one another. Thus, few economists would be astonished with *some* of these data. For instance, if an economy is 15.2 percent less productive than its neighbour, wages and income would normally be similarly lower. That average weekly earnings in Québec are only 7.1 percent lower than in Ontario instead of 15.2 percent, is probably a tribute to factors other than the theoretical ability of the economy to pay. These include factors such as unions, government regulations and other competitive imperatives. However, when we factor in the unemployed and those on welfare, we arrive at per capita personal income which is 13.3 percent lower in Québec, a figure relatively close to the 15.2 percent deficit in GDP. Thus, the average *Québécois* is in fact being *paid* an amount commensurate with the ability of the economy to pay.

How then does one justify the premiums paid to Québec's legislators? For instance, how does one justify paying members of the Québec Legislature a 28 percent premium over their Ontario counterparts when welfare recipients are receiving 25 percent less? Since Québec's economy is, in absolute

Table 8-1:	Report of the Manitoba Legislature		
	Québec Compared To Ontario		
GDP Per Capita	15.2	%	Lower
Personal Income	13.3	%	Lower
Weekly Earnings	7.1	%	Lower
Minimum Wage	7.8	%	Lower
Welfare Benefits	25.2	%	Lower
Provincial Legislature			
Members	28.1	%	Higher
Ministers	38.0	%	Higher
Premier	26.0	%	Higher

Source: Manitoba Legislature Committee on Compensation, 1994

terms, about 30 percent smaller than Ontario's, it is not because they have more to manage. On the other hand, since the Québec economy is 15.2 percent less productive than Ontario's, legislators in Québec may have more difficult jobs and thus deserve their premiums. Plausible perhaps except that the evidence shows that these politicians are largely responsible for this productivity gap. So why should they be paid a premium to solve problems of their own making?

Although members of the Québec Legislature have traditionally urged all *Québécois* to make financial sacrifices for the common good, they have clearly dispensed themselves from this noble invitation. To conclude that their salary premiums suggest lack of solidarity with other less fortunate *Québécois*, would of course be considered by them as an insult to all *Québécois*. This is not a surprising rejoinder since offended virgins predictably claim the moral high ground whenever they are caught with their pants down in the wrong places. Reminds me of the joke about the Irish priest who, when caught leaving the brothel, claimed that he was only trying to save the souls of the girls inside!

In the final analysis, it was the Manitoba Legislature that propelled me toward this polemic. As I dug further into the historical record, I discovered that the phenomenon described in the Manitoba report was not unique. The same conditions applied to many others among the *Québécois* élite. The élite, the people who urged the public to make sacrifices to safeguard and promote their unique culture, saw to it that the people, not the élite, made the sacrifices. Let's look at what else I found in the public record.

Wage Premiums: Public versus Private Sector

Using data from the 1991 Census, the Canadian Federation of Independent Business (CFIB) measured the wage gap between the public and private sectors in 1990. The jobs measured were loosely called office jobs: They included clerks, secretaries, economists and administrators but excluded occupations such as carpenters, plumbers and geologists. Not surprisingly, the CFIB found that all governments paid their workers a premium over their private sector equivalents. The Federal Government, for example, paid its workers an average premium of 13.9 percent over the private sector; provincial governments a premium of 9.8 percent; municipal governments a premium of 8.0 percent; provincial institutions a premium of 11.5 percent. Since the last three are directly or indirectly the responsibility of provincial governments, I have combined them to determine average premiums paid by provincial governments (Table 8-2).

It would appear at first blush that

Table 8-2: Wage Premiums	
Provincial Administration versus Private Sector	
Quebec	13.2 %
Manitoba	11.1 %
Saskatchewan	8.6 %
Ontario	6.3 %
PEI	6.2 %
NFLD	5.7 %
NB	4.8 %
Nova Scotia	4.0 %
Alberta	0.6 %
BC	0.6 %
Source: CFIB, Wage Watch, Nov. 1993	

the public sector was paid much more in Québec than in Ontario. Not so. According to the CFIB study, average public sector salaries in Quebec and Ontario were almost identical, $34,300 versus $34,555. On the other hand, the average private sector salary was 6.9 percent lower in Quebec than in Ontario, $30,275 versus $32,505. Thus, even though the average private sector wage in Quebec was lower than in Ontario, public sector workers in Québec were able to keep themselves abreast of their Ontario counterparts, 13.2 percent ahead of the Québec private sector. Not surprisingly, public sector unions in Québec have generally cosied up to their provincial government benefactor on matters of mutual interest: Secession and Ottawa bashing, for instance. Clearly, the various governments of Québec have been more effective than those in Ontario in shielding their public sector employees from competitive market forces.

Bloated Bureaucracies

Now let us consider the Québec public service from another perspective, how it fared relative to other claimants for public funds. That is, how did spending on public administration compare with spending on services to the public? If we express the 1993 provincial GDP in per capita terms, we find that the Provincial Administration GDP was 46 percent *greater* in Quebec than in Ontario while the Public Services GDP was 6 percent *lower*. These public services include such items as education, health and welfare.[1] If, as was established in the CFIB study, public sector salaries in these two provinces were roughly equal, it would appear that *Québécois* were being deprived of services to finance a bloated provincial administration. That is, *Québécois* were not only under serviced, they had to pay for a bloated provincial administration (46 percent overstaffed by the looks of it), each of whose members received a 13.2 percent wage premium over comparable jobs in the Québec private sector!

For how long, you may wonder, has this bloated condition afflicted the Québec provincial administration? In 1970 Quebec and Ontario were at par in per capita terms in this area. By 1976, Quebec had passed Ontario in absolute as well as per capita terms. In 1980, Quebec's per capita costs were 58 percent ahead of Ontario. Then, the spirit of moderation or fatigue at the trough must have set in because, by 1983, the excess was down to 47 percent. In 1990, the excess was down further to 36 percent. But, by 1993 it was back up to 46 percent![2]

University Professors

Now let us look at the wages paid to particular groups, starting with university teachers. Among academics, Quebec leads Canada in every category (Table 8-3). Since the Québec statistics do not include anglophone McGill University, these data can be taken as representative of francophone institutions in Quebec.

These wages are set by normal collective bargaining. In every

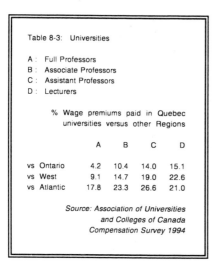

Table 8-3:   Universities

A :   Full Professors
B :   Associate Professors
C :   Assistant Professors
D :   Lecturers

% Wage premiums paid in Quebec
universities versus other Regions

	A	B	C	D
vs Ontario	4.2	10.4	14.0	15.1
vs West	9.1	14.7	19.0	22.6
vs Atlantic	17.8	23.3	26.6	21.0

Source: Association of Universities
and Colleges of Canada
Compensation Survey 1994

case, although the official employers are the universities, the effective employers are provincial governments. According to the record, the governments of Québec have been reluctant to control university spending. Something of the sacred cow syndrome at work, probably. Hence, those who find themselves at such bountiful troughs tend to nourish themselves with gusto. In Québec there has been an added incentive to keep the trough well stocked: Academics have tended to support the secessionist positions of the provincial government of the day. In fact, you will have to hunt far and wide before finding a *Québécois* academic willing to admit publicly that the secessionist emperor is naked. Apart from Pierre Trudeau who stepped forward in the mid-1960s and Stephane Dion in the mid-1990s, I see no obvious candidates.

Public School Teachers

When you step down the teaching ladder into primary and secondary schools, you see a similar picture (Table 8-4). The hourly rates indicated were derived from various collective agreements.[3] Here we see the results of the two quite different collective bargaining practices. In the provinces within column "A," teachers' unions bargain directly with only one employer, the provincial government; those in column "B" deal with individual school boards. For instance, there were 11 collective agreements in Alberta, 18 in British Columbia, 88 in Ontario and 6 in Manitoba.

Table 8-4: Public School Teachers

Wages ($ per hour) paid to
public school teachers in 1994

A		B	
Sask.	18.86	Alberta	21.24
Quebec	18.32	BC	21.19
Atlantic	17.80	Ontario	21.06
		Manitoba	19.82

Source: Labour Canada, Bureau
of Labour Information, 1994

Since the essence of collective bargaining is for the union to play one employer off against another, the greater the number of employers the better it is for the union. For example, before the process of collective bargaining with public school teachers' unions was centralized in Quebec in the early 1970s, there was great competition among school boards for teachers. Premiums were offered to entice teachers to leave one jurisdiction for another. I know personally of teachers who increased their salaries simply by moving from one school board to another within Montreal!

In Table 8-4, the average hourly rate was about 14 percent higher in column "B" than in column "A." This does not mean that the teachers in column "A" were underpaid; it may mean the reverse, that those in column "B" were overpaid; I make no claim for either option. However, I would argue that the wage premium in column "B" is in fact the extra cost to the taxpayer of allowing individual school boards to negotiate their own collective agreements, of allowing strong provincial unions to negotiate with relatively weak local school boards. Similarly, the lower wages in column "A" are the result of strong employers, provincial governments, dealing with weaker unions.

Suffice to say here that teachers in Québec are not under-paid, that they are instead paid at a rate competitive with those in other provinces with similar collective bargaining regimes.

Policemen and Firemen

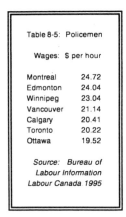

Table 8-5: Policemen

Wages: $ per hour

Montreal	24.72
Edmonton	24.04
Winnipeg	23.04
Vancouver	21.14
Calgary	20.41
Toronto	20.22
Ottawa	19.52

Source: Bureau of Labour Information Labour Canada 1995

The police form another interesting group. Here again Quebec leads the way (Table 8-5). Of particular significance is the 22 percent premium paid to policemen in Montreal relative to those in Toronto. Bear in mind that, at the conclusion of the next round of collective bargaining, it is quite likely that those on the lower end of the scale will cite those at the top to justify improvements in their relatively low rates. That is how the process works. It is clear, however, that policemen in Montreal have kept themselves more than competitive with their counterparts elsewhere in Canada ... sometimes using less than honourable tactics. Some may recall the infamous firemen's strike in Montréal in 1974 when policemen were also trying to negotiate a new collective agreement with the City of Montréal. I still retain a vivid memory of a fire set by thugs in the Griffintown area of Montréal as policemen stood by and watched! These policemen--and firemen--received substantial pay increases shortly thereafter. Sounds like the extortionists were rewarded.

Municipal Workers

And on it goes. Inside workers at the city of Montreal led the nation as well. In April of 1996, Premier Bouchard claimed that municipal workers were going to have to carry their share of the sacrifices required to bring public finances under control. He said that municipal workers were being paid 27 percent more than their colleagues working in the Québec public service.[4] Reporting on the impasse in labour negotiations between the city of Montréal and its 4,060 blue collar workers, *Le Devoir* noted that the union objected to the city's desire to reduce this total by the 1,000 workers it did not need.[5] Thus, Montréal not only had about 33 percent more blue collar workers than it needed, it was paying them 27 percent more than necessary. Consequently, the taxpayers of Montreal were paying about 60 percent more for blue collar services than was necessary! To be quite frank, slothfulness among municipal workers in Québec is legendary. Some readers may recall a news item in early 1996 where the mayor of Sillery, a suburb of Québec City, was required by the court to re-employ workers she demonstrably did not need. Others may recall the infamous news photos of municipal workers in Montreal asleep for hours in their City of Montréal truck parked outside a garage: They were waiting for someone to come and fix a flat tire! Had they paid the nearby garage--about 15 feet from the snoozers--to fix the tire, it would have cost the city about $50 instead of the thousand or so in wasted wages and truck down-time. It would also have saved Montréal the embarrassment of having the world giggle at this hilarious photo.

Private Sector

But, let no one conclude that it was only in the public sector that workers benefitted from government largesse in Québec: There were a few winners in the private sector, as well. Described earlier were hourly-rated workers in the construction industry, for instance, whose rates of pay were set by government decree: They earned about 10 percent more than their counterparts in Ontario. At the lower end of the hourly rated scale were those earning the government-imposed minimum wage rate, a rate greater than the equivalent rate prevailing in Ontario. That this relatively high minimum wage rate is coincidentally the cause of job losses is, of course, an unfortunate consequence.

Finally, there are those *Québécois* business executives whose positions were secured as a consequence of the ethnic cleansing policies of the government of Québec. Not a very nice way to advance one's career, but opportunity does not always knock in honourable ways.

Summary

During the period of Church hegemony, the economic lot of the people of Québec continued to improve despite the attempts of the clergy to keep the faithful *on the farm*. By their own efforts, the people managed to gradually reduce Québec's family income gap with Ontario. When the Church ceded the torch to secular nationalists in the 1960s, income from employment for the average Québec family was running about 11 percent below Ontario. In 1991, this had deteriorated to a 20 percent deficit. During the same 30-year period, the *Québécois* élite improved their economic circumstances considerably. Those in the public and para-public sectors, for example, were earning salaries in 1991 that put them up to 30 percent ahead of their opposite numbers in the Ontario public sector and in the Québec private sector. In addition, bloated public sector bureaucracies sucked scarce funds from other more worthy areas such as public education. Government-imposed wage rates also provided some private sector workers with wage premiums. Some private sector executives also benefitted from the consequences of ethnic cleansing.

Notes

1.　StatCan 15-203, 1984-1993.

2.　StatCan 61-202, 1983; 15-203, 1971-84; 15-203, 1984-1993.

3.　Bureau of Labour Information, Labour Canada, Special Report on Current Wages in Major Collective Agreements. March 7, 1995.

4.　CBC radio news April 1996.

5.　*Le Devoir*, May 16, 1996, p. A3.

9

SUMMATION TO THE JURY

It is now up to the jury to decide whether the *Québécois* élite are indeed patriots or scoundrels? If they are judged to be patriots, they deserve the highest public honours. On the other hand, if they are found to be scoundrels, they deserve something more appropriate to their status. Although tar and feathers come to mind, I will make more practical suggestions later in this summation. From the evidence presented here we must conclude that:

1. The Church and secular nationalists (the *Québécois* élite) have traditionally urged all *Québécois* to make financial sacrifices to advance their common cultural interests.

2. Because of the inadequate educational services provided by these élite, illiteracy and the level of education among *Québécois* are among the worst in Canada.

3. Because the public policies pursued by these élite discouraged job-creating business investment, the normal development of the Québec economy has been retarded. As a result, not only has family income in Québec lagged behind Ontario, even deteriorating between 1961 and 1991, the poverty rate in Québec is the worst in Canada.

4. As the policies pursued by these élite impoverished the people, they concurrently enriched the élite. For example, *Québécois* provincial politicians awarded themselves the highest salaries in Canada. Moreover, although *Québécois* workers were contending with relatively low wages and high unemployment, the *Québécois* élite, most of whom are employed in the taxpayer-supported public and para-public sectors, were being paid wages that were not only competitive with their Ontario equivalents, they exceeded substantially those paid for equivalent work in the Québec private sector.

5. To advance their secessionist agenda, these élite deliberately misled the people, enacted abusive language laws, resorted to ethnic cleansing and cheated at the polls.

6. The consequence of this secessionist agenda will likely be the partition of Québec into the independent state of Laurentia and the residual Canadian province of Québec. The poorest and least educated *Québécois* will find themselves in Laurentia while the best educated and most affluent will remain in Québec.

7. At partition, these élite will almost certainly remain in Montreal in the Canadian province of Québec, thus betraying their supporters by abandoning them to fend for themselves in the economically feeble state of Laurentia.

These are conclusions concerning which there can be no dispute.

Nor can there be much dispute concerning the obvious: Because of their collective responsibility for Québec's economic, social and political mess, these élite do not merit the patriot's mantle. But whether they all merit the scoundrel's horns is another matter. I urge the jury to award this designation to some and not to others. That is, although the responsibility of all of the élite for Québec's deplorable situation is clear, some are more responsible than others.

For instance, although the Church is clearly responsible for the origins of this malaise, I would argue that there is no point in seeking to punish it. For example, much as you might wish to, there would be no point heaping opprobrium upon your pet cat after it followed its instincts and devoured the canary: It did not know any better. Similarly, the Church should not be punished for having caused the faithful to remain under-educated and poor. In my view, because it was following its instincts, it simply did not know any better. If you doubt this, try convincing so-called true believers in any religion that God may not be on their side. Their faith simply makes them impervious to anything but their own interpretation of the word of God. Thus, the only remedy available is first, to ignore the Church from now on, and second, to ensure that it is never again permitted to care for the canaries. I would make much the same argument to excuse others among the élite, particularly those who found themselves too close to the public trough. For example, although I deplore the past tactics used by policemen and construction workers in Québec to extort their high salaries, their tactics were similar to those used by strong unions everywhere. In other words, they followed their instincts ... something like cats. So also with those working in Québec's bloated public sector bureaucracies: Why would they refuse well paying jobs?

But we cannot excuse those who, knowing better, nevertheless promoted the development and adoption of polices that impoverished the people, and who will certainly betray their supporters as they abandon them to fend for themselves after Québec is partitioned. Particularly contemptible are those who enriched themselves in the process. In this category I include:

*   Many *Québécois* nationalists.

*   Some *Québécois* journalists.

*   Most Québécois provincial politicians.

Since they all knew or should have known that the policies they were touting
could not advance the interests of the people, they of course merit special
consideration in the scoundrel sweepstakes. But even here I would distinguish
between those who actively promoted this charade and those who simply went
along with it. In the follower category I would include most *Québécois*
nationalists, an uncertain number of *Québécois* journalists and a few *Québécois*
provincial politicians. In the active and culpable category are:

*   *Québécois* nationalist leaders.

*   *Le Devoir.*

*   Leaders of Québec's provincial political parties.

Although these all deserve to be called scoundrels and dealt with appropriately,
those meriting particular attention are the province's political leaders. Not only
did they deliberately mislead and impoverish the people, they carried out a
program of ethnic cleansing, cheated at the polls, paid themselves and their
fellow travellers the highest salaries in Canada ... and sent the bill to the people
they were cheating, their own kin, people who are among the poorest in Canada!
Who but scoundrels would act this way?

Having established the proper credentials of the *Québécois* élite, the issue now
becomes: "*What is to be done about their disgraceful legacy, and by whom?*"
Well, it depends first, on who you are, and second, on your political perspective.
That is, first, are you a *Québécois* or a non-*Québécois* Canadian, and second,
what is your position on national unity? If you are a *Québécois*, you have a
special problem: Whether Québec ends up inside or outside of Canada, you
must decide what to do about the relatively poor quality of life that your élite
have foisted on you. In other words, if you are satisfied, do nothing. If, on the
other hand, you are not satisfied, you have no choice but to deal harshly with
these élite. As a strict minimum, I recommend that dissatisfied *Québécois*:

1.   In general, let their political leaders know that they, the people, are fed
         up with the self-serving bleating of *Québécois* nationalists and their
         mouthpiece, *Le Devoir*. That is, they must no longer allow the interests
         of the people to be subordinated to those of the élite.

2.   In particular, demand that the government of Québec (or Laurentia)
         make their public education system and business investment climate
         competitive with Ontario's.

Again, please note that this minimum stance by the people of Québec has
nothing to do with the potential secession of Québec from Canada. In other

words, unless the people's social and political environments improve, it will not matter whether they live in Québec, Canada or in the independent state of Laurentia: They will remain relatively disadvantaged in either case. That said, I would argue that if *Québécois* do not make common cause with other Canadians in the resolution of the so-called "Québec Question", they are not likely to realize even these minimum goals.

For those who have been spared exposure to this thorny item, the Québec Question is: "*What does Québec want, and how does Canada comply with its demands ... without having to repeal the laws of gravity?*" And, let us be clear: Québec's demands have everything to do with providing the *Québécois* élite with power and status and very little to do with providing the people with bread and butter. For example, designating Québec as a "*Distinct Society*" might do wonders for some nationalist egos, but it will not add one cent to the income of the average *Québécois* family, or reduce Québec's nation-leading poverty rate by one family, or reduce the number of school drop-outs by one student, or provide one iota of extra protection for Québec's allegedly fragile culture.

But, say some, "*Distinct Society*" status would convey new powers on the government of Québec that would permit it to do something about the poor economic condition of *Québécois*. Do what, pray? The relative poverty of *Québécois* has been caused by two factors for which the government of Québec has always been responsible: An inadequate education system that produced a relatively unskilled workforce, and a poisoned social climate that discouraged job-creating business investment. Clearly, Québec requires no new powers to deal with issues that already lie within its jurisdiction.

As an example of something that was high on image but low on practicality, consider the power to control foreign immigration to Québec that was transferred to that province by Ottawa. This was considered a major attempt to recognize Québec's unique need to favour francophone immigrants. Accordingly, officials now admit immigrants to Québec based on criteria determined by Québec. However, since Québec is still part of Canada, an immigrant refused entry there can still enter Canada legally in Toronto where Québec guidelines do not apply, get on a bus and in a few hours be in Québec ... legally! Clearly, Québec's control over immigration cannot exclude from that province any Canadian resident who wishes to live there. That this power serves no purpose other than to assuage the egos of *Québécois* politicians and their apologists should be obvious. Equally obvious is the fact that it does nothing to improve the living standards of the people of Québec. But then again, it makes a lot of sense to set up at Ottawa's expense the immigration service that will be required when Québec secedes from Canada.

Within this political environment, it is easy to see how failure to comply with any demand from the government of Québec is considered to be an attempt by Ottawa to humiliate all *Québécois*: This is the well known, impregnable, offended virgin defense. Since the record suggests that Québec refuses to be satisfied, the question then becomes "*Do we continue the charade or bring it to a close?*" The answer of course is: "*Close it, but how?*"

If you share the view of most federal politicians, you will do nothing except muddle along, tell *Québécois* that all Canadians love them, pay ever increasing tribute to Québec and hope for the best. Some may recognize this as the so-called Plan-A in the federalist arsenal. This is the same approach that led to two referenda on secession, the more recent coming within a whisker of seeing Canada destroyed. It is a no-brainer then to conclude that it will lead to a third Referendum in the near future when *Québécois* politicians will put another misleading question to the people, and then interpret an affirmative vote as one favouring the secession of Québec from Canada. And, based on past experience, we should expect a secessionist vote in excess of 50 percent next time, following which the government of Québec will unilaterally and illegally proclaim Québec's independence. Then, all hell will break lose, Canada will be thrown into disarray, our federal politicians will wring their hands in anguished dismay, and the *Québécois* élite will have proven once again that Canadian politicians really are impotent dummies.

If, on the other hand, you are able to discriminate between night and day, you will find that there are other options. But first, you must know with whom you are dealing. That is, when you ask "*What does Québec want?*" you must establish what Québec you are talking about. If you really mean "*What do Québécois politicians want?*" your answer is to be found in the historical record: Constitutional negotiations since about 1960 show that, short of granting Québec outright independence, nothing will satisfy them. And, the reason is simple: If the government of Québec is in the hands of the secessionists why would it accept anything short of independence; if so-called federalists are in power, they are so terrified of being called soft on Ottawa that they end up acting like secessionists anyway! So, there is no point wasting much time on Québec's provincial politicians! However, if you mean "*What do the people of Québec want and how do you deal with them?*", the answer is more complex. On the one hand, *Québécois* are like anyone else: They eat the same food, pay the same bills, have the same dreams, want the same opportunities to provide for themselves and their families, and so on. On the other hand, they are unique: Among other things, they have been duped for more than two-centuries by their élite.

So, how do you *undupe* them? "*Simple,*" say our federal politicians, "*Plan-A will provide them with the information needed to counter the lies told to them by Québécois politicians, intellectuals and teachers since 1960.*" So, in the four years or so between the last Referendum and the next, "villainous" Ottawa is going to turn the tables on the secessionists who control the schools and the media? Get real! Who but idiots, bleeding hearts and the intellectually infirm would support Plan-A? *Québécois* secessionists, obviously! Then, there is Plan-B, the so-called tough love approach. It could be very practical in *unduping* the people of Québec ... if there was anything tough in it.

So far, all I have seen is fluff. And, unless there is a ground-swell of outrage from concerned Canadians, we are not likely to ever see anything more substantial as Canada goes down the drain. On the other hand, an effective Plan-B would have to be based on experience-based wisdom. That is:

1   Unless the next Québec Referendum question is clear and unambiguous, *Québécois* secessionists will win the day.

2.   Since Québec's provincial politicians are not interested in resolving their demands within Canada, there is no point trying to appease them.

3.   Therefore, the government of Canada must appeal directly to the people of Québec with the unvarnished truth, especially as regards the unpalatable consequences of secession.

With these guidelines in place, we should be able to prepare an effective Plan-B with a clear objective and the procedures required to attain it.

My ideal objective is to retain all of Québec within Canada, my preferred approach Plan-A. Unfortunately, Canada lost the propaganda war in Québec by not competing with secessionists for the hearts and minds of *Québécois*. Hence, when the next Québec-sponsored Referendum takes place, Canada will not have had time to overcome the years of false advertising in Québec. As a result, the third Referendum will be a repeat of the first two with one notable exception: This time the secessionists will win. So much for that objective and Plan-A! Thus, I would conclude, first, that the government of Canada must control the next Referendum question, and second, that retaining all of Québec within Canada may not be possible. Hence, my practical objective is to save as much of Québec as possible; my procedure Plan-B with teeth. That is, the government of Canada must take the issue to the people in a national Referendum where it would propose amending our constitution to:

1.   Make promotion of secession in Canada a seditious act.

2.   Make illegal those laws, such as much of Québec's language laws, whose clear intent is (a) to interfere with people's legitimate personal freedoms, and (b) to cleanse inconvenient people from Québec.

3.   Provide the people of Québec with the choice of staying in Canada or leaving before items one and two are enacted.

If Canadians rejected these constitutional amendments, the government of Canada would then have no choice but to revert to the discredited Plan-A and prepare for chaos after the next Québec-controlled Referendum. Clearly, it is in Canada's interests that these constitutional amendments be approved. Then, the government of Canada should put the following question to the people of Québec in a federally controlled Referendum:

Do you want to secede from Canada to form an independent country?

Those ridings in Québec that voted to secede would thenceforth be considered foreign territory and be treated accordingly. On the other hand, the new Canadian province of Québec would include the three northern territories that were transferred to Québec by Ottawa in 1898, 1912 and 1927, as well as those ridings that rejected secession. The territorial integrity of the new Canadian province of Québec would be guaranteed by the government of Canada.

It is likely that the government of Québec, *Le Devoir*, assorted intellectuals and nationalist groups would organize a boycott. Let them. But, let the informed democratic will of the people of Québec prevail ... at last. Let the people decide whether they wish to continue following the self-serving dictates of their élite or start looking after themselves. The results will be decisive. Those who voted to leave and form the new state of Laurentia should be satisfied; those who voted to stay could then help the rest of us try to put Canada back together again. Although Canadians might be reluctantly satisfied with the results, how would the new *Laurentiens* feel? Betrayed probably.

In those areas of Québec with secessionist majorities in the 1995 Referendum, the average levels of education and economic well-being were the lowest in the province. On the other hand, the best educated and financially best off lived in those areas that rejected secession. Thus, under partition, the new state of Laurentia would include the poorest areas of the Québec Hinterland, Laval and Franco-Montréal; the new Canadian province of Québec would include the three northern aboriginal territories, all of Anglo-Montreal as well as the most affluent parts of the Québec Hinterland, Laval and Franco-Montréal. Ironically, many of the most influential secessionist leaders live in those areas of Montréal that would remain in Canada after partition. And, as argued earlier, they are not likely to leave Montréal for Laurentia. Thus, having sold the people of Québec a shoddy bill of goods, the *Québécois* élite will simply abandon them. Pointing this out to the people of Québec fits nicely into Plan-B.

But, however sound Plan-B may be, it contains one potentially fatal flaw: It is not likely to be implemented by a federal political party whose power-base is in Québec ... unless, of course, the party leader is called Trudeau. It will certainly never be implemented by leaders like Brian Mulroney, Joe Clark or Jean Charest. Since the partition of Québec would obviously cost some Québec federal politicians their careers, they are not likely to become willing proponents of a plan that might require some of them to commit political suicide. Moreover, since Plan-B would also require them to criticize some of the provisions of Québec's sacred language laws and challenge many *Québécois* myths, it would require of them a level of wisdom and courage not heretofore evident. Finally, since it is accepted conventional wisdom that no party can govern Canada without controlling the majority of seats in Québec, Plan-B may indeed be fatally flawed. In fact, not since 1917 has a political party held power in Ottawa that didn't also hold the majority of seats in Québec ... until the 1993 and 1997 federal elections, that is! Therefore, conventional wisdom is wrong: It *is* possible to rule without majority support from Québec ... if there is the will to do so. Sorting out this thorny issue is the challenge facing our federal politicians and the Canadian electorate.

Although there appears to be ample support among non-*Québécois* Canadians for this approach to resolving the Québec Question, it cannot be that straightforward for *Québécois*. For example, the historical record indicates fairly clearly that *Québécois* will follow the dictates of their leaders, no matter what the probable outcome; but the same record also indicates that, unless they free themselves from their self-serving leaders, they cannot improve their lot in life. So, unless something happens to cause the people to reject their élite, *Québécois* will remain disadvantaged either in the existing province of Québec or in the newly independent state of Laurentia. Since the partition of the existing province of Québec under Plan-B would have the effect of silencing this meddlesome élite, it would give some of the people a chance to pursue their own interests for a change. Thus, Québec urgently needs a new Moses to challenge its élite and lead the people from their misery ... within or outside of Canada. Failing that, it needs an external shock so dramatic that its impact would overwhelm the influence of the *Québécois* élite: Plan-B with teeth! That Plan-B would represent a clear, unambiguous choice is obvious. It would represent a departure from the past when ambiguity and misinformation were the norm; it would give the people the choice of overthrowing their élite or of continuing to succumb to them; for the first time, it would encourage the people to make an informed choice. If they chose to follow their current leaders, so be it; if instead they chose to overthrow, or to at least ignore them, God Herself will be pleased. Although hoping that they select the second option, I am prepared to live with either one. So also, I believe, are most Canadians.

This concludes the summation of the evidence and some of the remedies that flow from it. As a member of the jury, it is now up to you. What say you? Are the Québécois élite patriots or scoundrels?

===

30

POSTSCRIPT

Those interested in further study of Québec are fortunate to have a mountain of scholarship available to them: Much of it is worth reading. To provide a basis for separating the wheat from the chaff, I will recommend a few books that fairly reasonably describe the historical climate. Then, I will suggest a few current commentators whose views are worth noting. Remember that *worth noting* does not necessarily mean *worth accepting*.

The first book is <u>Feudal Society and Colonization: The Historiography of New France</u> by Roberta Hamilton (Langdale, 1988). To properly understand the underlying social and political currents in Québec, this short book is a must. Hamilton argues, first, that France's feudal structure was carried over to New France; second, that the main characteristic of this colonial feudalism was its hierarchical class structure; and third, that some of the effects of this hierarchical structure linger with us still. Some may trace the *Québécois* propensity to remain faithful to their leaders to these feudal tendencies.

The second book, also short, is <u>The Role of the Church in New France</u> by Cornelius. J. Jaenen (McGraw-Hill Ryerson, 1976). Though he credits the colonial Church with considerable clout, Jaenen nevertheless argues that its legendary influence was just that, legendary. In fact, the Church was constrained by the civil administration and bedeviled by the less-than-cloistered needs of a struggling frontier settlement. This book will put the Québec Catholic Church into proper historical perspective.

The third book is <u>An Abridgement of Lord Durham's Report: Report on the Affairs of British North America</u> by John George Lambton, Earl of Durham. Published in 1839, Durham's report dealt with his investigation of the turmoil in Britain's North American colonies in 1837. Edited by G. M. Craig, this short abridgement was published by Carleton in 1982/92. Although Durham is a bad word in Québec, his description of the social, economic and political scene in Québec (Lower Canada) at that time was brilliant in my view. That his forecast of the consequences of his assimilationist recommendations was wildly inaccurate is another matter, one that detracts not at all from the accuracy of his description of conditions at that time. Moreover, much of what Durham described then is echoed in modern Québec.

The fourth book is <u>Anglophobie: Made in Québec</u> by William Johnson (Stanké, 1991) where the history of Québec anglophobia is laid out. Johnson argues that anglophobia is a constant in the literature of Québec going back to the mid-19th century, the period described by Durham.

The fifth book is <u>The Traitor and the Jew</u> by Esther Delisle (Robert Davies, 1993). In this extract from her doctoral thesis, Delisle describes the antisemitism of the 1930s that was evident in *Le Devoir* as well as in the rants of Lionel Groulx and some nationalist groups in Québec. This may explain part of the xenophobia that still exists in modern Québec.

The sixth is William Johnson's <u>A Canadian Myth: Québec, Between Canada and the Illusion of Utopia</u> (Robert Davies, 1994). A sequel to

Anglophobie, this book describes how anglophobia was and remains at the core of public policy development in Québec. Johnson argues that "*although Québec freed itself from the tyranny of an anti-modern religion and anti-democratic educational institutions during the partial Quiet Revolution in the 1960s, many archaic attitudes survived the regenerative ferment, including anglophobia, which was quickly married to the vision of the ethnic state to become Québec's official ideology.*"

The seventh and final book is Reed Scowen's A Different Perspective: The English in Québec in the 1990s (Maxwell Macmillan, 1991). By describing the language-related environments faced by various Québec governments since 1960, Scowen provides a useful insider's view of the period.

After being properly fortified with this base, you might then consult the writings of *Québécois* historians such as Michel Brunet, Guy Frégault, Fernand Ouellet and Marcel Trudel. For those with a taste for the bizarre, the hagiography of the reverend Lionel Groulx might prove interesting.

Complementing any study of the history of Québec is the scribbling of a host of analysts and commentators who grace the pages of today's newspapers. Some are competent, most are tiresome, a few are not very nice.

If bleeding hearts turn you on, you will enjoy Gretta Chambers in the Montreal Gazette. Some refer to her affectionately as Gretta Chamberlain. But, if her musings are not available, you might enjoy the profound observations of David Peterson, former Premier of Ontario, or former Prime Minister Joe Clark. However, if you gag easily, you might prefer to avoid these stalwarts in favour of something more substantial: Constitutional trivia, for instance. Here, academics of every description are more than ready to bore you in the OpEd pages of any number of Canadian newspapers. But, when it comes to good, balanced analysis, the best probably comes from the pen of Don Macpherson of the Montreal Gazette followed by Jeffrey Simpson of the Globe and Mail. However, if a cut-the-crap approach is your preference, William Johnson of the Financial Post, Andrew Coyne of Southam and Janice Kennedy of the Ottawa Citizen are well worth reading. So is Mordecai Richler.

Among francophones, the range of choice is much narrower and the tone of analysis more predictable: They are all afflicted with some version of the Poor-Québec-Syndrome. As a result, the offended virgin wail tends to dominate their political analyses. Nevertheless, the most balanced is probably Lysianne Gagnon of *La Presse* and the Globe and Mail. Less balanced, but probably more interesting, is Chantal Hébert of *La Presse* and Southam. However, so Québec-centred is she that she would probably interpret the Second Coming in terms of Québec's constitutional interests! All the same, sometimes the quality of her comments rises above the predictable. But, if you wish to scour the bottom of the barrel, there is always Josée Legault. Her bitter anglophobia graces the editorial pages of *Le Devoir*. She also appears regularly on English radio and TV promoting Québec secession.

APPENDIXES

I   Regression Analysis

Regression analysis is a statistical procedure used to determine the degree of correlation between two or more items when the relationship between them, though probable, is difficult to determine. For example, it is generally accepted that obesity and gluttony are closely correlated: If you study, say, one-hundred people of differing weights, you will find that those who weigh more tend to eat more than those who eat less. That is, weight and food intake are closely correlated; or, stated another way, a change in weight is usually the result of a change in food intake. But scientists tell us that, since other factors also contribute to obesity, the correlation, although quite high, cannot be perfect.

Regression analysis requires two steps. The first is a qualitative test for reasonableness, the second a complex number crunching exercise to determine the technical degree of correlation. The test for reasonableness is simple: Does it make sense to expect a causal correlation between these two events? For example, if we wondered about the degree of correlation between the voting habits of Nova Scotians and the migration patterns of Monarch butterflies, we would be justified in rejecting this hypothesis out of hand because it makes no sense to presume a correlation between Nova Scotians and butterflies. This rejection would be valid even if the statistical correlation between the two was strong. Remember, there was a famous case of a near perfect statistical correlation between the sale of ice cream at Coney Island and the phases of the moon. This type of correlation is said to be technically perfect but spurious since it is not reasonable to presume a causal correlation between ice cream sales and the moon.

Once past the test for reasonableness, we can perform the technical test. The degree of correlation can vary between zero (no correlation) and one (perfect correlation). This correlation index is called R-Squared (R^2). When R^2 is 1.0, it means that the two elements are 100-percent correlated; when it is 0.8, they are said to be 80-percent correlated; and so on.

Now let us consider, by way of example, correlations between items where the correlation is known, for instance, between the perimeter of a square and the length of one of its sides. Our grade six teacher would remind us that it is reasonable to presume a causal correlation between the two since the perimeter of a square is in fact equal to four-times the length of one side. Thus, we would expect a change in the length of the perimeter of a square to be explained by a change in the length of one of the sides of that square. Then, crunching the data via regression analysis would determine the technical degree of correlation between the two, the value of R^2. Let

Regression Analysis	
Length of Perimeter Of Square	Length of One Side Of Square
8	2
4	1
100	25
20	5
40	10
16	4
$R^2 = 1.00$	

us pretend that we do not know that R2 in this case must equal 1.0. Let us assume that we only have the two series of data shown here: The lengths of one side of figures of unknown configuration and their related perimeters.

Our question is, to what extent is the change in the perimeter explained by changes in the length of one side of the figure; or, stated another way, how well correlated is the perimeter and the length of one side; or, stated still another way, how well correlated are the values in these two columns? When we subject these data to regression analysis (perimeter as a function of the length of one side), we find that R2 is in fact equal to 1.0. Surprise! Hence, we can declare that any change in the perimeter of the figure is 100-percent explained by change in the length of one side of that figure. Or, stated another way, changes in the values in the left-hand column are completely explained by changes in the values in the right hand column.

However, what if our data set was not composed of squares but of a mishmash of squares, circles, ellipses, parallelograms and other bizarre figures? Obviously, the correlation between the length of the perimeter and the length of one side (or diameter), would be less than 1.0. If, because of this mishmash, the correlation fell to, say 0.45, it would mean that changes in the perimeter of the average figure are 45-percent explained by changes in the length of one side (or diameter) of the average figure. With a value of R2 this low, I would conclude that the two sets of data are only weakly correlated and refrain from drawing any other conclusions. Bear in mind, however, that many researchers in the social sciences would kill for values of R2 in excess of 0.20.

II   Trudeau versus Bouchard

On Saturday Feb. 3, 1996, Pierre Trudeau, the former Prime Minister of Canada, published an article in two Montreal newspapers, *The Gazette* and *La Presse*, in which he accused Lucien Bouchard, the then secessionist leader, of having misled the people of Québec during the fall 1995 Québec Referendum campaign. One week later, Bouchard replied in *The Gazette*, *La Presse* and *Le Devoir*.

Trudeau's article took the form of (a) quoting Bouchard, (b) stating the relevant facts as Trudeau saw them, and (c) drawing appropriate conclusions. Although Bouchard did not appear to question Trudeau's facts, he did challenge his conclusions. He also opened a few issues not addressed by Trudeau. Below are a few of Bouchard's comments followed by my assessment.

1.   Bouchard wrote: "... *Pierre Trudeau considers only one acceptable reading of ... history: his own.*"

Clever but misleading. Although French and British historians might have different perspectives on the Battle of Waterloo, they would not dispute the facts: For instance, that the battle took place and that Napoleon was defeated. Since most of Trudeau's article was dedicated to a recital of the facts, and since Bouchard does not appear to dispute Trudeau's facts, I presume that Bouchard means that Trudeau's interpretation of the facts is not sacrosanct and may be challenged. Fair enough. I shall compare their respective interpretations and assess where reason lies. No blood here.

2.   Bouchard accused Trudeau of "*stirring up old arguments just when Quebecers and their government have agreed upon quite different priorities: jobs, education and public finances.*"

Disingenuous to say the least. Although jobs, education and public finances are extremely important issues that scream for attention, they were literally ignored during the PQ government's entire pre-Referendum mandate. During the Referendum campaign, Bouchard and company tried to win the vote by telling lies (Trudeau's thesis ... and mine) about his adversaries. Now, after the Referendum defeat, he expected his adversaries to forgive and forget--until he decides when to do it all over again! The man's gall is impressive. No points for Bouchard here.

3.   Bouchard wrote: "*Mr. Trudeau, who omits to mention his own role and that of Jean Chrétien in the failure of (the) Meech (Lake Accord), did not hesitate at the time to declare: 'Meech terrifies me ....'*"

True but trivial. Trudeau never denied opposing Meech. What he did in his article was answer Bouchard's statement that "*English Canada rejected the hand offered by Québec in 1990.*" He did so by detailing the opposition to Meech by *Québécois* nationalist groups, including the PQ, the party Bouchard currently heads. Advantage Trudeau.

4.   Bouchard wrote: "*... Mr. Chrétien and several leading federalists are showing enormous contempt for the intelligence of Quebecers*" claiming "*voters did not understand the (Referendum) question and did not know that by saying Yes, Québec would become sovereign.*"

According to public opinion polls before and after the Referendum, about one-third of those who voted for secession thought that Québec would still remain part of Canada, that residents of this independent state would still carry Canadian passports and receive unemployment benefits from Ottawa! This suggests that the voters were either confused or thick. Chrétien was simply quoting poll results. No points for Bouchard here.

5.   Bouchard wrote: "*... the word treason does not figure in my vocabulary,*"

... and, contrary to what certain federalist leaders ... maintain, I did not use it."

I remember seeing a TV news item where, during the Referendum campaign, Bouchard held up a newspaper photograph of Trudeau and Chrétien signing the 1982 Constitution. The headline in the French newspaper obviously pleased the smiling Bouchard: It declared Trudeau and Chrétien to be traitors. Moreover, anyone attentive to Bouchard's pronouncements in Parliament and elsewhere, before and during the Referendum campaign, could prepare a healthy list of epithets used by Bouchard and company to describe Chrétien and Trudeau. Many sounded a great deal like traitor. Bouchard's nose must have stretched more than a little as he composed this whopper.

6.   Bouchard wrote: "*... the Canadian prime minister who suspended civil liberties in 1970 ... is in no position to give lessons in democracy."*

Civil liberties in Québec were constrained by the War Measures Act that was imposed by Trudeau in 1970 at the request of the Premier of Québec and the mayor of Montreal. Pinnochio at work again.

7.   Bouchard wrote concerning the November 1981 First Ministers' Conference that had been called to discuss possible repatriation of the Canadian Constitution: "*Try to explain to any outsider that 11 first ministers were invited to a conference crucial to the country's future and that, during the final night, 10 of them got together to design an accord that, far from satisfying the 11th, took away part of what he already had. You will not find one who will believe that a democracy could act in that manner, regardless of circumstances or alliances."*

The facts, I believe, are as follows.

In May 1980, René Lévesque lost his Referendum on sovereignty: The voters of Québec decided to stay in Canada. As a result, Trudeau felt that Canada's constitution should be repatriated from Britain where it existed only as a law enacted by the British Parliament. Consequently, it could be amended only in Britain. Trudeau felt it was time to cut the colonial ties and repatriate it so it could be amended in Canada. He proposed that the repatriated constitution include a new Charter of Rights. Among other things, the Charter gave equal rights to French and English in all areas of federal jurisdiction as well as in education which lies in the provincial domain. All provinces except Ontario and New Brunswick, 8 of 10, opposed repatriation because of the proposed inclusion of the Charter, for reasons that need not concern us here.

When Trudeau said he would repatriate it unilaterally without provincial consent, three provinces, including Québec, asked the Supreme Court of Canada if Trudeau could act unilaterally. The Court said he could not, ruling that repatriation could only proceed with "*a substantial level of provincial consent.*"

To ensure that Trudeau would never get "*a substantial level of provincial consent,*" eight provinces, including Québec, signed an agreement in April 1981 in which Québec agreed that it was a province like all the others thereby giving up its historic veto on constitutional change. In return, the other provinces in this so-called Gang of Eight, agreed to oppose Trudeau's repatriation plans. Some might wonder why Lévesque would willingly give up Québec's historic veto on constitutional change. But there is no mystery here. If Lévesque's goal was to keep Québec in Canada, it was obviously a mighty blunder. But, since his goal was to have Québec secede from Canada, the right to veto the constitution of Canada, a foreign country, was of no value to him. No, Lévesque knew what he was doing. So those who wail that he was tricked into giving up Québec's sacred veto are either dense or mischievous.

To counter the agreement of the Gang of Eight, Trudeau proposed at a meeting of the ten First Ministers that the dispute be resolved by putting the question to the people in a national referendum where approval would be required in all regions. (Québec and Ontario are defined as regions for constitutional purposes.) Feeling very confident of defeating Trudeau's Referendum in Québec, Lévesque swallowed Trudeau's bait. He accepted Trudeau's offer and abandoned his signed agreement with the Gang of Eight. Thus, with Ontario, Québec and New Brunswick onside, Trudeau had his "*substantial level of provincial support.*" He could now proceed with repatriation. But then Lévesque withdrew his support for the Referendum. Back to square one for Trudeau. Moreover, Ontario and New Brunswick apparently withdrew their support for unilateral repatriation. Trudeau was on the ropes. He then struck a deal with the new Gang of Nine, all provinces save Québec, thereby reacquiring his "*substantial level of provincial support.*" The new deal was based on the original deal agreed upon by the Gang of Eight which included Québec. This was the genesis of the term the "*Night of the Long Knives,*" the night during which this new deal was struck, when Lévesque was allegedly betrayed by Trudeau and English Canada. Recognizing the potentially bad political optics in Québec, Trudeau, according to Jean Chrétien, offered to remove from the repatriation package the items offensive to Lévesque if Lévesque agreed to sign the repatriation agreement. Lévesque was trapped. As a secessionist, he could not approve Trudeau's package, no more than could a leopard change its spots. No surprise then that he refused Trudeau's concessions.

That Lévesque reneged on his signed deal with the Gang of Eight is clear. That the Gang of Eight betrayed Lévesque is ridiculous. That Trudeau betrayed Lévesque is nonsense. But that he outsmarted Lévesque is obvious. That Québec lost its historic veto on constitutional change due to trickery by Pierre Trudeau and the First Ministers from English Canada is not supported by the historical record: First, Lévesque gave up the veto voluntarily when he made his deal with the Gang of Eight; second, the Supreme Court effectively negated it with its decision on "*substantial level of provincial support,*" a decision sought and approved by Lévesque and company. Nevertheless, the legend of the "*Night of the Long Knives*" and its associated fairy tales live on in *Québécois* nationalist mythology. The offended virgins refuse to accept the obvious: Lévesque was not betrayed; he was outmanoeuvred by Trudeau; he was hoist by his own pétard; he bluffed and lost; he blew it, period.

Game, set and match to Trudeau.

III   Jacques Parizeau
THE Speech that Never Was/ THE Book that Was

Just before the Oct. 30, 1995 Referendum, the Premier of Québec, Jacques Parizeau, videotaped a victory speech that he intended to deliver on TV if his secessionist side carried the day on Oct. 30. Since he lost, the speech was never delivered. Instead, in an obviously impromptu and acrimonious speech on Referendum night, he blamed the loss on money and the ethnic vote. Some have wondered if the so-called soft sovereigntists would have voted for secession had they heard Parizeau's *victory* speech before they voted.

Below is a verbatim chronological summary of this speech. *In the statements in italics, Parizeau referred specifically to the 'new partnership' with Canada*; in other statements, he referred instead to Québec's imminent sovereignty. About 8 percent of Parizeau's text was dedicated to the '*new partnership*' with Canada, 92 percent to Québec's imminent sovereignty. Although Parizeau's supporters might argue that the whole text actually dealt with the proposed '*new partnership*' with Canada, that is not how I read it--in either French or English versions. Read on and decide for yourself.

In his speech, Parizeau said:

1.   A strong and simple decision was made today: Québec will become sovereign. Let a place be made ready for it at the table of nations. *And because Québec is now standing on its feet, it can first of all*

*extend a hand to its Canadian neighbour through the offer of a new
partnership, founded on the principle of equality between peoples.*

2. *In this spirit of coming together, the government will proceed, as we
    have indicated, to name new members to the committee that will guide
    and watch over the partnership negotiations with Canada.*

3. We also intend, in various forums, economic forums in particular, to
    call for solidarity between business and labour, so we can implement
    our social choices: the first of these will be a national strategy for job
    creation.

4. (We are committed) to respect and defend (anglophone) rights and to
    take all measures necessary to guarantee in Québec's new constitution
    that the identity of their community and their institutions is preserved.

5. New immigrants .... and refugees ... waiting for Canadian citizenship
    will be able, without further delay, to take advantage of their right to
    Québec citizenship at the time when sovereignty is declared.

6. Their (native people) rights will be enshrined in the new constitution
    of a sovereign Québec ....

7. The sovereignty of Québec will not be proclaimed right away. It can
    take as much as a year before the National Assembly makes that
    proclamation. This gives us the time we need to make proper
    preparations for the transition.

8. In the days to come ... our federal MPs will continue to represent us.
    Until we proclaim the sovereignty of Québec, in as much as a year.
    And that's when things are going to change, when things will become
    more simple. Until then, however, everyone will have time to get
    ready and see to it that the transition is made harmoniously, without
    disturbing services to citizens. There will be no upheaval, no legal
    vacuum. *What can proceed much more quickly, in contrast, are
    negotiations with Canada ... for a new economic and political
    partnership.*

9. And let me assure you (Canadians outside Québec) here and now: when
    Québec proclaims its sovereignty, it will mean that not one of your tax
    dollars will be paid to Québec. No transfer payments will be made to
    Québec.

10. We have resolved to keep the Canadian dollar as our currency.

11.   Of the 185 members of the United Nations, on the day Québec
       becomes sovereign it will be the 16th largest economic power. Our
       weight in the North American economy is considerable. We are the
       eighth largest economic partner of the United States. Québec firmly
       intends to remain an active and constructive partner within the World
       Trade Organization and within NAFTA.

Author's Comments:

This text is at least ambiguous. On the one hand, Parizeau speaks as if the
Québec electorate had voted in the Referendum for outright sovereignty,
sovereignty that would be proclaimed by the Québec National Assembly before
Oct. 30, 1996. On the other hand, he speaks of negotiating a "*new partnership*"
with Canada without relating the outcome of the negotiations to sovereignty.
The ambiguity is resolved only if we assume that Parizeau felt (1) that since the
affirmative Referendum vote was in fact a vote for secession, the negotiations
would take place between already sovereign countries, or (2) that the partnership
negotiations between the province of Québec and the government of Canada
would fail, thereby inducing sovereignty/secession by default.

      If the first assumption is valid, then, according to opinion polls,
about one-third of those who voted for secession in the Referendum were fooled:
They thought they were voting for something other than outright secession. If
the second assumption proves true, then Parizeau was simply acting out of turn:
It is one thing to assume an outcome, it is something else to act prematurely on
that assumption. The evidence will show (a) that, although he was willing to
play along for political reasons, Parizeau was sure that Canada would never
agree to the partnership terms set out in the Referendum documents, (b) that his
feeling was well founded: The partnership agreement could not possibly be
successfully negotiated, and (c) that he was prepared to proceed along the lines
of the first assumption.

      Item "a" (the assumption that Canada would never agree to the
partnership terms) was confirmed in a TV interview filmed before the
Referendum and released shortly afterwards. In it Parizeau declared that he
never believed that Canada would ever agree to the partnership terms set out in
the Referendum documents. Hence, he considered the Referendum vote a vote
on secession, thereby confirming item "c". To confirm item "b" (that Parizeau's
assumption was well founded) we must consider Parizeau's *victory* speech in the
context of the Referendum question which was:

> *Do you agree that Québec should become sovereign, after*
> *having made a formal offer to Canada for a new Economic*
> *and Political Partnership, within the scope of the Bill*
> *respecting the future of Québec and of the agreement signed*

on June 12, 1995?

The Bill referred to in the question is summarized below:

Bill number one (of the Québec National Assembly) declares that, since Québec is a distinct society, and since Québec has been very badly treated within the Canadian Confederation, Québec needs to become an independent country. Thus, Québécers will be asked in a referendum to approve the next step toward independence. After an affirmative referendum vote on Oct. 30, 1995, Québec will open negotiations with Canada to form a new economic and political union. If, by Oct. 30, 1996, a new union with Canada is not concluded, the National Assembly will unilaterally declare Québec independent.

Note that the proposed declaration of sovereignty on Oct. 30, 1996 is conditional on failure of negotiations with Canada to form a new economic and political union. However, in Parizeau's *victory* speech, the period between Oct. 30, 1995 and Oct. 30, 1996 is clearly identified as a time, not for negotiations, but as a time during which Québec would prepare itself for sovereignty. Consequently, sovereignty would be not proclaimed *after* Oct. 30, 1996, as set out in the Referendum question, but instead *no later than* Oct. 30, 1996. These different proclamation dates are obviously driven by different political imperatives.

The agreement referred to in the Referendum question was the June 12, 1995 tripartite agreement between Jacques Parizeau, Premier of Québec, Lucien Bouchard, leader of the *Bloc Québécois* and Leader of Her Majesty's Loyal Opposition in the Parliament of Canada, and Mario Dumont, head of *l'Action démocratique* in the Québec National Assembly. In this agreement were spelled out the procedural details for the post-Referendum negotiations with Canada. The new political union sought would include a parliamentary Assembly where Québec would have 25 percent of the seats, not unlike the current distribution in the Parliament of Canada. Overseeing this assembly would be a Council where Canada and Québec would have equal representation. Since each side would have veto rights, decisions of the Council would have to be unanimous. Yes, unanimous!

I develop a great headache reading this piece of sanctimonious and hypocritical trash. This political arrangement could never work. No wonder Parizeau assumed it would not fly. Except for the most mundane issues, the Council would be in continuous deadlock. If you need more than common sense to come to this conclusion, simply look around. You will not find anywhere a functioning representative system where unanimity is required. So why should it work here? Who would want to propose a political arrangement that was guaranteed to fail? Only those who wanted it to fail, of course: Messrs Parizeau,

Bouchard and Dumont. That is the nature of Referendum politics in Québec. How else does one convince trusting *Québécois* to vote for secession except by wrapping wolves in sheep's clothing!

I am neither astonished nor surprised by the contents of Parizeau's *victory* speech. His comments were consistent with what he had been saying for a long time, notwithstanding what the Referendum question asked. However, some voters may have been more influenced by the question than by what Parizeau had said. On balance, it seems reasonable to conclude that some of the so-called soft secessionists, the one-third who voted for secession, might have had second thoughts had they heard Parizeau's speech before the Referendum. But, make no mistake, during his *victory* speech, Parizeau was preparing to unilaterally proclaim the independence of Québec.

And then there was Parizeau's book.

In May 1997, in the middle of the federal election, Jacques Parizeau published his book *Pour un Québec souverain*. Although he flatly denied it, the *Québécois* media insisted that Parizeau claimed in the book that it was his intention to proclaim Québec's independence very soon after a successful Referendum vote. Here is a translation of the text that was taken as proof of Parizeau's intention to secede directly following the vote: Decide for yourself. I would argue that, coupled with his *victory* speech, it leaves little doubt that immediate secession was in fact his intent.

> *It was during this trip that (former French President) Valéry Giscard d'Estaing raised a question of which I had not, until then, understood the significance. It is essential, he said in essence, right after the Yes victory in the Referendum, in the hours or days that follow, that there be a solemn gesture taken by Québec to proclaim its sovereignty. Without that, no quick recognition, that is to say in a week or 10 days afterward, will be possible on the part of a foreign country.*
>
> *It was all well and good that we put off a declaration of sovereignty for six months to a year to leave enough time for negotiating with Canada or jointly draft a partnership treaty with Canada. But France, like other countries, only recognize countries. It doesn't recognize intentions.*
>
> *As far as negotiations with Canada are concerned, it can be seen that my speeches are written in a way to allow such a declaration of sovereignty. And I never committed myself, in public or in private, to not make a unilateral declaration of sovereignty.*

BIBLIOGRAPHY

Monographs

Notre question nationale. Montréal: Édition de l'Action Nationale, 1944.

Bercuson, D. J.   Colonies: Canada to 1867. Toronto: McGraw-Hill Ryerson, 1992.

Conrod, M. et al   History of the Canadian Peoples: Beginnings to 1867. Montréal: Copp, Clark, Pittman, 1993.

Delisle, E.   The Traitor and the Jew: Anti-Semitism and the delirium of extremist right-wing nationalism in French Canada, 1929-1939. Montréal: Robert Davies Publishing, 1993.

Durham, Lord   An Abridgement of Lord Durham's Report on the Affairs of British North America, 1839. Edited by G. M. Craig, Ottawa: Carleton University Press, 1982/92.

Garneau, F. X.   Histoire du Canada, 3. Montréal: 1859.

Goldhagen, D. H.   Hitler's Willing Executioners: Ordinary Germans and the Holocaust. New York: Vintage Books, 1997.

Gosselin, P. E.   Étienne Parent, 1802-1874. Ottawa: Fides, 1964.

Groulx, L.   Lendemains de conquête: Cours d'histoire du Canada, 1919-20. Montréal: l'université de Montréal.

Hamelin, L. E.   Évolution numérique séculaire du clergé catholique au Québec. Québec: Recherches Sociographiques, vol 2, Université Laval, 1961.

Hamilton, R.   Feudal Society and Colonization: The Historiography of New France. Gananoque: Langdale Press, 1988.

Harris, G. R. et al   Paying Our Way: The Welfare State in Hard Times. Toronto: C. D. Howe Institute, 1994.

Jaenen, C   The Role of the Church in New France. Toronto: McGraw-Hill Ryerson, 1976.

Johnson, W.   Anglophobie, L': Made in Québec. Montréal: Stanké, 1991.

A Canadian Myth: Québec Between Canada and the Illusion of Utopia. Montréal: Robert Davies, 1994.

Khouri, N   Qui a peur de Mordecai Richler?. Montréal: Balzac, 1995.

Lahaie, R., ed.   Le Devoir: Reflet du Québec au 20e siècle. Montréal: Éditions Hurtubise, 1994.

Lanctot, G et
Robitaille, G.   Canadiens français et leurs voisins du sud, Les. Montréal: Valiquette, 1941.

Legault, J   Invention d'une minorité, L': Les Anglos Québécois. Montréal: Boréal,
                    1992.

Lemelin, C.   "Éducation au Québec, L': La formation de base," dans Éducation et
                    formation à l'heure de la competivité internationale. Montréal:
                    Association des économistes québécois, 1990.

Mathieu, J et
Lacoursière, J.   Les mêmoires québécoises. Québec: Les Presses de l'université Laval,
                    1991.

National Council
of Welfare   Poverty Profile 1993. Ottawa: Supply & Services Canada, 1995.

                    Welfare Incomes, 1995. Ottawa: Supply & Services Canada, 1997.

Noel, J   "New France: Les Femmes Favorisées," Atlantis, VI, 2, Spring 1981.

Vaugeois, D et
Lacoursière, J.   Histoire 1534-1968. Montréal: Boréal, 1968.

Statistics

Annuaire Statistique de Québec, 1960. Québec: Gouvernement du Québec, 1961.

Canadian Advertising Rates and Data. Toronto: Sept. 1996.

Comparaison de la rémunération des emplois sans contrapartie, La: Réflexions et
orientations à partir de l'emploi d'enseignant. Québec: Institut de recherche et d'information
sur la rémunération, juin, 1993.

Diplomation par commission scolaire, juin 1993. Québec: Ministère de l'Éducation du
Québec, 1994.

Diplomes et accès aux diplomes dans les universités québécoises, 1976-80. Québec:
Ministère de l'Éducation du Québec.

Enquête salariale sur les emplois repères au Québec. Québec: Ministère du Travail du
Québec.

Enquête sur la rémunération globale des emplois repères au Québec en 1985. Québec:
Ministère du Travail du Québec.

Report on Private Giving, 1994-95. Montréal: McGill University Alumni Association.

Results of the Compensation Remuneration Study/Faculty and Other Related Professionals.
Ottawa: Association of Universities and Colleges of Canada, 1994.

Special Report on Current Wages in Major Collective Agreements, March 7, 1995. Ottawa:
Bureau of Labour Information, Labour Canada, 1995.

Statistical Abstract of Ireland, 1989. Dublin, Ireland: Central Statistics Office.

Statistics Canada, Various Reports. Ottawa: 1860 to 1995.

Statistics of the Catholic Church in Canada, 1992-93. Ottawa: Canadian Council of Catholic Bishops.

Statistiques de l'Éducation, 1992-93. Québec: Ministère de l'Éducation du Québec, 1994.

INDEX

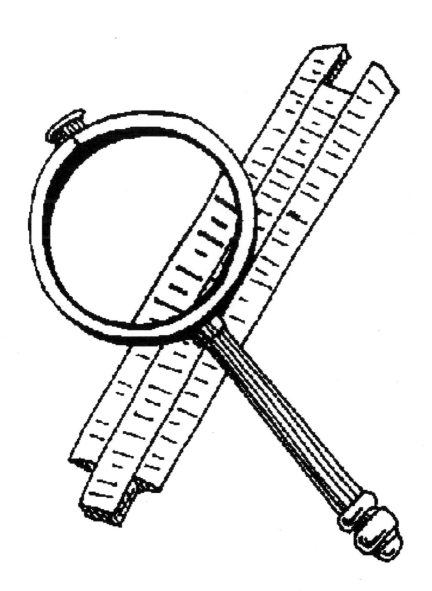

ABOUT THE AUTHOR

Robert Sauvé was born in 1934 and brought up in Saint Henri, a lower working class district of Montréal. As a young man, he received his secondary education from the Jesuits, a science degree from Loyola College and an engineering degree from McGill University. In his middle years, he obtained two degrees in history from the University of Ottawa. Most of his professional career was spent in the energy business in both the private and public sectors. Before the electors made him to come to his senses, he was also active in Québec politics. He and Lois Gallagher celebrated 40 years of married life together in 1998. They have four accomplished children and a pretty nice granddaughter.

The first Sauvé in New France was married in 1693. Some of his progeny married local Indian maidens, most married Europeans. The first of Mr. Sauvé's mother's ancestors, the Irish-speaking Stantons and O'Reillys, arrived in Québec in the 1850s. When two Stanton sisters married into the Sauvé family in the 1920s, the English-speaking wing of the Sauvés was born. According to some *Québécois* nationalists, English-speakers such as these should not participate in Québec elections ... either as candidates or as voters.

When he is not busy trying to wipe political correctness from the face of the earth, or commenting on matters political, Mr. Sauvé plays a great deal of golf.